"*Chinese scientists in America are caught in the crossfire of a war for talent between the United States and the PRC. David Zweig shows how they have been hurt by overreach on the part of Beijing and by overreaction from Washington. And he reminds us that the collateral damage is the scaling back of collaborative research to address global problems. His book is a timely corrective to the over-securitization of research in campuses across the western world.*"

— **The Honourable Yuen Pau Woo**, Senator, Parliament of Canada

"*David Zweig has written an important book. Against the context of many observers predicting outright war between the United States and China, everything in the relationship between the two superpowers has become contentious. With an understanding of history and the best data, Zweig analyzes the competition for human capital and intellectual property. His work, more astute than alarmist, is much needed.*"

— **Frank H. Wu**, President, Queens College, CUNY, and former Chancellor & Dean at University of California Hastings College of the Law

"*Professor Zweig, a long-respected scholar of Sino-American scientific cooperation and rivalry, offers not only an admirable perspective on developments to date but also a sophisticated analysis of the challenges this increasingly important field presents the next administration in Washington.*"

— **Jerry Cohen**, Adjunct Senior Fellow for Asia, Council on Foreign Relations

"*An outstanding piece of research. From a storehouse of material accumulated over 30 years, David Zweig has given us a detailed and well-balanced view of a contentious issue in Sino-American relations—the presence of large numbers of Chinese collecting valuable information in American universities and research institutes. This is an important book that should be read by all who are engaged with China.*"

— **B. Michael Frolic**, Professor Emeritus, York University

The War for Chinese Talent in America

The Politics of Technology and Knowledge in Sino-U.S. Relations

THE WAR FOR CHINESE TALENT IN AMERICA

THE POLITICS OF TECHNOLOGY AND KNOWLEDGE IN SINO-U.S. RELATIONS

David Zweig

Published by the Association for Asian Studies
Asia Shorts, Number 20
www.asianstudies.org

The Association for Asian Studies (AAS)

Formed in 1941, the Association for Asian Studies (AAS)—the largest society of its kind, with over 6,000 members worldwide—is a scholarly, non-political, non-profit professional association open to all persons interested in Asia.

For further information, please visit www.asianstudies.org.

Cataloging-in-Publication Data available from the Library of Congress.

ASIA
SHORTS

Series Editor: David Kenley
Dakota State University

ASIA SHORTS offers concise, engagingly written titles by highly qualified authors on topics of significance in Asian Studies. Topics are intended to be substantive, generate discussion and debate within the field, and attract interest beyond it.

The Asia Shorts series complements and leverages the success of the pedagogically-oriented AAS book series, Key Issues in Asian Studies, and is designed to engage broad audiences with up-to-date scholarship on important topics in Asian Studies. Rigorously peer-reviewed, Asia Shorts books provide cutting-edge scholarship and provocative analyses. They are jargon free, accessible, and speak to contemporary issues or larger themes. In so doing, Asia Shorts volumes make an impact on students, fellow scholars, and informed readers beyond academia.

For further information, visit the AAS website: www.asianstudies.org.

AAS books are distributed by Columbia University Press.

For orders or purchasing inquiries, please visit

https://cup.columbia.edu

COLUMBIA
UNIVERSITY
PRESS

My wife, Joy, has long wanted me to write a timelier and less academic book.

This one is for her.

About the Author

DAVID ZWEIG (Ph.D., The University of Michigan, 1983) is Professor Emeritus, Hong Kong University of Science and Technology (HKUST), Distinguished Visiting Professor of Taipei School of Economics and Political Science, National Tsinghua University, Taiwan, and Vice-President of the Center for China and Globalization (Beijing).

He was a Postdoctoral Fellow at Harvard in 1984–85, and in 2013–2015 received the Humanities and Social Sciences Prestigious Fellowship, Research Grants Council of Hong Kong.

For fifteen years, he directed the Center on China's Transnational Relations at HKUST.

Over 40,000 students have signed up for his two courses on Chinese politics and China and the world, both on Coursera.

He has retired to New York City where his wife, two children and dog live.

CONTENTS

TABLES AND FIGURES

Tables

Tables in the Statistical Appendix

Figures

Acronyms and Abbreviations

AAJC	Asian Americans Advancing Justice
ACP	Association of Chinese Professors
AI	Artificial Intelligence
BJUT	Beijing University of Technology 北京科技大学
CAS	Chinese Academy of Sciences 中国科学院
CAST	China Association for Science and Technology 中国科技协会
CDM	Center for Disease Modeling
CHTZ	Chengdu High-Tech Zone
CI	China Initiative
CIHR	Canadian Institute of Health Research
CJSP	Changjiang Scholars Plan 长江学者计划
CJVP	Changjiang Visitors Plan
CLGCWT	Central Leading Group Coordinating Work on Talent 中央人才工作协调小组
COC	conflict of commitment
COI	conflict of interest
CRISP	Chief of Research Security and Policy
CSCSE	Chinese Service Center for Scholarly Exchange 中国留学服务中心
CSET	Center for Security and Emerging Technology
CSIS	Center for Strategic and International Studies
DHS	Department of Homeland Security
DKNs	Diaspora Knowledge Networks
DOD	Department of Defense
DOE	Department of Energy

DOI	Director of Outside Interests
DOJ	Department of Justice
ECI	Ethnic Collaboration Index
EEA	Economic Espionage Act
FTTP	Foreign Thousand Talent Plan
GAO	Government Accountability Office
HKUST	The Hong Kong University of Science and Technology
HHS	Department of Health and Human Services
IMS	Institute for Medical Science
IP	Intellectual Property
ITMS	Investigations and Threat Management Service
JCORE	Joint Committee on the Research Environment
LKSF	Li Ka Hsing Foundation
MOE	Ministry of Education 教育部
MOHRSS	Ministry of Human Resources and Social Security 人力资源和社会保障部
NCI	National Cancer Institute
NIH	National Institute of Health
NSD	National Security Division (under the DOJ)
NSF	National Science Foundation
NSFC	Natural Science Foundation of China 中国自然科学基金
NSPM	National Security Presidential Memo
NSTC	National Science and Technology Council
NYUSoM	New York University School of Medicine
OCAO	Overseas Chinese Affairs Office 侨务委员会
OECD	Organization for Economic Cooperation and Development
OIG	Office of the Inspector General
OSTP	White House's Office of Science and Technology Policy
PIs	Principal Investigators

PLA   People's Liberation Army 人民解放军

PKU   Peking University (Beida) 北京大学

PRC   People's Republic of China 中国人民共和国

RGC   Research Grants Council

R&D   Research and Development

SAFEA   State Administration of Foreign Experts Affairs
           国家外国专家局

SEDC   State Education Commission 国家教育委员会

SHUFE   Shanghai University of Finance and Economics
           上海财经大学

SWUFE   Southwest University of Finance and Economics
           西南财经大学

SSCI   Social Science Citation Index

SSTC   State Science and Technology Commission
           国家科技委员会

USCSTA   US-China Science and Technology Agreement

STEM   Science, Technology, Engineering, and Math

SUSTech   China Southern University of Science and Technology
           中南科技大学

TMUCIH   Tianjin Medical University Cancer Institute and Hospital
           天津医科大学肿瘤医院

TTP   Thousand Talents Plan 千人计划

UAF   University of Arkansas at Fayetteville

UBC   University of British Columbia

UCSD   The University of California at San Diego

UFWD   United Front Work Department 统战部

UNC   University of North Carolina at Chapel Hill

USTR   United States Trade Representative

UTK   University of Tennessee, Knoxville

WMU   Wenzhou Medical University 温州医学大学

WRSA   Western Returned Scholars Association 欧美同学会

Preface and Acknowledgments

This book is comprised of what were to be the last two chapters of a larger book on China's "reverse migration." I have been working on the topic of "brain drains" and "returnees" (海归派) for over thirty years, having interviewed in 1991 and 1992 the first cohort of academics and scientists who went abroad in the late 1970s and early 1980s and then returned to China.[1] The bigger book involves four case studies: on entrepreneurs, academics, scientists in the Chinese Academy of Sciences (CAS), and the bevy of young people who largely went abroad for various master's degrees and then returned in large numbers to look for a job.

Initially, those four case studies were to be followed by two more chapters. The first was about "China's diaspora option"—that is, the policies instituted by the Chinese party/state to gain the maximum value it could from the million or more China-born academics and businesspeople who chose to stay abroad and not return to their "homeland." An earlier version of the chapter analyzing this topic appeared in the journal *Science, Technology, and Society* in 2006.[2]

The second, and what was intended to be the last chapter of the larger book, was a study of the "China Initiative" (CI) instituted by the US Department of Justice (DOJ) under then President Donald Trump. I first presented a draft of that chapter at a conference at the Duke-Kunshan University campus in Kunshan, Jiangsu Province, in central China. I then published it through the Center for Strategic and International Studies (CSIS) as one of their occasional papers on China.[3]

However, as I dug deeper into those events, the chapter on the CI kept getting longer. My insights and information about the CI increased when I became an "expert witness" on behalf of two Chinese academics who were charged by the DOJ and the National Institute of Health (NIH). One case was brought against a world-class cancer specialist working in one of the top medical schools in the US. In my view, his so-called "crimes" were minimal, yet under pressure from the NIH, the university fired him from his tenured position based on a decision by a closed tribunal; his case has still not seen the light of day. And his case was not alone, as perhaps 150 ethnic Chinese scientists lost their jobs for misdemeanors that, before the CI, would have been handled by the universities internally. It became obvious to me, and many others, that the FBI, the DOJ, and the NIH were engaged in an attack on ethnic Chinese scholars and businesspeople in the US that had the aura of a new round of McCarthyism.

The enlarged chapter also explored the impact of the CI on Sino-American scientific collaboration, which is the largest project of cross-national copublications in the world. In particular, the CI has had enormous repercussions for collaborative work on cancer research, which, during the Obama presidency, became a major bilateral effort—supported by the NIH and the Chinese government—to end this scourge on humanity.[4] Eventually, the chapter on the CI reached over 105 pages, even with a smaller font and line spacing.

I realized that I could not present what the manuscript had become to a publisher. Also, the new information on China's efforts to access Western technology and the CI called out for a quicker publication than the time involved in publishing a large manuscript with an academic press. Now that it was so long, it might take two years to come out. So I peeled off the last two chapters and turned them into this shorter, timelier, and less academic book, something my wife has wanted me to do for years.

I owe enormous thanks to numerous people to whom I want to express my appreciation.

First, my coauthor in the CSIS publication, Dr. Kang Siqin, my former MPhil student who gained a PhD in government and public administration at the University of Hong Kong, is currently an assistant professor at the Chinese University of Hong Kong in Shenzhen. His creativity and statistical analysis have been critical to several of my more successful publications.[5]

Thanks to my long-term co-researcher, Professor Chen Changgui, formerly of the Huazhong University of Science and Technology in Wuhan and then later a professor in the School of Education at Sun Yat-sen University (中山大学) in Guangzhou. We worked closely for a decade, interviewing China's new diaspora in the US.[6]

A second important collaborator and coauthor is Stan Rosen of the University of Southern California. He organized the research in California that went into our book on China's brain drain to the US. For many years, he has edited *Chinese Education and Society*, which translated many articles about brain drains, brain gains, and the policy toward them.[7] We also co-authored several widely cited articles and book chapters.

Third, Dr. Shao Wei, deputy director of the Chinese Service Center for Scholarly Exchange (CSCSE) under the Ministry of Education (MOE), invited me to join a CSCSE delegation to Japan in 2006, where I carried out over twenty interviews with Chinese who remained in Japan after college or training programs. That research in Japan was carried out with Dr Shao's colleague, Ms. Zhang Ying. Thanks, too, to Dr Shao's colleagues at the CSCSE, Che Weimin and Wei Zuyu, for their assistance and intellectual support.

I was very fortunate to have the opportunity to work with Dr. Alwyn Didar Singh, who for many years directed the Federation of Indian Chambers of Commerce and Industry (FICCI), a nongovernmental organization supported by the Indian business community, which lobbied for their interests. Together, we researched India's "diaspora option" and the attitude of the Indian state toward the reverse migration of its overseas population.[8] Dr. Didar Singh and I traveled to Silicon Valley and met with the Indus Entrepreneurs (TIE), one of the world's leading diasporic organizations, which diligently helps India, and many young Indians, develop. He also arranged a meeting with the Indian consul general in San Francisco.

I owe a debt to Dr. Wang Huiyao, president, and Dr. Miao Lu, vice president and secretary general, of the Center for China and Globalization (CCG) in Beijing, who brought me into China's "personnel system" (人事系统), giving me the chance to observe how the government managed all aspects of the development of talent in China. Once I entered that system, I frequently worked with the Ministry of Human Resources and Social Security and its think tank, the China Research Institute on Personnel. Dr. Wang also introduced me to Miao Danguo, who compiled and shared with me the most comprehensive collection of documents, speeches, essays, and meetings related to China's overseas study and reverse migration.[9] Also, after I became a vice-dean of the CCG center in Guangzhou, called the South China Global Talent Institute, I created a team composed of undergraduate students in Guangzhou, who, under the direction of Dr. Kang Siqin, built a dataset from public records of full- and part-time returnees under the Changjiang Scholars Plan (长江学者计划), and the Thousand Talents Plan or TTP (千人计划), which I use in this book. That information showed that most of China's best overseas talent was remaining in the diaspora.[10]

Through other channels, I was invited to speak to the Organization Department of the CCP at the national, regional, and local level, particularly the Talent Office of the Organization Department in Beijing—all of which taught me much about China's Thousand Talents Plan (TTP). I greatly appreciated their interest in my work and in my views. In 2012, I attended a meeting run by the central Organization Department, where, in a small group setting, I told its director—whose reform agenda was of great importance to the development of talent in science, technology, and education—that the personalistic talent system, run by bureaucrats who jealously protected their power and who dominated the universities and the CAS, was undermining his TTP.

All this research needs funding, which I got from several sources. Funders included the Research Grants Council of Hong Kong; the Asia-Pacific Foundation of Canada in Vancouver; the Japanese External Trade Organization in Hong Kong (and its director general, Mr. Kuniyasu Funaki); the School of Humanities and Social Sciences at The Hong Kong University of Science and Technology (HKUST); the Hang Lung Institute at HKUST's School of Business Management; my friend, Paul Thiel; and the Chang Tseng-Hsi Foundation of Hong Kong, chaired by Ronnie Chan of Hang Lung Property, who helped me set up the Center for China's Transnational Relations, through which much of my research was done. Assistance also came from the Chiang Ching-kuo Foundation for International Scholarly Exchange in Taiwan, and the Research and Conference Fund of the Department of Foreign Affairs and International Trade, the Government of Canada. Those grants paid as well for the administrator of my center, Ms. Meggy Wan, who for many years managed all logistical and nonacademic aspects of my research.

A few other individuals who have been extremely helpful include Jeremy Wu (APA Justice), who recommended me to be an expert witness for two cases under the China Initiative, Beth Margolis, Huang Chuanshu's lawyer who also introduced me to case study six in the book, Drew Ledbetter and Simon Ang, Mike German, Peggy Blumenthal and Leah Mason of IIE, James Lee, Chen Wenhong and Barry Wellman, Hans Jiang Ao, Chia Jingyin (JC), Gerry Postiglione, Scott Kennedy, Denis Simon, Cong Cao, Michael Lauer, Rebecca Keiser, Huang Chuanshu, Sam Meng Sun, Didi Kirsten Tatlow, Pete Suttmeier, Yojana Sharma, AnnaLee Saxenian, Xie Yu, Wu Jianhong, Liu Mingyao, Tian Guoqiang, Gan Li, Sheridan Prasso, Kevin Kramer, Carol Lam, Hu Anming and Phil Lomonaco, Xi Xiaoxing, Chung Siu Fung, Zha Qiang, and particularly, Jon Wilson, who was my hands-on editor at Asia Shorts, and the Asia Shorts series editor, David Kenley.

Finally, I thank my children, Rachel and Aaron, and most importantly, my wife, Joy, who worries when my books are too full of theories and regression analyses. This one is for her.

Summer 2024

New York City

1

BRAIN DRAINS, BRAIN GAINS, AND THE DIASPORA OPTION

Human resource development in nonindustrialized states faces the loss of talent due to the "brain drain." By this process, educated, talented, and entrepreneurial people in developing countries have been "pushed" out of their homelands by political instability or by rampant corruption, economic limitations, and a sense that greater opportunities exist for them and their families abroad. According to El-Saati, the existence in the West of specific criteria for evaluating performance and achievement, which decrease the importance of personal ties in affecting incomes and promotion, makes the West more appealing to people from more traditional states that lack such connections.[1] Huang found a significant relationship between a nation's lack of political freedom and its citizens' desire to stay in the US.[2] Some see the roots in the global economy, lower-quality educational institutions, and the inappropriateness of the educational training in the schools created by colonial and neocolonial powers.[3] At the same time, talented people are "pulled" into the industrialized world by better educational institutions for themselves and their children, higher salaries, a better quality of life, increased opportunities, and a host of other forces.[4] According to G. L. Rao, it is the "comparison of the potential migrant's situation in his country of origin with the situation of his peers in the country of destination that is critical to the decision of the potential migrant."[5]

As states struggle to limit this loss of talent, two strategies have emerged. First, developing states can invest money and policy energy to trigger a "reverse brain drain," where talented, home-country nationals bring back the knowledge and the enhanced human capital they acquired abroad and put it to work for their home country (and for themselves).

Numerous studies have analyzed this "reverse migration," including the activities of scientists,[6] academics,[7] political elites,[8] and entrepreneurs.[9] Those findings suggest that reverse migration can mitigate some problematic aspects of the brain drain, such as the loss of talent in the fields of health care, biotechnology, tertiary education, entrepreneurship, and scientific discovery. More widely, returnees can affect many sectors of their home country's economy and society and bring the world's newest scientific and technological developments back home.

And in fact, people do return. Rosenzweig estimated that in four out of six Caribbean countries, at least 70 percent of migrants educated in the US returned home.[10] South Korea,[11] Hong Kong,[12] and Taiwan[13] have succeeded in triggering a significant reverse brain drain. The same goes for India.[14]

Second, of great relevance to this book, many of the policy innovations or reforms needed to bring talented people home are also key components of the "diaspora option," a policy that is easier to implement than pulling talented people back. This strategy sees the outflow of scientific personnel less as a permanent exodus but more as a form of "brain circulation,"[15] where people in the diaspora share a collective identity linked to their ancestral home and a common commitment to improve the situation there.[16] So they transfer scientific and economic information, capital, skills, or business opportunities back to their country of origin and find ways to participate in the economic and scientific development of their former homeland.[17] This way, scientific, academic, or business collaboration ensues without people in the diaspora uprooting their lives and moving back home full-time.[18]

The Extent of the "Brain Drain" Globally

The "Human Flight and Brain Drain—Country Rankings," which considers the economic impact of human displacement and its consequences on a country's development, finds that the global average for 2022, based on 177 countries, was 5.21 index points, running from a low of zero to a high of ten (where a higher index number signified a higher level of human displacement). The highest value was in Samoa (ten index points) and the lowest value was in Australia (0.4 index points).[19] China ranks 144, with a score of 3.2, suggesting only limited disruption from the brain drain.

The Institute for Employment Research created a dataset that shows the flow of talent from developing countries to those in the Organization for Economic Cooperation and Development (OECD).[20] It divides the quality of education of the migrants into low, medium, and high, with the high including some tertiary education beyond high school. The data are measured in five-year cohorts. I have utilized their data to create table 1.1.

Country	1990–95			1995–2000			2000–2005			2005–2010			1990–2010 (Totals)		
	High Talent	Total Migrants	% High Talent	High Talent	Total Migrants	% High Talent	High Talent	Total Migrants	% High Talent	High Talent	Total Migrants	% High Talent	Total High	Total Migrants	% High Talent
Philippines to Canada	37260	56165	66%	49500	73305	67.5%	74170	98845	75.0%	97768	121100	80.7%	258698	349415	74.0%
Philippines to US	218192	329167	66%	276716	403918	68.5%	398224	549691	72.4%	443406	601969	73.7%	1336538	1884745	70.9%
Philippines to UK	1304	4732	28%	3819	7402	51.6%	4552	7881	57.8%	7203	11246	64.0%	16878	31261	54.0%
Philippines to France	195	781	25%	373	1206	30.9%	445	1204	37.0%	922	3299	27.9%	1935	6490	29.8%
Philippines to Australia	13555	18311	74%	17047	22952	74.3%	18793	24599	76.4%	20817	26371	78.9%	70212	92233	76.1%
Philippines to Germany	1948	3521	55%	2100	3530	59.5%	791	2901	27.3%	951	2446	38.9%	5790	12398	46.7%
Total	272454	412677	66%	349555	512313	68.2%	496975	685121	72.5%	571067	766431	74.5%	1690051	2376542	71.1%

Country	1990–95			1995–2000			2000–2005			2005–2010			1990–2010 (Totals)		
	High Talent	Total Migrants	% High Talent	High Talent	Total Migrants	% High Talent	High Talent	Total Migrants	% High Talent	High Talent	Total Migrants	% High Talent	Total High	Total Migrants	% High Talent
India to Canada	55500	105875	52.4%	76170	140015	54.4%	119540	194910	61.3%	157573	230499	68.4%	408783	671299	60.9%
India to US	208439	254435	81.9%	310501	375441	82.7%	563280	664439	84.8%	666595	778907	85.6%	1748815	2073222	84.4%
India to UK	51474	186802	27.6%	70421	192940	36.5%	83934	196520	42.7%	132822	267839	49.6%	338651	844101	40.1%
India to France	1361	5943	22.9%	1849	7434	24.9%	2207	7231	30.5%	3966	13491	29.4%	9383	34099	27.5%
India to Australia	22838	31257	73.1%	29630	39982	74.1%	32666	43063	75.9%	36183	46435	77.9%	121317	160737	75.5%
India to Germany	2794	19556	14.3%	3602	19651	18.3%	5797	21264	27.3%	9355	24063	38.9%	21548	84534	25.5%
Total	342406	603868	56.7%	492173	775463	63.5%	807424	1127427	71.6%	1006494	1361234	73.9%	2648497	3867992	68.5%

Country	1990–95			1995–2000			2000–2005			2005–2010			1990–2010 (Totals)		
	High Talent	Total Migrants	% High Talent	High Talent	Total Migrants	% High Talent	High Talent	Total Migrants	% High Talent	High Talent	Total Migrants	% High Talent	Total High	Total Migrants	% High Talent
China to Canada	37710	102020	37.0%	69435	137475	50.5%	114170	184615	61.8%	150494	219273	68.6%	371809	643383	57.8%
China to US	134213	249629	53.8%	187713	336723	55.7%	288624	507076	56.9%	308889	550991	56.1%	919439	1644419	55.9%
China to UK	2564	9305	27.6%	7801	14861	52.5%	9298	15780	58.9%	14714	22480	65.5%	34377	62426	55.1%
China to France	2643	9075	29.1%	3192	11624	27.5%	3809	11295	33.7%	9014	25612	35.2%	18658	57606	32.4%
China to Australia	29942	43374	69.0%	35455	53645	66.1%	39087	56686	69.7%	43296	58312	74.2%	147780	211417	69.9%
China to Germany	10143	18335	55.3%	12581	21148	59.5%	7771	28504	27.3%	21506	29952	71.8%	52001	97939	53.1%
Total	217215	431738	50.3%	316177	575476	54.9%	462759	803356	57.6%	547913	906620	60.4%	1544064	2717190	56.8%

Table 1.1. Male Brain Drain, Developing Countries
to OECD Countries, 1990–2010

This table has two goals: (1) to compare China's loss of talent to six members of the OECD—Canada, the US, the UK, France, Australia, and Germany—with that of the Philippines and India; and (2) to show the scale of the transfer of higher-quality talent from China to the US.

These three countries have lost an enormous amount of talent to the six OECD countries. Between 1990 and 2010, the Philippines lost 1.69 million talented people, India lost 3.4 million, and China lost 1.54 million talented people. Among the destination countries, the benefits to the US are outstanding. The US received 1.336 million talented people from the Philippines, 1.748 million people from India, and 919,439 talented people from China, giving the US four million talented people from just these three countries!

Second, between 1990 and 2010, China lost 1.544 million highly talented people to these six countries. Most of that loss has been to the US and Canada, with the US gaining 59.5 percent of China's talented outflow, while Canada received 24.0 percent.

Third, the absolute number of Chinese migrants to the US is significantly greater than that of any other recipient country. From 2005 to 2010, the US took in over 550,991 Chinese immigrants, of whom 308,889 were high-quality talents, making up 56.1 percent of the total inflow. As mentioned above, from 1990 to 2010, the US facilitated the immigration of 919,439 Chinese with some tertiary education. In comparison, from 2005 to 2010, Chinese immigration of high-quality talent to Australia, the UK, France, and Germany, relative to the US, was 14.0, 4.7, 2.9, and 7.0 percent, respectively.

Finally, China's loss of high-quality talent in the twenty years between 1990 and 2010 was less than the losses suffered by the Philippines and India. The three countries lost a total of 5.882 million high-talent people. Yet while the Philippines lost 28.7 percent of that total and India lost 45.0 percent, China's loss was only 26.2 percent. Thus, India lost much more talent than China. In total numbers, China's loss of high talent to the US is only 52.5 percent of India's.

Still, because of the enormity of its talent outflow to the US, China has focused a great deal of its attention since the late 1980s—and continues to today—on generating a wave of reverse migration from the US. And where that effort has failed, China has focused much of its effort on promoting the diaspora option from within the boundaries of the US.

Indeed, China needs these returnees. In 2008, when Li Yuanchao launched the Thousand Talents Plan (TTP), the CCP's preeminent recruitment program for overseas talent, China had 2.11 R&D researchers per 1,000 employees, compared to the average of OECD countries at 7.34, the US at 7.55, and Taiwan 10.58. As of 2020, China was still far behind, averaging 3.22 R&D researchers per 1,000 employees, as compared to the OECD average of 9.64, the US at 9.95, and Taiwan at 14.22.[21] According to the World Bank, while the OECD countries averaged 3,883 R&D researchers per million people in 2015, China had only 1,176 R&D researchers per million people.[22]

The Diaspora Option and Its Benefits

For developing countries that face a large brain drain, the "diaspora option" may narrow their scientific gap with the West and improve their economic, scientific, and social development.[23] Writing in 2003, Dickson argued that the high cost of the brain drain, and the difficulty of triggering a "reverse brain drain" in the third world, makes the "diaspora option" a moral necessity.[24]

Originally, the emphasis on the diaspora's role was on remittances, capital, and foreign investment, the theme of a 2004 World Bank conference that was organized to promote African development.[25] The bank encouraged governments to increase the flow of such funds back home by deregulating the process and cutting the costs of such transmissions.[26]

However, from the late 1990s, the focus shifted to human capital. In his 1998 Prebisch Lecture, Joseph Stiglitz, then chief economist of the World Bank, argued that development strategies needed to be geared toward creating capacities to absorb and adapt knowledge—a process that could be achieved through investments in human capital and technologies that facilitated the dissemination of knowledge and local knowledge creation.[27]

In 2010, the Migration Policy Institute analyzed how the diaspora could promote trade, tourism,[28] equity markets,[29] and economic growth in developing states by recycling to their homeland the "wealth of diasporas," including the savings, retirement funds, stocks, bonds, and trust funds that members of the diaspora had accumulated overseas.[30] And with the world engaged in a talent war, where scientific knowledge becomes a key component of national power, the diaspora can strengthen developing states by transferring patents, inventions, and research outputs.[31]

Network analysis highlights the importance of the diaspora.[32] Diaspora scientists cooperate largely with those in the home system, so the strengthening of China's scientific base through state investment in domestic research and development (R&D) has created strong incentives for diasporic Chinese to collaborate with China and for scholars in the PRC to seek overseas collaboration.[33]

Boyle and Kitchin outline six ways a diaspora can promote development: as aid donors, financial investors, knowledge networks and brokers, international market facilitators, brain circulators, and goodwill ambassadors.[34] This list highlights most of the key players—individuals, diaspora knowledge networks

(DKNs),[35] business, academic, alumni, or student associations, international organizations, universities, overseas scholars and entrepreneurs, and even second-generation migrants who transfer knowledge, finances, wealth, and technology on their own.

Focusing on the dissemination of knowledge, governments and international agencies bring nationals of a country back for short visits to transfer skills, information, and technology to the homeland. For example, the United Nations Development Plan's TOKTEN program, which stands for the "transfer of knowledge through expatriate nationals," was established in 1977 to help country nationals transfer their knowledge back to their homeland.[36] The Colombian Network of Scientists and Engineers Abroad—the "Caldas Network"—showed how a government could link with scientists overseas to improve science and technology development.[37] According to Meyer and Wattiaux, these DKNs "subverted the traditional 'brain drain,' migration outflow into a 'brain gain' of expatriates' skills by converting lost human resources into a remote though accessible asset of expanded networks."[38]

Many DKNs emerge spontaneously, driven by expatriates who desire to share their knowledge, business acumen, and overseas contacts with aspiring entrepreneurs back home. Possessing a strong ethnic identity, members of DKNs donate time and energy to attack development dilemmas in their homeland. They may also want to make some money. When these DKNs link with groups of people in the home country, they become what Faist calls "transnational social spaces."[39]

A particularly influential organization is the Indian TIE (The Indus Entrepreneurs), which has chapters all over the world and in six Indian cities. TIE helps Indian entrepreneurs set up shop in the US, transfers funds and know-how directly by setting up branch plants in India, and gives aid to poorer regions. It brings young Indian entrepreneurs to the US to enhance their business acumen.[40]

What else can states do?

Some states create new ministries or government departments dedicated to forging closer ties with their émigré populations. Consular or embassy officials may encourage or facilitate members of the diaspora to work with the homeland. Entrepreneurs and venture capitalists can set up companies, supply capital, or invest in existing firms in the homeland. Saxenian found that Indians, Israelis, Taiwanese, and mainland Chinese who had set up shop in Silicon Valley engaged in these efforts.[41]

Political factors are important if overseas citizens are to consider engaging with their homeland. A stable government, the rule of law, and good governance signal to the diaspora that the state will help them maximize their investments. In this vein, corruption is a hugely negative phenomenon. Local Indian officials are jealous of those who succeed overseas and feel no compunction against squeezing bribes from foreign investors,[42] an issue articulated by Indian entrepreneurs in Silicon Valley.[43] But by creating investment zones for diasporic capital, the government may shelter investors from the vicissitudes of the domestic bureaucracy.

States must simplify the mobility of members of the diaspora across their national boundaries, particularly those who have adopted foreign citizenship. In this regard, the Indian government demonstrated great flexibility.[44] In 2002 and 2005, India began offering Person of Indian Origin and Overseas Citizen of India cards, respectively. India allows Indians who maintain their Indian citizenship, but are residents in another country, to vote in elections and own property (other than agricultural land). One Chinese blogger heralded the prospect of an overseas Chinese card, noting that among Indians, the "11 million cards [as of 2010] have greatly promoted the return and circulation of talented Indians abroad."[45]

Conclusion

The diaspora option mitigates the brain drain of talented human capital because people who settle abroad gain knowledge that is unavailable in their home country or that would be extremely costly for their country to purchase. With this knowledge, they can promote their own careers in their host or home country. Without an outbound population that gained these skills by studying in OECD countries, working in overseas companies, or creating their own enterprises in the West, these developing countries would never have gained access to these new technologies at such a low cost.

However, this process carries risks for the economic and military security of the OECD countries and can generate anger if the foreign students and scholars, whom the advanced countries educate in the most up-to-date technologies, transfer those innovations to their home countries, creating products that challenge the OECD countries' economic or national security.

Little wonder, then, that the US government under Donald Trump created an initiative to stop that flow. But as we will see, that effort disrupted innocent Chinese who were living in the US and threatened Sino-US educational, scientific, technological, and medical exchanges.

2

CHINA UTILIZES ITS DIASPORA OPTION

Persons who are studying and working in other countries are, by various ways and means, serving China with the advanced science and technology and management knowledge they have acquired and are making contributions to our country's socioeconomic development. . . . The term, "overseas students serving China" means participation in various activities to promote China's economic and social development by overseas students who are presently studying abroad or who have completed their course of studies and are now working abroad, as well as by overseas student professional bodies.

> — 关于鼓励海外留学人员以多种形式为国服务的若干意见 ("A Number of Opinions on Encouraging Overseas Students to Provide China with Many Different Forms of Service)," *Renfa* (人发), no. 49 (2001).

"Overseas Chinese students are an important component of the ranks of talent (人才队伍)" and "also a new focal point of United Front work (也是统战工作新的着力点)."

> — Xi Jinping speech at the Chinese Communist Party United Front Work Department meeting, May 20, 2015.

China's Brain Drain

In 1978, Chinese leaders decided that if they wanted to catch up to the West, they needed to send people to the West to gain access to modern science, management, and technology.[1] The goal was to transform China quickly into a "powerful socialist country." As Deng Xiaoping said, "One must learn from those who are most advanced before one can catch up with and surpass them."[2] So Deng proposed sending ten thousand students abroad each year. However, due to resistance from the Ministry of Education (MOE), the policy was set at sending three thousand students a year for five years.[3] In 1984, China's cabinet, called the State Council (国务院), instituted a new regulation, which allowed anyone (except current graduate students) who could get foreign funding to study overseas, triggering a "fever" to study abroad that to this day has never abated.[4]

The West welcomed such an opening. In 1984, the US allowed spouses of Chinese students to join their partners, so students who were already overseas were able to apply for more advanced degree programs, as their spouses could support their studies.[5] In 1987 and 1988, many publicly funded Chinese students and scholars in the US found ways to shift from the more restrictive J-1 visa to the more flexible F-1 visa, allowing them to extend their stay almost indefinitely. In 1989 and 1990, the US, Canada, and Australia gave permanent residency to about one hundred thousand Chinese students in the wake of the June 4 military crackdown in Beijing (henceforth referred to as the Tiananmen Crackdown). In 2006, the US secretary of state, Condoleezza Rice, told US consulates worldwide to give out more student visas to increase funding for America's universities.[6] In 2013, the Netherlands, Denmark, and Sweden introduced scholarships to target talent and create opportunities to stay after graduation, while the Canadian government stipulated that the last two years of study in any degree program at a Canadian university could constitute the first two years—out of a total of five—needed for permanent residency.[7] Across the board, foreign universities, funding agencies like the Ford Foundation, international organizations like the World Bank, and foreign governments encouraged this outbound flow of talented Chinese.[8]

In 1978, Deng recognized the dangers of a "brain drain," but he miscalculated the potential loss of brain power that would occur. For him, a 10 percent loss would not be a problem. But the easier foreign governments made it for Chinese to stay abroad, the harder it became for China's government to bring them home.

China's own policies intensified the brain drain. In the early years of the opening, as funding for Chinese students from foreign organizations increased, China decreased its funding. In 1979, the People's Republic of China (PRC) government supplied 54 percent of the financial support for J-1 visa holders; however, that share dropped to 25 percent by 1984, and after 1985, the government's share hit 17 percent.[9] The conscious decision to underfund students and scholars "sent by the state" forced overseas students to seek assistance in their host countries, increasing their interactions with overseas institutions, which increased their tendency to stay.[10] A US government policy paper in 1988 decried the fact that "the consistent under-funding of officially sponsored Chinese students forces them to seek financial assistance elsewhere, rather than continue as PRC government funded students, and thus may contribute to development of ties which encourage them to remain abroad."[11]

Data show that the Chinese government left many of its own students and scholars on their own. In a survey, Chen Xuefei (陈薛飞), a professor of education at Peking University, asked 1,500 state-sponsored students who had returned to China about the source of financial support for their overseas education or research.[12] Among "government sponsored" scholars who were selected and approved by the MOE or the State Science and Technology Commission (SSTC), 62.3 percent of their funding came from China's government, while 33.3 percent came from foreign universities or donors, such as the World Bank. Students and scholars sent by their work units (called "publicly sponsored by units," or 单位公派) relied primarily on overseas agencies (70 percent), while their Chinese units only paid 18.7 percent of these scholars' costs.[13] In many cases, this may have been the price of the air ticket. For all 1,500 scholars, overseas agencies supplied 57.8 percent of the funds these people used to gain their overseas education, while China supplied only 30 percent. According to this report, "although people going overseas to study as state-sponsored scholars benefited from holding the title of 'state led,' they still relied primarily on foreign supplied funds as their major source of funding when they were overseas."[14] Thus, by 1985, the US was paying three times what the Chinese government was paying to train Chinese students abroad.

Political events exacerbated the problem. Following student protests in China in December 1986 and January 1987, and the purge of Hu Yaobang, a liberal reformer and general secretary of the CCP, in January 1987, hardliners in the CCP launched the "Campaign against Bourgeois Liberalization," which attacked Western values and freedoms in China. This campaign suggested to Chinese students in the US that Maoist-style political campaigns were not a thing of the past. The MOE, with the support of Deng Xiaoping, also introduced new regulations to constrain the outflow of students, particularly to the US.[15] The MOE stipulated that those who had been abroad for five years could only get a one-year extension on their passports; if they did not return, the passports would become invalid. In response, Chinese students in the US delivered a protest letter to the CCP.[16] The number of people applying for extensions increased in 1987 by 22 percent over 1986, the largest increase of any year between 1983 and 1991.[17]

The "brain drain" triggered an important policy debate in 1988 among leading officials and bureaucracies, which had significance for China's new diaspora.

According to an official who defected from the Chinese embassy in Washington due to the Tiananmen Crackdown, four perspectives were presented at a meeting in November of 1988 concerning how to deal with this problem.[18]

The MOE foolishly advocated that the government call back all students. The Ministry of Personnel, worried because returnees were having problems finding appropriate jobs, opposed any policy that would increase the return rate. The Overseas Chinese Affairs Office (侨务委员会) of the State Council, which was responsible for ties with the diaspora, hoped that some students would become US citizens, positioning them to influence the overseas Chinese community's perceptions of China. Finally, the SSTC wanted people to stay abroad and gain access to American high-tech, which they could eventually bring back to China.

According to this report, Zhao Ziyang, the liberal leader who had been elevated to the top post of CCP general secretary the year before, characterized scholars remaining abroad as part of a strategy of "storing brain power overseas." In his view, which was shared by the SSTC, these overseas PhDs would, over time, gain access to Western science and technology, which would make its way back to China.

The Tiananmen Crackdown of June 4, 1989, greatly exacerbated the brain drain (figure 2.1). Including scholars and their dependents, in the US, Canada, Australia, as well as other OECD countries, over one hundred thousand people received permanent residency. The Bush administration passed the 1992 "Chinese Student Protection Act," under which the US government gave out fifty thousand green cards. Canada gave permanent residency to eleven thousand Chinese students in Canada, while Australia gave residency to thirty-six thousand Chinese students.[19]

Data from Chinese sources in 1997 show that from 1978 to 1997, China's return rate was only 32 percent. The return rate for students "who had paid for their own studies" (自费) or received overseas funding was only 3.9 percent, which was a good measure of the brain drain since this cohort comprised 52.6 percent of all students or scholars who had gone abroad in those years. Among "sojourners" who had received some support from their home unit, 43.5 percent had not returned either. Finally, even among those fully funded by the Chinese government, who were called "state sponsored" (国家公派) sojourners, 17 percent had not returned. Overall, eight thousand state-sponsored scholars, forty thousand unit-sponsored, and 148,000 self-paying students and scholars, for a total of 196,000 students (66.9 percent), were still abroad as of 1997.

The brain drain persisted in the new millennium. A 2011 survey of 652 undergraduate, master's, and PhD students in the US found resistance to returning.[20] Among PhDs, 29.9 percent were definitely not returning, with 34.2 percent sitting on the fence. Thus overall, 64.1 percent were either not planning to return or were ambivalent about this decision.

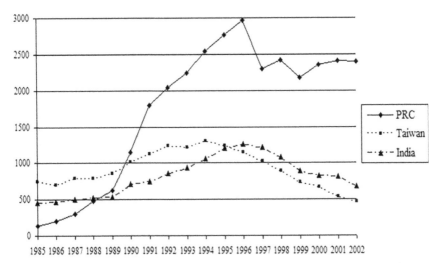

Figure 2.1. Non-US Citizens Awarded Doctorates in Science and Engineering: PRC, Taiwan, and India, 1985–2002.

Source: Science and Engineering Doctorate Awards, 2002 (SRS Home Page), October 2023.

Finn and his co-researchers, as well as the US National Science Board, have calculated the "stay rate" of Chinese students with PhDs in science and engineering (table 2.1).[21] The most recent data are for 2017. The assumption is that PhDs who were still in the US five years after receiving their PhD were likely to stay longer and form part of China's diaspora. And although the five-year stay rate among Indians surpassed China's in 2013 (85 percent versus 84 percent), the number of Chinese remaining in the US in 2013 was double the number of Indians—12,300 versus 6,300. Interestingly, the ten-year stay rate for Chinese, as of 2013, was greater than both India's and China's five-year rate, so as of 2013, there were at least eighteen thousand mainland Chinese working in the US.

What about the brain drain among the most valuable talent? According to the Center for Security and Emerging Technology (CSET) at Georgetown University, the long-term stay rates of PhDs in Science, Technology, Engineering, and Math (STEM) subjects is high.[22] In February 2017, approximately 90 percent of Chinese nationals and 87 percent of Indian nationals who completed STEM PhD programs in the US between 2000 and 2015 were still living in the country, well above the average of 77 percent for all STEM graduates. A plurality of Chinese graduates who completed their degrees between 2004 and 2011 gained permanent residency by February 2017, and among those who graduated before 2004, nearly half were naturalized US citizens. CSET estimates that as of 2018, return rates of Chinese with a PhD in a discipline related to artificial intelligence (AI) was still under 10 percent—the same as in 2014—leaving over 90 percent of all Chinese with a PhD in AI overseas, with most of them remaining in the US.[23]

Country/Region	2001	2003	2005	2007	2009	2011	2013	2015	2017
China	98	93	95	94	89	85	84	85	83
India	89	90	89	83	79	82	85	83	83
EU	53	63	67	67	60	62	63	64	71
Canada	66	63	60	56	53	55	-	-	-
South Korea	22	36	44	42	42	42	-	66	57
Japan	24	39	41	33	40	38	-	-	-
Taiwan	41	48	52	43	37	38	-	-	-
Mexico	31	22	32	33	35	39	-	-	-
Brazil	26	26	31	32	33	37	-	-	-
All Countries	58	64	67	63	62	66	70	70	71

Table 2.1. Five-Year Stay Rates in the US for Foreign Students on Temporary Visas Receiving S/E Doctorates, for Selected Countries, 2001–2017.

Source: For 2001–2013, see Michael Finn, *Stay Rates of Foreign Doctorate Recipients from US Universities, 2013* (January 2014), Oak Ridge Institute for Science and Education, https://www.osti.gov/biblio/1425458. For 2015, see National Science Board, *Science and Engineering Indicators, 2018*, https://www.nsf.gov/statistics/2018/nsb20181/report/sections/science-and-engineering-labor-force/immigration-and-the-s-e-workforce. For 2017, see National Science Board, *Science and Engineering Indicators, 2019*, https://ncses.nsf.gov/pubs/nsb20198/immigration-and-the-s-e-workforce.

Still, data show that China's problem is not less severe than many other countries. An index that measures the impact of the lost brain power on economic development (table 2.2) shows that China's index is well below the average index score for all countries and that 136 countries suffer more than China.

Country	Ranking	Index
Cambodia	62	6.3
Indonesia	75	6.0
India	98	5.2
Philippines	103	5.1
Vietnam	108	5.0
Mexico	114	4.6
Malaysia	118	4.4
China	137	3.5
Russia	142	3.5

Table 2.2. Brain Drain Data for Several Asian and Large Countries, 2022.

Note: The average score for 2022 based on 177 countries was 5.21.

Source: www.theglobaleconomy.com/rankings/human_flight_brain_drain_index/.

The Size of China's "New Diaspora"

The size of China's "new diaspora"—which is composed of Chinese who, since 1978, went abroad to study or work, or for internships, job transfers, or for family reunification, and chose not to return—is unclear. In 2001, Xiang estimated that there were 344,032 overseas Chinese professionals in the world, with 59 percent of them in the US.[24] According to the Ministry of Education (MOE), at the end of 2019, 5.86 million Chinese had studied abroad since 1978; 4.32 million had completed their studies, while 3.65 million had returned. By this calculation, 710,00 people who had gone abroad to study joined the diaspora.[25] Compared to 2018, the diaspora in 2019 had increased by thirty-eight thousand people. This number would not include those who went to work, who went for family reunification, or who just migrated. Wang Huiyao, president of the Center for China and Globalization, estimates that as of 2018, one million skilled or educated former mainlanders were living abroad.[26] Drawing on table 1.1 in the previous section, one can calculate that, as of 2010, the total number of former mainlanders with some tertiary education in the six OECD countries was 1.544 million.

The Chinese government waxed proudly about an overall rate of over 85 percent in 2021.[27] Still, the diaspora could be growing 20 percent a year, which is the gap between the number of students going overseas and those returning. Moreover, among the returnees in 2015, 80.7 percent were short-term MA students, rather than the valuable and scientifically adept PhDs, who made up only 9.5 percent in that year.[28] Thus, as Finn, the US National Science Bureau, and CSET have shown, many of the most talented Chinese being trained abroad are remaining abroad.

The Quality of Researchers in the Diaspora

The China-born scholars who live in the diaspora are remarkable. They comprise four of the top five—and five of the top ten—scientists doing material science in the US, though the share of China-born scientists declines as we look at the top twenty or top fifty.[29] Using the names of Chinese scientists written in pinyin to differentiate those born in China from those born elsewhere, Xie and Freeman argued that despite being relatively few in number, Chinese diaspora researchers accounted for a substantial proportion of journal articles, had a presence on many more articles, gained above average citations and publications in top journals, disproportionately coauthored with researchers in China, and were a key node in the flow of citations between China and the rest of the world.[30] Between 2000 and 2015, over 55,000 Chinese citizens graduated from STEM doctoral programs at American universities, accounting for nearly one-third of all international graduates. As of February 2017, approximately 50,000 of these graduates (90 percent) were still residing in the United States.[31] They also make up a very significant part of America's scientific research community. National Science Foundation (NSF) research indicates that out of the 6.75 million people working in the US science and technology sector around 2021, approximately 452,000 held doctoral degrees, and around 22.4 percent of these individuals, or over *one hundred thousand people*, were born in the PRC, a rather amazing number.[32]

China's "Diaspora Option": Serving the Nation from Abroad

As discussed in chapter 1, states hoping to utilize their diasporas need to invest in R&D that enhances the research conditions for those who remain in the diaspora but want to establish themselves back home. China has clearly done just that (table 2.3). The numbers in the brackets, which signify the share of investment for each country relative to US gross expenditure on R&D (GERD) in the same year, show that China has cut the gap with the US dramatically since the beginning of the 21st century. In 2001, China's spending was only 21 percent of American spending, but reached 52 percent by 2011, jumping to 72 percent four years later. As of 2021, it had reached 82 percent of US investment, getting much closer to parity. Such massive investments in infrastructure and education mean that researchers in the diaspora can access new modern laboratories and equipment and work with graduate students in China who can serve as inexpensive research assistants.

	1997	2001	2005	2009	2011	2015	2017	2019	2021
European Union	157.9 (0.74)	160.9 (0.57)	251.7 (0.77)	330.3 (0.81)	361.6 (0.84)	340.5 (0.67)	386.6 (0.68)	448.0 (0.66)	474.1 (0.59)
Japan	122.3 (0.57)	127.9 (0.46)	151.3 (0.46)	168.9 (0.42)	200.0 (0.46)	168.5 (0.33)	166.6 (0.30)	172.3 (0.25)	177.4 (0.22)
Republic of Korea	12.7 (0.06)	12.5 (0.04)	23.6 (0.07)	29.7 (0.07)	45.1 (0.10)	76.9 (0.15)	90.3 (0.16)	104.0 (0.15)	119.6 (0.15)
China	6.1 (0.03)	12.6 (0.04)	29.9 (0.09)	85.0 (0.21)	134.5 (0.31)	366.1 (0.72)	420.8 (0.74)	526.2 (0.74)	667.6 (0.82)
US	212.7	280.8	328.0	406.9	430.3	507.4	565.7	677.9	806.0
India	0.84 (0.003)	1.92 (0.006)	N/A N/A	6.36 (0.015)	7.2 (0.016)	10.44 (0.02)	12.36 (0.02)	15.0 (0.02)	15.2 (0.018)

Table 2.3. Global Expenditure in R&D
(GERD, current USD in billions), 1997–2021.

Notes
[1] The calculations are in 2015 USD.
[2] The value in parenthesis is the ratio of a country's GERD to US GERD in the same year.

Sources:
1. All data from 1997 to 2021, other than India, are from https://data.oecd.org/rd/gross-domestic-spending-on-r-d.htm.

2. For India, the source is *Research & Development Statistics at a Glance, 2022-23*, Department of Science & Technology, Ministry of Science & Technology, Government of India, https://dst.gov.in/document/reports/rd-statistics-glance-2022-23. Thanks to Vivek Kulkarni, CEO of Brickworks in Bangalore, India, for clarifying the Indian data. India saw a 46 percent increase in GERD between 2021 and 2022.

Ministries, commissions, and leaders have also introduced a plethora of policies targeted at persuading Chinese in the diaspora to help the nation, short of returning home (table 2.4). The following section describes some of the most important policies since the early 1990s.

Date	Agent	Content
1991	K.C. Wong Foundation	Starting in 1991, the KC Wong fellowship sponsored Overseas Chinese Professionals to return to China for work for at least two months. The program was expanded in 2003.[1]
10/1992	Jiang Zemin	At Fourteenth Party Congress, Jiang "warmly welcomed people who are studying overseas to use various ways to express concern, support and to participate in the motherland's modernization."[2]
02/1993	Central Committee and the State Council	First time put forward twelve-character slogan: "Support overseas studies, encourage returnees to China, grant the freedom to come and go."[3]
04/1996	MOE	Established "Spring Light Program" (春晖计划)[4]
10/1997	CCP General Secretary Jiang Zemin	At the Fifteenth Congress of the CCP, Jiang called for people to return even for a short visit and serve the country from overseas.[5]
1998	MOE	Enlarged the "Spring Light Program."
08/1998	MOE	Changjiang Scholars Program (长江学者) offered Chinese scientists living abroad a chance to return for one year in strategic research areas.[6]
11/2000	MOE document, no. 81	Agreed to pay overseas scholars up to five times their overseas salaries for returning during summer vacation.
05/2001	Ministries of Education, Science and Technology, Personnel, Finance, and Public Security (doc. 49)	"Serve the nation" (为国服务) without "returning to the nation" (回国服务), a policy to encourage Chinese who remained abroad to help China.[7]
04/2002	PSB, MOFA, MOE, MOHRSS, Labor, Foreign Trade, OCAO, etc.	Regulations simplified entry and exit for highly talented mainlanders and investors holding overseas citizenship.[8]

12/2003	China Association for Science and Technology (with MOHRSS and CCP-OD)	"Help our Motherland through Elite Intellectual Resources from Overseas Program" (海智)[9]
2006	MOHRSS	"Project to Introduce Talents in Academic Disciplines to Universities," also called "111 Project"[10]
2009	MOE and SAFEA	Chunhui Cup Competition (春晖杯)[11]
2009	MOHRSS	"Homeland Serving Action Plan for Overseas Chinese"[12] (海赤)
2010	Organization Department, CCP	Part-time Thousand Talents Plan
2010	State Council and Central Committee	Outline for the National Medium and Long-term Talent Development Plan (2010–2020)[13] called on the state to create databases of overseas talent (for targeting and recruitment) and promote technology transfer "using overseas talent."
11/2013	CCP General Secretary, Xi Jinping	At the one hundredth anniversary of the WRSA, he said that the CCP must ensure that "those who stayed abroad have a pathway to serve the state."[14]
05/2015	CCP General Secretary, Xi Jinping	"Overseas Chinese students are a new focal point of United Front work."[15]
2018	CCP General Secretary, Xi Jinping	Xi spoke of new concept of talent "that does not seek that they are here, only that they act." Called on CCP to "mobilize talents to engage in offshore innovation in foreign countries."[16]

Table 2.4. Key Statements and Policies to Mobilize the Diaspora, 1991–2018.

[1] Xiang Biao, *Promoting Knowledge Exchange through Diaspora Networks (The Case of People's Republic of China)*, ESRC Centre on Migration, Policy, and Society, University of Oxford, a report written for the Asian Development Bank, March 2005, 34.

[2] Jiang Zemin, 江泽民文选: 第一转 (Selected Works of Jiang Zemin: Volume One; Beijing: Renmin chubanshe, 2006), 234, cited in 崔晓麟, 张君 (Cui Xiaolin and Zhang Jun), "中国共产党吸引海外留学人员回国工作政策考察, 1978–1992" (Survey of CCP's policies on attracting overseas personnel to return to work in China), 三峡大学学报 (*Journal of Three Gorges University*), 第 39 卷, 第 4 期 (no. 39, vol. 4) (July 2017): 22.

[3] Miao, *Sixty Years of Overseas Study*, 371.

[4] 赵峰, 苗丹国, 魏祖钰, 程希 (Zhao Feng, Miao Danguo, Wei Zuyu, Cheng Xi), eds., 留学大事概览, 1949–2009 (An Overview of Overseas Study, 1949–2009). 北京: 现代出版社, 2010, 86.

[5] Miao, *Sixty Years of Overseas Study*, 881.

[6] https://en.wikipedia.org/wiki/Changjiang_Scholars_Program.

[7] Ministries of Personnel, Education, Science and Technology, Public Security and Finance. See "人事部, 教育部, 科技部, 公安部, 财政部关于印发 "关于鼓励海外留学人员以多种形式为国服务地若干意见" 的通知" (Number of Opinions on Encouraging Overseas Students to Provide China with Many Different Forms of Service), 14 May 2001 (人发, No. 49, 2001), in *Chinese Education and Society*, vol. 36, no. 2 (March/April 2003): 6–11.

[8] Miao, *Sixty Years of Overseas Study*, 889.

[9] Miao, *Sixty Years of Overseas Study*, 483.

[10] Spear, in Hannas and Tatlow, 31–32.

[11] 第十七节 '春晖杯' 中国留学人员创新创业大赛真是启动 (The Seventeenth Round of the Competition for the "Chunhui Cup for Innovation and Entrepreneurship" is Officially Announced), April 24, 2021, https://www.cscse.edu.cn/cscse/index/xwdt/2022042108450125636/index.html.

[12] https://chinatalenttracker.cset.tech/static/cset_chinese_talent_program_tracker.pdf, p. 6, and Spear, "Serve the Motherland While Working Overseas," 25.

[13] The list of key components of the Talent Development Plan is from Jeffrey Stoff, "China's Talent Programs," in Hannas and Tatlow, 41.

[14] 习近平在欧美同学会成立100周年庆祝大会上讲话（全文）(Xi Jinping's speech at the 100th Anniversary of the Western Returnees Scholars Association, 新华网 (*Xinhuanet*), October 21, 2013, http://www.chinanews.com/gn/2013/10-21/5406110.shtml.

[15] 习近平: 巩固发展最广泛的爱国统一战线 ("Xi Jinping: Consolidate and Develop the Broadest Patriotic United Front"), Xi Jinping speech at the CCP United Front Department meeting, May 20, 2015, https://www.xinhuanet.com/politics/2015-05/20/c_1115351358.htm, found at Wayback.

[16] "习近平在全国组织工作会议的讲话" (Xi Jinping speech at National Organizational Work Conference), July 3, 2018, www.12371.cn/2018/09/17/ARTI1537150840597467.shtml, found at Wayback.

In 1987, Hong Kong entrepreneur Wang Kuancheng (K. C. Wong) supported lectures in China by scientists in the diaspora, and in 1991, he established the K. C. Wong Education Foundation Fellowship for Short-term Returnees. Managed by the Chinese Academy of Sciences (CAS), its goal was to encourage collaboration between China-based scholars and overseas Chinese researchers by funding return visits to China to work for at least two months. In 2003, the number of beneficiaries increased 25 percent (from approximately seventy to ninety-five people a year), with total funding of RMB 1.5 million (USD181k).[33]

Three years after the Tiananmen Crackdown, Deng's visit to the south of China transformed the post-Tiananmen environment. The idea of utilizing the talent in the diaspora emerged in 1992, when Chen Shujin, a researcher at the Chinese Academy of Social Sciences, writing in 科技导报 (*Science and Technology Review*), called on the government to translate and publish in China important articles written by overseas mainlanders who were not returning to China. He also called on their original home units in China to invite the Chinese staying abroad back to speak.[34]

In March 1993, the Fourth Plenum of the Twelfth Party Congress outlined a twelve-character principle to govern overseas study and relations with diasporic researchers: "support overseas study, encourage them to return, but give them the freedom to come and go" (支持留学, 鼓励回国, 来去自由). Thereafter, people abroad became more interested in visiting to see whether China had indeed improved, and the state began to introduce policies focusing on getting Chinese overseas to "serve the country."[35]

Between 1992 and 1995, the MOE brought 1,200 people back to "serve the country" (为国服务) in some form.[36] At the Eighth National People's Congress in spring 1993, Prime Minister Li Peng's work report welcomed overseas scholars to use "a variety of methods" (多种形式) to participate in rebuilding the motherland. And in February 1996, Li, a conservative on the issue of sending students abroad, recognized that some people remained abroad because they had good jobs. "This," he said, "was all understandable."[37]

The "Spring Light Program" (春晖计划) was the first government policy to mobilize the diaspora. On April 25, 1996, an enlarged MOE, then called the State Education Commission (SEDC), published a document called "Implementation Measures for Special Funds for Overseas Students Studying Abroad Returning to China for Short-term Work."[38] Reportedly, in early 1995, Chinese students in Germany proposed to the SEDC that they visit China, so in May 1995, the SEDC brought a delegation of students back from Germany for consultations about how to encourage more people to return.[39]

During their visit, they donated a plaque embossed with a passage from a famous Chinese poem that asked how a small child, nourished like young tender grass, can ever repay their parents' love, which shines upon them like the "springtime sun."[40] So, the Spring Light Program became official policy in 1996; in 1997, six hundred scholars visited China, and funding increased in 1998. While Wei Yu, writing in 2000, said that the Spring Light Program was part of the state's strategy to convince overseas students to return full-time, it was the forerunner of the May 2001 policy encouraging "serving the nation from abroad," rather than being pressed by the CCP to return full-time.[41]

In April 1996, following the successful visit of the students from Germany, the Foreign Affairs Bureau of the MOE set out the terms of the Spring Light Program,[42] and in November 1997, the first official delegation of overseas mainlanders visited China under this program.[43] While six hundred students and scholars came in 1997, in 2000, the program was expanded by encouraging people to come during their summer break.[44]

In 1996, Lin Qitan of the State Council's Development Research Center in Shanghai called on Shanghai to tap what he called the "Think Tank of Overseas

Chinese" to promote the city's development.[45] CCP General Secretary Jiang Zemin reinforced this position in October 1997 when, at the Fifteenth Congress of the CCP, he called for people to return even for a short visit to serve the country.[46] In 1999, Wang Xi, a professor at Indiana University of Pennsylvania, argued that many overseas mainlanders were working on "bellwether projects" and were willing to exchange information with friends and colleagues in China. He advised the government to create a data bank of students abroad, establish long-term stable exchanges with them, and collate their research achievements that were in the public realm.[47]

Other programs also mobilized people in the diaspora. In May 1998, Jiang Zemin gave a significant speech at the Great Hall of the People in Beijing, commemorating the one hundredth anniversary of the founding of Peking Univerity,[48] and in October, the MOE introduced the Changjiang Scholars Plan (长江学者计划, or CJSP) in collaboration with Li Ka-hsing's Cheung Kong conglomerate in Hong Kong, which included a part-time component as part of its original program.[49]

The State Administration of Foreign Experts Affairs (SAFEA) brought foreign specialists to work in China, and since the vast majority of SAFEA participants from Canada were born in China and had studied and stayed in Canada, this program morphed into another form of "brain circulation."[50] In 1994, China's Natural Science Foundation (国家自然科学基金, or NSFC) began giving twenty to thirty awards a year—some as high as RMB 500,000 or USD 95,500)—to mainlanders living abroad, calling them "exemplary young researchers"; the stipulation was that they had to spend the money in China.[51] In November 2000, an MOE document promised overseas scholars as much as five times their overseas salaries if they returned during the summer, and at the end of 2000, the Ministry of Foreign Affairs issued multiple entry visas to overseas students and scholars so they could travel back and forth easily.[52] According to another report, between 1996 and May 2003, the Chinese government helped over seven thousand individuals and over fifty groups of overseas mainlanders come back to "serve the country."[53]

Writing in 2000, the then deputy minister of education encouraged people to work overseas for a long period of time if they were on the front lines of scientific research, improving their access to information, funding, and advanced research conditions.[54] Also, by returning to work even for a short term, they could help China's research "walk along" (同步) with world-class research. In his eyes, this strategy was irreplaceable, though he might really have been defending the part-time component of the CJSP, which had emerged, along with the full-time program, in 1998. This policy was also presented as the outcome of the "twelve-point slogan," which offered the opportunity to "come and go freely."

Finally, he supported researchers having "two bases" (两个基地), one abroad and one in China, rather than picking one or the other location. This idea would become highly problematic around 2018, when the US and the NIH saw having academic posts in both the US and in China as "double dipping" that was likely to lead to technology transfer that the US government wanted to constrain.

Many other organizations in China joined the fray, organizing visits to encourage talented mainlanders living abroad to see how China had changed since June 4 and to find partners for research projects with organizations in China.[55] A world-class specialist on Alzheimer's in my Vancouver focus group told me that in 1999, after she had been out of China for over ten years, the Overseas Chinese Affairs Office (OCAO) brought her to a conference on psychiatry.[56] Amazed by the positive changes that had taken place in China, she returned a few times that year and thereafter returned about ten times per year.

After encouraging so many people to come to visit or return part-time, China was ready to focus on the benefits of "brain circulation" rather than the costs of the "brain drain."[57] This way, "brains" that had been "drained" overseas could serve "national self-strengthening" through a new form of engagement.

So, in May 2001, China introduced a new policy that incorporated China's "new diaspora" into the national development strategy. Document 49 (2001), authored by the Ministries of Personnel, Education, Science and Technology, Public Security, and Finance, encouraged people and their organizations in the diaspora to participate in China's scientific and academic development "in numerous ways" (多种形式).[58] It called for mainlanders overseas to "serve the nation" (为国服务), even if they did not "return to the nation to help" (回国服务). Boyle and Kitchin define this "diaspora-centered development" as "a formal and explicit policy initiative or series of policy initiatives enacted normally by a sending state, or its peoples, aimed at fortifying and developing relationships with expatriate communities, diasporic populations, and foreign constituencies who share *a special affinity*" (emphasis added).[59] In adopting this perspective, China joined many developing countries that, through the "diaspora option," encourage citizens who have settled abroad to help their motherland.[60]

This policy encouraged seven types of activities:

1. utilize the advantages of their professional bodies;

2. hold concurrent positions in China and overseas;[61]

3. engage in cooperative research in China and abroad;

4. return to China to teach and conduct academic and technical exchanges;

5. set up enterprises in China;

6. conduct inspections and consultations; and

7. engage in intermediary services, such as running conferences, importing technology or foreign funds, or helping Chinese firms find export markets.[62]

China called on organizations of overseas students to "give full play to their collective advantages in developing various activities in the service of China."[63] Miao says this document shifted previous government efforts to encourage reverse migration into an "unprecedented" (空前) era.[64] In Eastern Europe, in 2001, China employed "united front" (统战) tactics to encourage overseas students and scholars to contribute to the motherland, mobilizing people to join pro-mainland organizations, meeting regularly with these associations, informing them about changes on the mainland, and asking them to help China.[65] To show that their view of people who refused to return had changed, they called members of the new diaspora "patriotic." Still, the Chinese education consul in Los Angeles in 2004 argued that people in the diaspora would cooperate with China only in their own self-interest, not out of patriotism.[66]

Consuls in the education and science sections of consulates in the West began encouraging overseas mainlanders to participate in research projects at home.[67] For example, in December 2001, the science consul in China's Los Angeles consulate led a delegation of thirty-four overseas professors from the Chinese American Professors/Scholars Network to the Fourth International Science-Tech Convention for Overseas Scholars and Professionals in Guangzhou.[68] Chen and Liu, believing that consulates were critical tools for utilizing former students in the diaspora, called for the expansion of the education sector in Chinese consulates.[69] In 2003, consular officials organized meetings where delegations from China described conditions on the mainland, introduced delegations to student organizations, or arranged meetings with successful overseas scholars.[70]

This new policy yielded results. In 2002, Shu Huiguo, the vice minister of personnel, said that one hundred thousand students and scholars had helped the motherland develop without resettling.[71] In 2003, Chen Xuefei et al. estimated that 25 percent of China-born ethnic professionals working abroad were "serving the country" in some form.[72] Xiang, writing in March 2005, looked at the curriculum vitae of 130 overseas Chinese professionals randomly selected from more than twenty thousand CVs held by the OCAO and found that 52.7 percent had "stable academic or commercial connections with China-based institutes," almost 15 percentage points higher than the 38.9 percent reported by the OCAO.[73] In 1993, seven years before this policy, Zweig and Chen had found that only 21.4 percent of 197 China-born students and scholars interviewed in the US exchanged research data with their former work unit.[74] Clearly, the 2001 policy on serving the country from abroad had led many more people to help.

In June 2010, China's leaders introduced a new plan to promote human talent called the Outline for the National Medium and Long-term Talent Development Plan, 2010–2020 (国家中长期人才发展规划纲要).[75] For several years, Chinese officials had been developing a "strategy for creating a country that is powerful in talent" (人才强国战略), so when this plan was rolled out, all of China's top leaders attended the meeting. The plan committed to spending 15 percent of GDP promoting talent, including getting overseas talent to establish businesses in China, continuing recruitment programs and replicating them at local levels, creating databases of overseas talent "for targeting and recruitment," and promoting "technology transfer using overseas talent."

The Strategies

This section shows how China implements its policy on "serving from abroad."

Holding Fairs in China for Diaspora Researchers and Entrepreneurs

One way was to encourage overseas researchers and entrepreneurs to attend talent fairs around the country.

The Overseas Chinese Scholars Fair in Guangzhou (广州海外华人学者交流会) was begun by the local government in 1997, but under the MOE, it became the largest annual event linking thousands of overseas entrepreneurs with domestic firms and high-tech zones. Following the establishment of the TTP in 2008, the fair was organized by the CCP's Organization Department, with continued involvement by the MOE. The twenty-first meeting of the fair in 2019 included over two thousand overseas researchers from over thirty countries, including the US, the UK, Canada, Australia, Japan, Germany, France, and Russia, who brought with them 1,761 projects.[76] Domestic participants included 126 government delegations, 116 universities, and research institutes and firms, which were looking for talented people to fill 14,790 positions. At this event, and at similar fairs around the country, overseas researchers post the fruits of their research on bulletin boards for domestic participants to see. Face-to-face meetings are then scheduled.

Pudong's Zhanjiang high-tech zone has been running an annual program for more than a decade, reflecting Shanghai's effort to tap into the diaspora. The high-tech zone was established in 1992. In 2007, the zone established a Returnees' Association, which runs the fair.[77] According to the association's director, Chen Dong, three hundred people from overseas applied to attend the fair that year. Although he had planned to limit participation to the fifty best people and the fifty best projects, intense demand led him to expand attendance to eighty people. The program had been relatively successful; over the previous eight years, 18 percent of attendees (eighty out of 450) had opened a company in Pudong. If one included the firms established elsewhere in China, the success ratio was close to 50 percent, as many attendees who wanted to be in that region of China, but who found costs in Shanghai prohibitive, set up shop in one of two zones in nearby Suzhou.

As start-ups may fail, Director Chen only recruited entrepreneurs with established companies overseas. Among attendees from these firms, 15 percent were the founder or chairman of the board, 16 percent were the chief executive officer or general manager, 26 percent were vice chairs, 26 percent were the chief technical officer who facilitated technology transfer, and the rest made up another 11 percent.

Director Chen preferred people who were forty-five or older, and he did not want recent postdocs who would have limited experience creating start-ups. Fifty eight percent had PhDs, 30 percent had MAs, 2 percent had been postdocs, and 10 percent had only an undergraduate degree. Seventy-seven percent came from North America, 12 percent from Europe (including the UK), 3 percent from Australasia, and 8 percent from Southeast Asia. The program gave RMB 6,000 to those coming from North America or Europe, RMB 3,000 to participants from East Asia, and RMB 1,000 to those from within China. The district promised tax breaks to new firms, and anyone investing over USD 50,000 was promised permanent residence status.

The name of the game was networking. At one event, overseas attendees sat down in a large ballroom and carried out one-on-one discussions with domestic venture capital firms or local companies who were looking for projects. Over several hours, people rotated, discussing their plans and, of course, exchanging business cards, or cellphone connections, such as *Weixin*.

One attendee I chatted with hated the CCP but felt it incumbent to consider moving some of his businesses back to China. A second participant was a citizen of an EU country who traveled frequently to Beijing, where the company for which he worked had relocated its technology. His wife too worked for an EU company in Beijing, so they were exploring a possible return to China. Still, he felt settled in Europe and worried about working closely with the Chinese government if he returned. A third attendee had recently moved to Guangzhou after twenty-two years in the US, where she worked for a company that uses genome technology to produce cosmetics for celebrities in Beverly Hills. She was planning to set up a company in Shanghai.

Director Chen was particularly interested in medical innovations and cutting-edge medicines, as Pudong had set up a "Medicine Valley" (药谷). The sectoral breakdown of attendees mirrored this strategy, with 14 percent in the biomedical sector, 5 percent in physical materials, 10 percent in IT, 56 percent in finance, 8 percent in microelectronics, and 5 percent in energy and environment.

Business Engagement and Technology Transfer

Entrepreneurs were invited to invest in China, expand its exports, or transfer technology developed abroad back to China. As of 2004, 42 percent of Chinese—including mainlanders, Hong Kongers, and Taiwanese—who ran their own businesses in Canada were "transnational entrepreneurs" who built their businesses in Canada by trading goods, services, technology, knowledge, and culture between Canada and their home region. The businesses included trade, finance, telecommunications, tourism, education, media, and immigration services.[78] As ethnic entrepreneurs, they were willing to be bridge builders, matchmakers, or intermediaries between Canada and their home region. Chinese local governments sometimes paid for their visits and accommodations. As one informant reported:

> Within one year, I visited more than twenty cities and met at least eight leaders at the highest level, including governors and ministers. . . . They rolled out the red carpet for us. Wherever we went, there were always motorcycle escorts, welcoming parades, and huge banquets. All these made us feel very excited.[79]

Gaps in the market in China motivated business engagement. One of Chen's informants told her, "I am excited to see that the data mining industry in China is almost blank. . . . I sense there is a niche for me."[80]

By the turn of the century, overseas students had accumulated the financial or technical wherewithal to invest in China. The Chinese government saw these people as more willing than other foreigners to set up firms in China, partly because of the ethnic comfort of doing business with their former (and maybe future) homeland, and they were more willing to transfer technology back to China, a target of the program to "strengthen the country through science and education" (科教兴国). Some overseas mainlanders who designed a technology, but whose employers owned the technology, ignored patent laws, setting up shop in China to benefit from their own creativity.[81] These firms annually saved China billions by introducing technology that otherwise would have been imported or whose patents would otherwise had to have been purchased. Likewise, because they possessed leading overseas technologies, many firms had comparative advantage in China's domestic market.

To see how businesspeople in the diaspora promoted China's modernization at the turn of the millennium, I use data compiled in 2001 by Dr. Annalee Saxenian of the University of California, Berkeley, who, through contacts with immigrant associations in Silicon Valley, obtained responses from 386 Chinese entrepreneurs and employees about their links with the mainland.[82] While the data are old, they suggest who is likely to serve China from abroad today.

Among this group, 69 percent had come to the US between 1990 and 1999, and another 19.4 percent had come in the 1980s. The vast majority (79 percent) had attended college in the US and stayed on, while 9 percent had been brought to the US by American companies. Eighty-nine percent had scientific, technical, or engineering degrees, and 82 percent had earned their highest degree in the US. Two-thirds were technical professionals in nonmanagerial positions.

Those who owned their company, were more willing to share technology with China. Among all the respondents, 19.5 percent "regularly" exchanged technology, with 28 percent of company owners doing so, as compared to 15.8 percent of nonowners, while another 56.5 percent of owners "sometimes" shared technology, showing that if mainlanders owned a company, some of their technology flowed back to China. Additionally, those considering setting up a company in China engaged more, with 23 percent "regularly" exchanging technology with colleagues on the mainland, much more than the 9 percent who were not considering setting up a company.

Among respondents, 33 percent had helped "bridge" business contacts in China, with 61 percent of company owners and 22 percent of nonowners having done so. Among company owners, 32 percent had consulted for Chinese companies, but only 8 percent of nonowners played this role. In these early days, overseas mainlanders were not yet an important source of capital for China. Among 117 company owners, 15 percent had invested once in a start-up in China, while 14 percent had invested more than once. Out of 267 nonowners, only 3 percent had invested in a start-up.

The "Servers"

Who in Silicon Valley was "serving China" (为国服务)? I broke those who engaged in activities mentioned by the Chinese government in its 2001 policy into four groups based upon the number of activities they carried out. I also compared "servers" and "non-servers" and sought differences among the "servers." Of the 386 respondents, 179 (46 percent) had responded that they carried out one of four types of engagement, with one hundred employing one mode, forty-eight employing two, nineteen doing three, while twelve partook in four.[83]

"Servers" were older; in the cohort ranging from thirty-six to fifty years old, "servers" outnumbered "non-servers" by 10 percent. Fewer women were "servers," and the percentage of women declined among those who were more active. Immigration status was important; US citizens comprised 40 percent of "servers" and only 29 percent of "non-servers," but among those holding US permanent residency, 40 percent were "non-servers," while only 30 percent were "servers." MBAs and PhDs were more likely to engage China than other degree holders, while managers or executives in corporations were more likely to work with China than those with professional or technical skills. Among ninety-two executives and managers, 72 percent "served" China, while 28 percent did not.

Participation in professional associations made one more likely to serve China, either because the organization encouraged involvement or because those who wanted to work with China joined such organizations. Among those "servers" using two or more modes, 41 percent attended professional meetings once or more a month, while 60 percent attended meetings at least four times a year.

Owning a company increased the likelihood of being a "server," while 60 percent of people planning to open a company engaged China versus 46 percent of "non-servers." Likewise, those considering returning to China were actively building relationships that could help them if they returned. Among those who said they are "quite likely to return," 21 percent were serving, while non-servers comprised only 8.5 percent of this group. Among the twelve people who were most active, ten were "quite likely to return." Knowing a returnee made one more likely to serve—perhaps these returnees formed the channels through which the "servers" served.

A New Young Business Diaspora

In 2018, when I visited Silicon Valley, the United States Trade Representative under the Trump administration was investigating if Chinese firms in the US were illegally transferring proprietary technology to China, making a survey impossible. In fact, the heads of Chinese business associations refused to meet. But a new group in the Chinese diaspora that emerged after 2010, composed of young people who went abroad in their mid-twenties to get an MA/MSc/MBA in the West and stayed on, were willing to chat. These younger mainlanders are part of a growing population of people with excellent skills who enhance the cooperation of Western companies with China. Some also help Chinese companies establish a foothold in the West.[84] In 2018, I met a China-born informant in Silicon Valley, who went to college in the US, worked for an Iranian American entrepreneur and hosted companies from China that were looking for start-up technology firms in which to invest in Silicon Valley.[85]

Another entrepreneur I interviewed in April 2018 earned an MA in electrical engineering and a second degree in computer science in the US. She graduated in 2010, and while working with IBM and Goldman-Sachs, she created her own software at night. When I spoke with her by phone from her home in New Jersey, she and her partner were having difficulties raising funds from China for their project, because Chinese investors wanted to see "traction" first.

Another interview was with a thirtysomething entrepreneur who had graduated with an MBA from Stanford University. He had been traveling to China for ten years, but with a young child and a Taiwanese wife, he had no plans to move back. He believed he is most valuable in the diaspora, where he can build a client base, but he needs to frequently return to learn from China about how to link the apparel business to e-commerce. He helped his buyers in the US upgrade China's "just-in-time" apparel manufacturing. Interestingly, he would not join any Chinese business associations, believing that they encourage their members to deviate from proper business norms.[86]

Organizing Overseas Organizations

After "serving the country" became national policy in 2001, ministries and national organizations, including the MOE, the Ministry of Human Resources and Social Security (MOHRSS), the China Association for Science and Technology (CAST), and the SAFEA brought technology produced by Chinese researchers in the OECD countries to industrial enterprises or to high-tech zones in China.[87] These efforts probably intensified after China introduced its "Made in China, 2025" policy in early 2015, so most of the transferred technology was to improve China's position in global production chains, although some technologies had both industrial and military applications.

In 2006, the Chinese Service Center for Scholarly Exchange (中国留学服务中心— CSCSE) established a link between overseas entrepreneurs and top projects with local enterprises, which became the "Chunhui Cup" (春晖杯). In 2019, supervisors shortlisted 301 projects, mostly from the US (eighty), the UK (forty-two), Australia (twenty-eight), Canada (twenty-four), France (sixteen), Japan (fourteen), Germany (thirteen), Singapore (ten), and Switzerland (ten). Most projects were in automation, new materials, new energy, and biotech. From 2006 to 2018, 2,628 projects were short-listed, of which 448 (17 percent) relocated to China, and by 2023, the program had selected 3,424 "excellent" projects.[88]

Under the "Program of Introducing Discipline-Based Talent to Universities" (高等学校学科创新引智计划—the 111 Project), which SAFEA and the MOE launched in 2006, China would establish one hundred innovation bases at top universities by gathering one thousand overseas scholars from the top one hundred universities and research institutions worldwide.[89] The project included 143 innovation bases (126 formal bases and seventeen seed bases) from seventy-two universities. Each base received RMB 1.8 million (USD 269,000) annually for five years. China planned to invest RMB 600 million (USD 90 million) in the project. China may have recruited 4,120 foreign intellectuals.

Cai Hongxing describes three "innovation bases" established in 2006, 2007, and 2008 at Peking University under the 111 Project, in the School of Life Sciences, Peking University Health Science Center, and the College of Chemistry and Molecular Engineering, respectively.[90] Recruitment occurred through three channels: (1) distinguished, overseas Chinese scholars were identified by domestic universities and experts and then contacted directly; (2) some were found haphazardly through international conferences; and (3) some were found through alumni and former colleagues' relationships. Fifty-five percent of participants (twelve out of twenty-two) on the Chinese side had an overseas PhD.

Under the 111 Project, the faculty at the Peking University centers and their overseas collaborators published over fifty papers in international journals, which was due in part to the creation of a world-class research environment. In 2008 and 2009, over two hundred overseas experts visited one center and gave 170 lectures; this center hosted sixteen international and bilateral conferences; over twenty China-based faculty members visited overseas institutions.[91]

Spear sees the 111 Project as a strategy to get overseas scholars to share their knowledge on strategic issues with military-linked academic institutions in China. Several projects he cites are run at universities that foreign intelligence agencies believe have close ties to the People's Liberation Army (PLA) and whose graduates are now barred from doing research in the US.[92] One project set up a base on advanced materials for aerospace propulsion at Beihang University (北航大学), which has close ties to the PLA.[93] The base at Harbin Engineering University (哈尔滨工程大学) researched advanced ceramics and deep-sea engineering, both of which have military applications.

In December 2023, during a trip to Beijing, I questioned the participation of the above-mentioned institutions, i.e., Beihang University and Harbin Engineering University, in Project 111, suggesting that their close ties with the PLA, and the scope of the research, raised troubling questions about whether Project 111, and some of its cooperative projects, were being utilized for military modernization. The director of a Chinese research center told me that such linkages were no longer a problem, as SAFEA had been absorbed into the Ministry of Science and Technology (科学技术部 or MOST), and that Project 111 had ended. However, the project was very much alive. The unit which drafted the "2020 National Foreign Expert Project Application Guide" was the Bureau of Foreign Expert Services (外国专家服务司) which, as of June 2020, was still managing applications for Project 111, despite being absorbed into the MOST in March 2018. The program was still called the "Higher Education Curricula Innovation and Intellect Recruitment Program (111 Program)" (高等学校学科创新引智计划 [111计划]), and the main application units were central and local institutions of higher education.[94] And while the project's guidelines emphasized that foreign and Chinese units would engage in "high-level talent training, and high-quality academic exchanges to promote the establishment of 'world-class curricula' (一流学科)," the project was also expected to "carry out high-level cooperative research, and enhance the technological innovation capabilities" of institutions of higher education.

In December 2003, CAST, with the help of the MOHRSS and the CCP's Organization Department, established the "Help Our Motherland through Elite Intellectual Resources from Overseas Program" (海外智力为国服务行动计划), also called the "HOME Program" or "Haizhi" (海智).[95] As of 2017, this program had links with ninety-six science and technology groups overseas, forty-seven of them in the US. According to Spear, as of that year, CAST had held 1,012 "intellect recruitment docking activities," yielding 1,099 signed cooperation agreements, and had negotiated 5,928 start-up projects, of which 1,267, or 21.4 percent, relocated back to China from overseas. It had also sent 232 groups overseas to recruit potential participants.

A second phase of this program promotes technological innovation overseas in "Offshore Innovation and Entrepreneurial Bases for Overseas Professionals," and then monetizes it once it is transferred to a commercial enterprise in China.[96] This model was tested in five cities in 2014, then expanded to five more in 2016. An article on the CCP's United Front Work Department's (UFWD) website emphasized the protection of the property rights of these products.

According to the director of personnel of the high-tech zone in Chengdu, Sichuan Province (CHTZ), home to one of the first five bases, "The overseas talents will not have to stay in the Chengdu high-tech zone. They can just do research overseas and achieve their scientific research at the high-tech zone's overseas centers."[97] The zones will also subsidize the overseas work, commercialize the product, and manage the firm for the Chinese counterpart. As of 2016, the CHTZ had four overseas bases, with one in Frankfurt, Germany, and one in Copenhagen, Denmark. By July 2019, the CHTZ had reportedly established thirty-one overseas centers in Korea, Japan, the US, and the EU linked to its "innovation and entrepreneurial base" within the larger zone.[98] An overseas center linked to the CHTZ in San Diego focuses on biotechnology and medical instruments, with the biotech projects managed by a Chinese professional association based in San Diego, while the equipment projects are administered in San Diego by an overseas subsidiary of a Chinese company in Guangzhou.

Under the "Homeland-Serving Action Plan for Overseas Chinese Project" (海外赤子为国服务行动计划), the MOHRSS encourages overseas students and experts to return to China for short-term visits and work.[99] First raised in 2009, and officially launched in 2010, the program attracts over one thousand overseas graduates and experts annually, and since its inception, has involved as many as one hundred thousand individual projects. "Overseas talent connection stations" (海外人才联络站) help promote this program.

The plan's six subcategories function at different administrative levels from Beijing, at the provincial and municipal levels and through self-organized groups of overseas students sponsored by MOHRSS. Initially, these "homeland-serving projects" focused on poverty alleviation but then began to include projects in more high-tech industries (linked to "Made in China, 2025") and projects under Xi's massive overseas investment and development project, the Belt and Road Initiative.[100]

The MOHRSS provides these projects with special benefits and guidance. In 2016, Ningxia Province held an "homeland-serving project" forum to attract more young professionals and overseas students to work on a Belt and Road Initiative.[101] The Ningxia project covered a wide range of topics including high-tech industries, international trade, online transactions, green agriculture, social welfare, and youth responsibility.[102] A special fund under the MOHRSS pays their travel costs while supplying professional information and helping them to get visas.

Many provincial and city-level governments have detailed records on what programs the "homeland-serving project" supports. Beijing had a project in 2010 to upgrade its industry. Hebei Province, in 2015, invited experts from the University of Tennessee to solve pollution problems. Still, few records outline the levels of local engagement.

One source in 2018 showed that the "homeland-serving project" had, up to that point, supported 502 projects with a total value of RMB 114.8 million,[103] while my own data show that the number of projects each year remains between thirty and forty-two, while the number of participants fluctuates from one thousand to twenty thousand annually.[104] In total, I found that over seventy-three thousand people participated through 267 projects.

As mentioned above, the OCAO encouraged overseas China-born researchers to cooperate with colleagues in China. When I met a professor of psychology in 2008 from the University of British Columbia, she had four projects, with several under the rubric of the Canadian Institute of Health Research (CIHR). One project brought thirty Chinese students to Canada for PhDs. As a Changjiang Scholar, she had established a research lab on medical genetics at South Central Chinese University in Changsha, Hunan Province, which employed eighteen students.[105]

Professional associations in academic disciplines such as economics, political science, history, agriculture, computer science, or IT built bridges between East and West. Foreign donors such as the Ford or Rockefeller Foundations supported some associations, while others were supported by China's government.[106] As mentioned above, Saxenian's data showed that around 2001, entrepreneurs who were members of organizations in Silicon Valley were more likely to collaborate with China than those who were not members.[107]

In their analysis of 208 Chinese professional associations, Fedasiuk and Weinstein focused on their role in technology transfer.[108] One-third of these associations were in the US, with the remaining two-thirds operating across twenty-one countries, including Germany (13.5 percent), Canada (8.7 percent), France (7.9 percent), the UK (6.3 percent), Japan (4.8 percent), Australia (4.0 percent) and South Korea (3.2 percent).[109] These 208 associations had 145,000 members. The technology that was transferred involved trade and investment (22.4 percent), engineering (19.7 percent), biomedical development (18.4 percent), energy and environment (14.5 percent), and information and communication technology (13.2 percent).[110]

These associations were up front about their technology transfer to China, with 126 associations (61 percent) advertising their efforts on their association's website. Among these groups, 102 associations (49 percent) advertised exchanging technical information with China, 67 associations (32 percent) publicized bringing overseas scientists to China, and 27 associations (13 percent) reported how they helped China's talent plans by encouraging members to apply to state-run competitions that recruit overseas talent or that involve top overseas technology. Often, however, only the Chinese language websites announced that they had transferred technology.

One organization, the Overseas Chinese Science and Technology Organization Federation, which was founded in China in 2015, hosts overseas delegations along with the Investment Promotion Agency of the Chinese Ministry of Commerce. Their goal is to integrate "international technologies and talents with domestic industries, capital, and markets," and to support technology indigenization across various industries.[111]

Some organizations bring new enterprises that use cutting-edge overseas technology designed by their members to industrial and high-tech parks in China that are established for overseas entrepreneurs. As of 2016, at least sixty-three (30.3 percent) overseas professional associations had reportedly signed 103 strategy documents, contracts, and cooperation agreements with these zones.

Individual Talent Programs

To overcome the deleterious impact of the brain drain, some states create programs which reward their talented nationals who had settled abroad if they return home to work. These awards include, among other benefits, additional research funds, higher salaries, research facilities, and housing allowances. Canada's Ministry of Foreign Affairs created the Canada Research Chairs Program to keep top scholars from moving overseas or to attract top Canadian academics working abroad back home.[112] It also was used to attract talented researchers who previously had no contact with Canada. It included a salary supplement of CDN$40,000 as well as CDN$50,000 per year for research for seven years. According to Zha Qiang, many countries have such initiatives.[113] The Presidential Young Investigator Award and the Presidential Early Career Awards for Scientists and Engineers in the US provide up to USD 640,000 over a five-year period for junior researchers; the Federation Fellowship Program in Australia offers AUS 221,000 per year; the Marie Curie Program in the EU offers EUR 410,161 per year; and the Humboldt Research Awards in Germany are valued at EUR 60,000 over a one-year period. Clearly, China is not unique.

The targets of such individual recruitment programs were usually scientists or professors below 55 years of age—though most of these programs preferred people in their mid-40s, with well-established positions overseas, with in-depth knowledge in a key aspect of scientific research, with experience running research teams and experience at raising funds, but who were still in a creative stage of their scholarship. The key programs in this category include the CAS' 100 Talents Plan (百人计划 or HTP), the NSFC's National Science Fund for Distinguished Young Scholars (中国杰出青年 or NSFDYS), the MOE's Cheung Kong (also called Changjiang) Scholars Program (长江学者 or CJSP), and the well-known (and somewhat infamous) Thousand Talents Plan (千人计划 or TTP) run by the Central Leading Group for the Coordination of Work on Talent (中央人才工作协调领导小组) under the Organization Department of the CCP.

Table 2.5 below shows the comprehensiveness of China's effort to gain technology through programs targeted at individuals and professional organizations. Still, before 2008, and the emergence of Li Yuanchao as director of the CCP's Organization Department, the rolling out of all these programs was not coordinated. According to Wang Huiyao, one of the main problems in China's overall effort to recruit its overseas talent was that, despite the decision in 2003 to place all talent plans under CCP leadership,[114] until 2008, no one individual directed this effort. Each ministry or government bureau put forward these programs on their own initiative. Thus, as of 2019, six national ministries or agencies were operating 13 talent programs; and local governments had initiated at least 183 programs to attract international talents.[115] Table 2.5 provides the year initiated, the target population, the managing agency, and the total number of participants for each program. Table 2.6 presents some of their incentives.

Programme	Agency in Charge	Target of the Programme	Year Initiated	Total Number
Hundred Talent Program	CAS	Scientists under 45 years of age[a]	1994	1,930[b]
National Science Fund for Distinguished Young Scholars	NSFC	Academic leaders under 45 years old; frontier sciences and technology	1994	3,454[c]

Chunhui Program and Chunhui Award	MOE	Chinese expatriates for short-term service	1996	3,424 (15,000)[d]
Changjiang Scholar Program	MOE	Endowed professorships for under 45 years old; extended to 55 years old in social sciences and humanities	1998	2,948
111 Program	MOE and SAFEA[e]	1000 foreign scholars from top 100 universities and research centres	2005	201 bases[f] (as of 2017)
Thousand Talent Program	CLGCWT	1000 academics, corporate executives, and entrepreneurs under 55 years old to return from overseas	2008	7-8000[g] 2,629 in US
Young Thousand Talent Program	CLGCWT	Academics under 40 years old with three plus years of post-doctoral research	2010	3,535[h]
Science Fund for Emerging Distinguished Young Scholars	NSFC	Researchers under 38 years old to work in academia	2011	2,398[i]
New Hundred Talent Program	CAS[j]	Renewal of Hundred Talent Program	2014	n.a
Young Cheung Kong Scholar Program	MOE	Endowed professorships for young scholars at Chinese universities	2015	440[k]

Table 2.5: Major Programs Focusing on Overseas Talent, 2018.

Notes: MOE—Ministry of Education; NSFC—Natural Science Foundation of China; SAFEA—State Administration of Foreign Expert Affairs; CLGCWT—Central Leading Group for the Coordination of Work on Talent; CAS—Chinese Academy of Sciences.

[a] Initially the 100 Talents Plan included part-time participants, but the CAS changed that policy around 2004 when too many people accepted the award and the funding, but rarely appeared at the CAS. See Hao Xin, "Frustrations Mount over China's High-Priced Hunt for Trophy Professors," *Science*, Vol. 313, 22 (September 2006): 1721–1723.

[b] "Two-decade Development of the Hundred-Talent Program," https://english.cas.cn/bcas/2015_1/201503/P020150324534612618850.pdf, reported that 90 percent of the 2,145 awardees were from abroad. This is the number as of 2005. Today, the number is surely well over 2,000. See *People's Daily*, on 科学网 (Web of Science), 百人计划 (Hundred Talents Plan), https://baike.baidu.com/item/百人计划/7597351.

ᶜ 刘 彬, 乔黎黎, 张依 (Liu Bin, Qiao Lili, and Zhang Yi), 生命科学领域国家杰出青年科学基金 项目资助状况及影响力分析 (Analysis of the Funding Status and Achievement Impact of National Science Fund for Distinguished Young Scholars in Life Sciences), 中国科学基金 (China Science Fund), 第 2 期 (issue no. 2) (2016), 122–131.

ᵈ By the end of 2009, the Spring Light Program had brought to China over three hundred delegations, comprising fifteen thousand overseas mainlanders who established over one thousand projects. 赵峰, 苗丹国, 魏祖钰, 程希 (Zhao Feng, Miao Danguo, Wei Zuyu, Cheng Xi), eds., 留学大事概览, 1949–2009 (An Overview of Overseas Study, 1949–2009). 北京: 现代出版社, 2010, 86.

ᵉ SAFEA was closed in 2018 and reconstituted under the MOST. See 2017 Budget of the Former State Administration of Foreign Experts Affairs, CSET, Washington, DC, https://cset.georgetown.edu/publication/2017-budget-of-the-former-state-administration-of-foreign-experts-affairs/.

ᶠ "An introduction to China's '111 Project,'" British Council, March 15, 2017, https://opportunities-insight.britishcouncil.org/news/market-news/introduction-china%E2%80%99s-%E2%80%9C111-project%E2%80%9D-0. This website posted the name of all the project bases in China.

ᵍ At the end of 2014, there were 4,128 awardees; in 2015 alone, 1,028 talents came to China via the TTP. "China's TTP has attracted 5,206 high-end overseas talents" (中国 '千人计划' 引进 5,206 名海外高层次人才), accessed March 10, 2020, http://www.gqb.gov.cn/news/2016/0107/37723.shtml. The Chinese media estimated 8,000 TTP awardees in 2018. 深度解读: 国家 '千人计划' 人才项目申报 ('In-depth interpretation: 2018 national TTP application'), accessed October 2, 2019, http://www.sohu.com/a/236432599_100103651. For the number in America, see Anthony Carpaccio, "US Faces 'Unprecedented Threat' from China on Tech Takeover," https://www.bloomberg.com/news/articles/2018-06-22/china-s-thousand-talents-called-key-in-seizing-u-s-expertise.

ʰ "An Analysis of the 2015 Youth Thousand Talents Program" (in Chinese), http://www.1000plan.org/qrjh/article/60547. Cao accessed it on July 20, 2017, but it is no longer accessible.

ⁱ Cong Cao, Jeroen Baas, Caroline S. Wagner, and Koen Jonkers, "Returning scientists and the emergence of China's science system," Science and Public Policy, 47, 2 (2020): 176, doi: 10.1093/scipol/scz056, present a similar table, but mine is more comprehensive. See also Cong Cao, "China's Approaches to Attract and Nurture Young Biomedical Researchers," A report for the Next Generational Researcher Initiative, US National Academies of Sciences, Engineering, and Medicine (March 2018), http://sites.nationalacademies.org/cs/groups/pgasite/documents/webpage/pga_184821.pdf.

ʲ The Chinese Academy of Sciences, "Global Recruitment of Pioneer 'Hundred Talents Program' of CAS," http://english.cas.cn/join_us/jobs/201512/t20151204_157107.shtml (accessed on July 20, 2017).

ᵏ Shi, D., Liu, W. & Wang, Y. "Has China's Young Thousand Talents Program been successful in recruiting and nurturing top-caliber scientists?" Science, 379, 6627 (2023): 62–65.

While the original goal was to bring these people back from the diaspora, the sponsors of these programs knew that getting top scholars who were established overseas to give up their jobs abroad and return full-time was no easy task. So, both the CJSP and the TTP established part-time programs. The CAS had originally offered part-time affiliation but abandoned it around 2014, when too many participants signed up without ever showing up. As of 2006, the CAS had cancelled 166 contracts out of a total of 1,005 recruits and demanded the money back.[116]

Given the controversy that would emerge during the "China Initiative" (CI) about how China-born scholars in America were transferring technology from the US to China, and the attacks on them by the FBI, the Justice Department, the NIH, and the US Congress, why did China-born scholars in the US join such programs? Were they driven by personal gain, patriotism, or perhaps by a willingness to spy for China, as alleged by some US government officials and politicians? The director of the FBI, on numerous occasions, as well as former President Trump, accused the China-born scholars and students in America of being spies.[117]

However, Chinese PhD candidates in the US, Canada, and Australia, who interviewed China-born scholars for their own dissertations, found that culture, and a desire to help Chinese science reach world-class standards, and in this way pay back China for their earlier education, underlay these efforts. These programs also offered China-born scholars working overseas very nice incentives, though part-timers received much smaller benefits than those who returned on a full-time basis.

Joining a part-time talent program, such as the Changjiang Visitors Plan (CJVP) and the TTP, allows individuals in the diaspora to contribute to China, resolving some of the guilt they might feel about not returning full-time. But participation brought summer salaries, prestige, and an opportunity to do subsidized research funded by the NSFC back in China, often in collaboration with former colleagues or mentors, and with inexpensive and talented graduate students as research assistants. Or they might receive the support of graduate students or postdoctoral fellows who may temporarily join their laboratories or programs overseas and help these China-born professors embellish their research and publications, and help them get tenure. Table 2.6, on the following page, shows some of the financial subsidies proffered by these talent programs.

Program	Start-Up Research Funds	Settlement Allowance	Extra Salary	Housing
Hundred Talents Plan	> RMB 2 million	RMB 8–9 million	RMB 400,000/ year	(depends on the institute)
HTP Pioneer Initiative	7 million RMB salary and 1 mil. RMB for Team Building[a]			(depends on the institute)
Changjiang Full-Time	Usually > RMB 2 million	RMB 500,000– 1 million	RMB 200,000/ year	100–200 square-meter apartment
Changjiang Part-Time	~RMB 300,000	None	RMB 30,000/ month when in China	Supplied an apartment
TTP Full-Time	RMB 3.5 million	RMB 1–1.5 million	RMB 400,000/ year	none
TTP Part-Time	RMB 500,000	None	RMB 30,000/ month while in China	Supplied an apartment

Table 2.6. Subsidies under Three National Talent Programs.

Source: David Zweig, Wang Huiyao, and Kang Siqin, "'The Best Are Yet to Come': State Programs, Domestic Resistance, and Reverse Migration of High-Level Talent to China," *Journal of Contemporary China* 29, no. 125 (September 2020): 776–91.

Notes.[a] "Academic Leaders" get the funds listed above. A second tier, "Technological Excellence," get 1–2 mil. RMB as salary and .6 mil RMB from the CAS for infrastructure construction. For tier three, "Young Talents," in the first two years, the CAS allocates 0.8 million RMB in salary and the institute provides start-up funding of no less than 0.5 million RMB. After two years, they are reviewed and selectively recruited into the "Hundred Talent Program" with a salary of 2 million RMB and infrastructure construction funding of 0.6 million RMB. http://www.demoe.org/upload/1450689915_file2_1450689915.pdf.

The CJSP had its roots in President Jiang Zemin's speech honoring Peking University's one hundredth anniversary. Driven by the goal of "establishing world-class universities," the MOE launched both the "985 Program" (九八五计划) and the CJSP in 1998. The former program gave large grants to twenty top universities in China, with 20 percent of the grant to be used to bring talented academics working overseas to their universities. The latter program was funded by the MOE but also by Hong Kong tycoon Li Ka Hsing, who gave RMB 60–70 million in August 1998. In 2008, on the tenth anniversary of the establishment of this program, the Li Ka Hsing Foundation (LKSF) announced that the program had received RMB 454 million since 1998, of which RMB 124 million came from the LKSF, and RMB 330 million from the MOE.[118]

Participants fell into two categories: (1) 'distinguished professors' who returned full-time, and (2) 'chair professors' who signed up for short-term visits, usually in the summers. In the first five years of the program (1998–2003), the ratio of the two cohorts was over ten to one (488 versus 43), with the smaller number being the 'chair professors.' But the number of part-time participants increased. As of 2003, the ratio between full- and part-time returnees jumped to three to two (960 versus 615), thereby accepting many more people who remained abroad.[119]

The recipients of the "Chair Professor" Award, what I call the CJVP, are among the best China-born professors in the diaspora. My data set of CJVP awardees comprises 190 "chair professors," who are impressive along numerous dimensions, such as where they received their PhDs, the schools where they taught, and their research productivity. They are widely cited, with an average of 15,900 citations, which is quite high. A plurality (36.3 percent) are engineers, reflecting China's commitment to acquiring technology. Given China's desire to promote medical research as a core business, another 15.8 percent were in medical sciences. Natural scientists comprised 16.8 percent; 12.6 percent were in formal science, such as mathematics, computer science, logic, or statistics; 10.5 percent were in humanities and social science, and 7.9 percent worked in business schools, which in some universities included the Economics Department. Most had an overseas PhD (158 out of 190, or 83.2 percent), while thirty-two had received their PhD in China and then probably got a job overseas after working abroad as a postdoctoral fellow.

Most were in the US—126 (67.4 percent) were working there after 109 of them (57.7 percent) got their PhD there. Over thirty received an MA in the US as well. Four had received a joint US-China PhD, while six had a joint US-China MA. Other countries of note include the UK, with twelve PhDs and fourteen employees; Canada, with thirteen PhDs and twelve employees; Japan, with nine PhDs but only two employees; and Hong Kong, with only four PhDs but sixteen employees. No one in my sample worked in Germany, though six worked in Singapore.

Their ages followed the guidelines of the program. Sixty-four (33.7 percent) were forty-five or younger, among whom twenty-one (11.1 percent) were under forty, so the program was attracting young scholars. Another thirty-four (17.9 percent) were forty-six to forty-nine years of age, forty-five (23.7 percent) were fifty to fifty-four years old, while only seven (3.7 percent) were fifty-five or older.

An important political question was whether these scholars informed their universities that they had taken on commitments with institutions in China. As we will see in the next chapter, some China-born scientists working in the US who had not listed their participation in the TTP on their CVs, or on grant applications to US funding agencies, were investigated by the US government or the National Institute of Health (NIH) during the China Initiative (CI) between 2018 and 2022, and in some cases, such secrecy, when discovered, became grounds for firing them.

But the same phenomenon among participants in the CJVP was not an issue for the West, perhaps because it was run by the MOE and not the CCP.

Disclosure could occur in two ways: researchers could list it on their overseas CV or in a PDF on their university's website. The latter shows whether the university knew about their affiliation, and unfortunately, only 132 (69.5 percent) had not. As for posting it on their publicly available CV, which can be found through various search engines, forty-one (21.6 percent) had done so, two had listed it only on their Chinese CV, and 138 (72.6 percent) had not, again displaying a lack of transparency to Western institutions and colleagues by these China-born scholars who were working in America.

Comparing Full-Time and Part-Time Returnees

Were part-time participants in this program who remained in the diaspora better scholars than people who returned full-time? In other words, did this talent program give China access to better researchers than the people they attracted back? To answer this question, I compare the 191 academics who had been awarded the Changjiang Scholar's "Chair Professor" Award (CJVP) between 2011 and 2016 with 292 scholars who had joined the full-time program (CJSP) between 2012 and 2017.

Statistical analysis of these scholars shows that the part-time participants in the CJVP are almost twice as influential as their full-time colleagues in the CJSP because their work is cited much more frequently (see statistical appendix, table A.1). And when I combined all the part-timers and full-timers under both the TTP and the CJSP, I found again that part-time participants had significantly more scholarly impact than the full-time participants (see appendix, table A.2). This fact was true in terms of the frequency with which their papers were cited, the quality of the journals in which they published, and the number of papers they published.

These findings make sense. Academics working overseas should have a better international network, giving them access to better projects than those who returned. They may be less encumbered with administrative affairs than full-time returnees who often take on leadership positions. In fact, one senior researcher at the University of Toronto I interviewed in 2016 said that returnees often lose their aggressiveness for scientific research, preferring power and money.[120] Likewise, scholars in the diaspora need not spend as much time building "relationships" with senior academics or administrators, whose support is a necessity if they want to get ahead in China.

The fact that my measure of success is based on refereed publications outside of China, the Social Science Citation Index (SSCI) journals, there is a built-in bias in this analysis. Part-time participants, who compete in the Western academic world, mostly publish in international journals, while full-time returnees may publish both internationally and in local journals, so their work may be cited less by international researchers.

Finally, full-time returnees in Shenzhen and Beijing confirmed that, for many years, returnees to China had great difficulty getting grants because they lacked allies in the senior ranks of China's academy who could go to bat for them.[121] All these problems undermined their research and publications. Additionally, lower-quality scholars may be predisposed to return full-time, while the best scholars stay abroad, following Lien's argument that proffering incentives, such as awards, higher salaries, or housing, increases the return of moderate-quality, but not top-quality, talent.[122]

The difference in the quality of the universities where they received their PhDs could affect the quality of their training and, therefore, the impact of their research. Shanghai Jiaotong University's ranking system for universities shows that the mean ranking of the foreign schools where the CJVP awardees received their PhD was 170.3, while the mean ranking of the universities where full-time participants in the CJSP received their PhDs was significantly lower at 225.7. This finding may result from the fact that, as mentioned above, 86.3 percent of the part-time participants in the Changjiang program had overseas PhDs, as compared to 16.4 percent of the full-time returnees. According to this measure, too, the best talent remained abroad.

Li Yuanchao and the Thousand Talents Program (TTP)[123]

When Li Yuanchao (李源潮) picked up the reins of the CCP's Organization Department and became chair of the Central Leading Group on Coordinating the Work on Talent (中央人才工作协调小组—CLGCWT) in October 2007, following the Seventeenth Congress of the CCP, policy on returnees took on a liberal direction. In December 2007, several ministries, led by the Organization Department, drafted three documents about returnees, focusing on improving their working conditions back in China, awarding special privileges to improve the returnees' livelihood, and finding short-term methods for increasing the flow back to China.[124] The documents emphasized that attracting China's overseas talent was "absolutely necessary" if China was "to raise its global competitiveness" and become "an innovative society." Then, in December 2008, the CLGCWT, composed of representatives of approximately fifteen ministries, bureaus, and the Organization Department, proposed a program to convince two thousand highly talented people to return to China full-time over the following five to ten years, which became the Thousand Talents Plan (千人计划 - TTP).[125]

Li believed he could increase the number of top-quality returnees by throwing the full authority of the CCP behind this issue. In fall 2009, "Leadership Offices on Talent" in cities around the country were ordered to study the meaning of "talent" and find ways to attract more overseas talent. Party secretaries of universities around the country pressed senior faculty to persuade former students or colleagues working abroad to join the TTP.[126] Participants in the part-time program who were living in the US described how academics and university administrators in China applied for the award on their behalf because it would bring money from the CCP to their institutions.[127]

Yet, few academics and scientists were willing to return full-time. Among 501 TTP participants my research assistant could find online, 73.5 percent of the 374 scientific and academic researchers who joined the program (A-innovative) did so on a part-time basis, meaning that they held on to their overseas post (table 2.7). Those who joined state-owned enterprises (B-innovative) were much more likely to return full-time (80 percent), as were entrepreneurs who needed to be in China to protect their intellectual property and run their businesses themselves.

Type of Returnee	Full-Time	Part-Time	Total
A-innovative	99 (26.5%)	275 (73.5%)	374 (74.7%)
B-innovative	36 (80.0%)	9 (20.0%)	45 (9.0%)
C-entrepreneur	73 (89.0%)	9 (11.0%)	82 (16.4%)
Total	208 (41.5%)	293 (58.5%)	501 (100%)

Table 2.7. Part-Time versus Full-Time Returnees,
by Categories of Returnees, TTP, 2011.

Note: Initially, China released 350 names online, and my research assistant found another 150 online. As of 2011, the number of returnees under the TTP was 1,510, so we found one-third of the participants.

Source: Data collected by Meng Sun, Sam at HKUST.

While the program became much more secretive after Li Yuanchao left the post of director of the Organization Department in 2012, I found the annual number of participants of the various programs under the TTP through 2018 (table 2.8).

Year	Total Number of Recipients	Innovation Scheme	Entrepreneurs Scheme	Young Talent	Foreign Talent
2018	Approx. 8000[1]	Approx. 4400	N/A	3586[2]	N/A
2015[3]	5208 (1028)[3]	2358 (202)[3]	808 (121)[3]	2367 (1226)[3]	244 (48)[4]
2014	4180 (861)[5]	2156 (301)[5]	687 (97)[4,6]	1141 (396)[4]	196 (67)[3]
2013	3319 (526)[6]	1855 (132)[5,6]	590 (154)[6]	745 (151)[4]	129 (89)[6]
2012	2793 (1283)[7]	1723 (562)[7]	436 (87)[5,7]	594[4]	40[6,7]
2011	1510 (367)[8]	1161 (281)[8]	349 (86)[8]		
2010	1143 (537)[9]	880 (454)[9]	263 (82)[9]		
2009	607 (263)[10]	426 (204)[10]	181 (59)[10]		
2008*	326[11] [344][10]	222[10]	122[10,11]		

Table 2.8. Annual and Accumulated Number of
Thousand Talents and Its Sub-Categories, 2008–2018.

Note: *There is a slight discrepancy in terms of the Total Number of Recipients for 2008 between sources ten and eleven below. I list them both in the sources, putting the number from source number ten in square brackets. The annual number under the Total Number of Recipients is in parenthesis. The number of Innovation Scheme awardees in 2012, 2013, and 2014 was calculated by Dr. Kang Siqin.

Sources:

[1] http://www.gqb.gov.cn/news/2016/0107/37723.shtml, and http://www.sohu.com/a/236432599_100103651, accessed on 2 October 2019 and 10 March 2020. These two webpages have been erased.

[2] For the "Young Talent," see Shi, et al. "Has China's Young Thousand Talents Program been successful in recruiting and nurturing top-caliber scientists?"

[3] I have data for 2015 but cannot find my original source. Nevertheless, I present these numbers: for entrepreneurs, the number is 121, totaling 808 as of 2015. An additional 1,226 Young Thousand Talents were added in 2015, totaling 2,367, and there were an additional forty-eight Foreign Talent awardees, totaling 244 by 2015.

[4] 关于公布第十批 "千人计划" 创业人才，青年人才入选资格名单公告 (Announcement of the Name List of the Tenth Batch of Entrepreneurial Talents and Young Talents Qualified for the "Thousand Talents Program"), http://www.1000plan.org/qrjh/article/51267. Found at Wayback, July 31, 2023.

[5] 引七成海外学子 "回家" (70 Percent of Overseas Scholars Are Attracted to "Return Home"), 人民日报海外版, 2/6/2014, (Overseas edition of the *People's Daily*, June 2, 2014), http://paper.people.com.cn/rmrbhwb/html/2014-06/02/content_1435643.htm. Found at Wayback, June 29, 2023.

[6] 江苏 "千人计划" 特聘专家分布情况分析" (An Analysis of the Situation of the Distribution of the Recruitment of the "Thousand Talent Plan" in Jiangsu), November 18, 2013, http://qrjh.jshrss.gov.cn/fwdt/201311/t20131118_129039.html. Found at Wayback, June 29, 2023.

[7] 全国已分8批共引进 2793 名海外高层次人才 (The Eighth National Recruitment of High-Quality Talent Already Brought in 2,793 people), http://www.js.xinhuanet.com/2012-08/26/c_112848404.htm. No longer available.

[8] 激发海外人才回国热情 "千人计划"对中国影响深远 (Be Excited about the Deep Influence of the "Thousand Talent Plan" that Generated Enthusiasm about Talent Returning to China), http://www.chinanews.com/lxsh/2011/09-28/3360365.shtml. Found at Wayback, July 30, 2023.

[9] 千人计划2010年为止已引进海外人才1143名. 其中创新人数占880人, 创业 263 人 (As of 2010, the Thousand Talent Plan Had Already Pulled in 1,143 Talented People from Abroad, including 880 Researchers and 263 Entrepreneurs), http://politics.gmw.cn/2011-01/17/content_1551348.htm. Found at Wayback, June 29, 2023.

[10] 千人计划第一至三批 (2008–2010) 名单 (The Name List of the First to the Third Groups for the Thousand Talents Plan, 2008–2010), http://blog.renren.com/share/49053086/4334094101. Found at Wayback, July 30, 2023.

[11] "千人计划" 已引进326名海外人才 建立 67 家海外人才创新创业基地 (The Thousand Talents Plan Has Already Attracted Back 326 Overseas Talents and Established Sixty-Seven Bases for Overseas Talented Researchers and Entrepreneurs), http://news.xinhuanet.com/politics/2009-09/25/content_12111209.htm. Found at Wayback, July 30, 2023.

The secrecy came both from the CCP and the participants. The former may have feared that disclosing that participation was mostly on a part-time basis would show that the policy had failed. Also, China would be seen to be encouraging people who had jobs and commitments to organizations abroad to work for China, even as the overseas organization was footing their salary. "Double-dipping" and "conflict of commitment" were criticized during America's CI between 2018 and 2022. Some awardees wanted secrecy, as they were worried that colleagues and administrators at their home universities would question their loyalty to their employer. So, when I asked the director of the Higher-Level Talent Office at a top university in China's northwest for the names of the school's TTP recipients so I could interview them, she refused, even though she was very candid in our discussions about the program. She said that the TTP participants wanted anonymity.[128] Likewise, some TTP participants were holding two full-time jobs concurrently, one overseas and one in China, and they did not want their overseas employers to find out. According to Cong Cao, "so many of the recruits hold concurrent positions at Western institutions, the disclosure could embarrass them and even cause them to lose their permanent positions overseas, which are more secure."[129]

How good are these people? Hirsch argues that scholars with an h-index from twenty to forty are "good," those with a score between forty and fifty-nine are "outstanding," while those with scores of sixty and above are "exceptional."[130] Using the h-index of 174 part-time participants in the TTP, who joined the program between 2008 and 2013, I find that one-third were "good," 31.6 percent were "outstanding," and 7.5 percent were "exceptional." The 27.6 percent of this group with an h-index of under twenty would be seen as quite ordinary.

How Do Overseas Chinese "Serve the Nation?"

In 2001, the Chinese state outlined the seven ways mainlanders in the diaspora could "serve the nation." Four focused on academic engagement: (1) collaborative research (which could involve joint research, shared funding, and co-publications); (2) lecturing in China; (3) holding joint positions in China; (4) and training mainland students, postdocs, or visiting professors either in China or by bringing them abroad—what Bozeman and Corley call "mentoring."[131] These mechanisms could all improve research in China. The list did not mention joint laboratories or directing a laboratory in China, a contentious issue under the CI, but joint laboratories could fall under the category of collaborative research.

Collaborative Research and Joint Publications

Cross-national collaboration on publications is a worldwide trend. Between 2006 and 2016, the percentage of articles in science and engineering that were coauthored by people in different countries increased from 16.7 percent to 21.7 percent, with the international collaboration rate reaching 37 percent for US researchers in 2016, up from 25 percent in 2006.[132]

Katz and Martin list ten reasons scholars collaborate, among which I highlight seven: (1) changing patterns or levels of funding; (2) the desire of researchers to increase their scientific recognition; (3) escalating demands for the rationalization of scientific manpower (an increased division of labor); (4) the requirements of ever more complex (and often large-scale) instrumentation (the need for sophisticated equipment); (5) researchers hoping to make breakthroughs must pool their knowledge; (6) the need to train apprentices effectively; and (7) the need to work with others in close physical proximity to benefit from their skills and knowledge.[133] One might add that given the transnational nature of epidemics and disease, cooperative research should become a necessity.

One reason for the explosion in cross-national collaborative research is more co-ethnic publications,[134] driven in part by the human need for "homophily,"[135] where contact among people of similar backgrounds occurs at a higher rate than among dissimilar people. For example, Bozeman and Corley found women collaborate more than men, and usually with other women.[136]

Jin et al. created an "ethnic collaboration index" (ECI), drawing on the 3,602 articles published in over one hundred SSCI journals that had at least one mainlander who was residing abroad as a coauthor.[137] The index shows the share of international collaborative papers published by mainland Chinese that were written with an overseas Chinese, as a share of total collaborative publications with that country. The ECI per country between 2001 and 2005 was quite stunning, demonstrating that even in those early years of web technology, Chinese on the two sides of the Pacific were deeply involved in collaborative research and publications.

As the data show (table 2.9), 72.1 percent of all co-publications between Chinese in the PRC and scholars in the US between 2001 and 2005 were written with ethnic Chinese in the US, while over half the co-publications between scholars in Canada (55.1 percent) and Australia (56.1 percent) involved a China-born academic who had moved to those two countries. Thus, without publishing with China-born scholars in the diaspora, scholars in the PRC could have had difficulty getting recognition. Moreover, Jin et. al. asserted that the ECI was increasing over time, especially for the US, England, and Canada.

Country	ECI	Country	ECI	Country	ECI	Country	ECI
USA	0.72	Canada	0.55	Japan	0.48	France	0.30
Australia	0.56	England	0.48	Germany	0.40	South Korea	0.28

Table 2.9. Ethnic Collaboration Index (ECI) by Country, 2001–2005.

Source: Jin, et al., "The Role of Ethnic Ties in International Collaboration."

The "overseas Chinese phenomenon" in China's international collaboration in science and technology has developed from a deep social basis. Chinese scientists leaving China permanently or temporarily are influenced by Chinese traditional culture and have close social relations with China. One interviewee in Australia spoke of a shared culture and a "sense of Chinese being and identity."[138] Some overseas mainlanders who felt undervalued and insufficiently connected to the scientific community in their host country might look to China for a sense of belonging, while others spoke of how working with China enhanced their personal and professional fulfillment.[139]

Suttmeier found that the number of papers by Chinese in the US and China increased enormously between 1995 and 2005,[140] while according to Jonkers, around 2008, 22 percent of PRC scholars' publications in SSCI journals were co-published with international partners, of whom 75 percent had ethnic Chinese surnames.[141] Looking at examples of Chinese-American collaborative papers in about one hundred journals, Jin et al. found that among 3,603 papers, 72.3 percent had at least one author working in the US who was of Chinese descent.[142] They, too, attributed increased collaboration between Chinese inside and outside China to homophily. So, without the diaspora, "China's contribution to international collaboration would not be as high as it is today."[143]

Zhu Hong found similar emotional ties among her interviewees in the US.[144] "First, we are Chinese. It is hard to get rid of our roots. . . . No matter if one stays or returns, he can hardly get rid of his Chinese roots."[145] Cai's informant named Dai said that Chinese always hope to connect with the place of origin and want to make a "contribution" (贡献) to China.[146] A senior administrator of a major medical program in Toronto told me that he promoted more ties between his institute and China "because I am Chinese."[147]

According to Cai, diasporic scholars help domestic scientists publish their work overseas out of a sense of loyalty or responsibility and their sense of belonging to a great civilization. As one commented, "I am especially grateful for the completely free education I received in China, and my status is built on that. I owe China so much and think it's my obligation to repay this to the best of my ability."[148]

Other than mentoring graduate students,[149] getting grants, and the need for a "division of labor" for large international projects, motivate the search for partners whose skills and equipment will help a project succeed.[150] Thus, a scholar in Australia wanted to mentor mainland students and scholars who spent time in Australia.[151]

All four respondents in Canada interviewed by Zhang in 2014, who had suffered during the Cultural Revolution, expressed a stronger sense of obligation to China than those who had not been through such difficult times. Once they got tenure, they wanted "to do something for China. It is the emotion from the bottom of my heart."[152]

Interest in collaboration is not a one-way street driven totally by Chinese in the diaspora. Mainland academics who want to publish in good journals often cannot do it themselves; hence, they collaborate and coauthor papers. As one local scholar in China told Cai, their research group had a very good paper that they wanted to publish but did not know where or how to do it successfully. Their overseas collaborator told them to ask the journal to exclude two specific examiners when the paper was reviewed and helped them revise the paper according to the editor's feedback. Their successful publication was regarded as a breakthrough for Mainland scholars.[153]

One Peking University professor saw diasporic scholars as a bridge, bringing state-of-the-art knowledge to China and promoting the work of domestic scientists in the global community. This Peking University professor's overseas colleague used his extensive relationship with scholars around the world, to build a strategic relationship between the Peking University lab and foreign research groups led by his former colleagues. He also publicized their lab when he attended international conferences, so that "now more and more people know there is such a lab at Beida."[154]

Yet some Western universities were ambivalent about their faculty collaborating so much with Peking University. One part-time Changjiang scholar, who went to Peking University three or four times a year and spent more than two months there each year, was told by his home university that he should spend more time in his lab and with his research fellows.[155] A second overseas professor who became dean of a program at Peking University reported that his university president in the US "wouldn't allow me to leave campus for as long [a time] as before. . . . You can't be a full professor at Beida but only an adjunct professor of our university."[156]

Overseas Academics and the Diaspora Option in the New Millennium

The PRC's policy of "serving China from abroad" began in 2001, but by 2005, interviews and online surveys in the US, Hong Kong, and Canada, showed that many in the "new diaspora" were engaged with China. In total, I received information from ninety-four professors in the US, ninety-eight in Hong Kong, and sixty in Canada. The largest group from all three countries were in the natural sciences (43 percent in the US sample, 31 percent in the Hong Kong sample, and 31 percent in the Canadian sample). Engineers composed 28 percent, 13 percent, and 28 percent from the US, Hong Kong, and Canada, respectively. The Hong Kong sample was weighted toward business and management (19 percent) and social science (21 percent). In both the US and Canada, 37 and 39 percent held administrative posts (there was no such data from Hong Kong). Almost half the respondents from the US and Canada were assistant professors, while more than half the respondents from Hong Kong were associate professors.

Participants selected the two or three most important reasons for interacting with China from a list emailed to them (table 2.10). I only include those responses that were selected by 5 percent of the people or more.

Reasons for Collaboration	US %	Canada %	Hong Kong %
Improve the quality of research in China	45.0	32.6	23.2
Make China stronger	14.5	17.4	8.7
Attract Chinese graduate students	11.1	10.0	13.3
Quality of collaborators is high	4.0	11.6	11.8
Establish personal relationships	8.8	16.3	9.5
I study China, so I need to collaborate	5.6	3.4	20.3
Research costs are cheaper	5.0	5.3	5.3

Total number of selections[1]	531	380	693
Sample size	98	60	70[2]

Table 2.10. Why Collaborate with China? Academics in the US, Canada, and Hong Kong, 2004–2005.

Notes:

[1] Respondents in the US and Hong Kong could only make a first and second choice; the Canadian group had a third choice. For the first reason, I multiplied the number of times the response was selected by five, the second reason was multiplied by three, and the third reason was multiplied by one. I summed the total for each item and show the percentage of the selections.

[2] The Hong Kong face-to-face interviews in 2001 and 2002 did not include this question about collaboration. So, the total number of Hong Kong responses is seventy, based only on the online survey.

Source: Interviews with mainlanders in Hong Kong, 2004; web-based survey in the US and Canada, 2005.

When I began these surveys, I was skeptical that when mainland scholars explained their motives for collaboration, they would prioritize "serving the country" to appear patriotic and avoid being accused of betraying their motherland. So, I did not include this option in my questionnaire in Hong Kong. But in 2002, a senior colleague at HKUST complained that my questions excluded the option of "improving the quality of research on the mainland."[157] He felt that he, and many colleagues, having had the chance to go overseas and benefit from a Western PhD, were strongly motivated to improve the research skills of their colleagues who had been unable to go abroad. This idea fits with the assertion that those who collaborate want to improve the quality of human capital in China.[158] Thereafter, I included this option in future surveys. He also felt that getting good graduate students from China prepared a new generation of mainland professors who would be more skilled than the current crop.

Thus, the most important reason in all three locations was "helping promote the quality of research." In the US and Canada, "making China strong" was the second-most important reason, though in Hong Kong, it only ranked fifth. Perhaps some academics in Hong Kong feared that a stronger China could threaten Hong Kong. Attracting good Chinese graduate students was a powerful motivation, particularly in Hong Kong, where the parents of local Hong Kong students discouraged their children from engaging in research, making it necessary for professors in Hong Kong to bring graduate students from the mainland.

Survey respondents were also asked about the frequency of their interactions with China over the previous five years. Mainlanders in Hong Kong interacted the most, with 3.3 interactions each. Mainlanders in Canada were second, with 2.5

interactions, significantly above those in America who averaged 2.0 interactions a year. Among scholars in Hong Kong, 28.1 percent carried out "most" or "all" of their research with colleagues on the mainland, with 48.1 percent doing half or more of their projects there, demonstrating the high degree of interaction between Hong Kong and the mainland. For Canada and the US, 14 and 16 percent of the people who were surveyed, respectively, did at least half their projects with colleagues on the mainland. From a reverse perspective, only 19.4 percent of mainlanders in Hong Kong had "almost no" or "no" collaborative projects on the mainland, while 60 and 52 percent of Canada-based and US-based mainlanders, respectively, had "almost no" projects or no projects at all. The close link between Hong Kong and mainland academics was due, in part, to policies such as the RGC-NSFC Joint Research Scheme to encourage cross-border collaboration. In 2022/23, the RGC gave US$80.7 to 50 projects.[159]

Joint or Adjunct Positions in China

In the early 2000s, joint positions in China were colloquially called the "dumbbell model" (魔灵模式) or the "double location model" (两个基地模式), and China-born scholars working overseas were strongly interested in such arrangements. In 2005, an amazing seventy-seven of my ninety-three (83 percent) survey respondents in the US wanted such an opportunity. Of the sixty respondents surveyed online in Canada, 90 percent were interested in a joint position, even though only 11 percent tried to find a job on the mainland. Among fifty-five professionals interviewed by Xiang in Europe in 2004, around one-third were interested in a joint position, and of those, 40.7 percent already worked as a "special-term professor or researcher."[160]

Professors holding an adjunct position can maintain a Western lifestyle, educate their children abroad, access research opportunities, gain social status, and receive some of the benefits of being a "returned" scholar. Chinese universities were keen to grant adjunct positions to these talented overseas researchers because they were counted when the MOE calculated each university's publications, which affected their funding. Adjunct professors were far more likely to co-publish with scholars in China.[161] And those in our US sample who wanted a joint position in China were much more likely to engage in some manner with China (table 2.11) than those who did not care about being an adjunct. Thus, 62.5 percent of people who did not want a joint appointment had zero interactions, while among those who wanted a joint position, 80 percent had one or more interactions. Clearly, the many people who wanted an adjunct post in China were strongly inclined to interact with China.

Levels of Interaction with China	Yes to a Joint Post[1]	No to a Joint Post[1]	Total No. and Column %[2]
None	15 (19.4%)	10 (62.5%)	25 (26.8%)
1	27 (35.1%)	4 (25%)	31 (33.3%)
2–3	24 (31.2%)	1 (6.3%)	25 (26.8%)
4 or more	11 (14.3%)	1 (6.3%)	12 (12.9%)
Total Respondents	77 (100%)	16 (100%)	93 (100%)

Table 2.11. Interactions with China, by Joint Position Preference, US, 2005.

[1] Percent in parenthesis for first four rows in columns 2 and 3 shows percent of people in the column who said "yes" or "no" at each level of interaction with China. Thus, among those who wanted an adjunct position in China, only 15/77 or 19.4 percent had no interactions, while 10/16 or 62.5% of those who did not want a position in China had no interactions. [2] This column has the total number and percent of the 93 survey respondents for each level of interaction. $p < 0.05$.
Source: Web-based survey of China-born professors in the US, 2005.

According to Xiang, engagement in "knowledge exchange and network-building activities" occurred most frequently among junior and senior faculty.[162] In his view, middle-rank professors were preoccupied with establishing their careers overseas. No doubt senior faculty had easier access to grants, research assistants and graduate students, administrative help to arrange trips to China or for hosting visitors from China, and other time-consuming activities necessary to manage such interactions. However, the US survey of 2005 (table 2.12) showed that 80.4 percent of the lower-ranked, assistant professors had one interaction or less, while 73.7 percent of full professors had two or more interactions. Thus, a female academic I interviewed in Toronto in 2016 told me that in her early years on the job, she was too busy establishing herself in her field and getting tenure to have the time to cultivate strong ties with colleagues in China.[163] The data on administrative posts also show that those with such posts were more likely to interact with China.

No. of Interactions	Assistant Prof.	Associate Prof.	Full Prof.	Total No. and Column %[1]
None	19 (41.3%)[2]	4 (14.8%)[2]	1 (5.2%)[2]	24 (26.1%)
1	18 (39.1%)	9 (33.3%)	4 (21.1%)	31 (33.7%)
2–3	7 (15.2%)	8 (29.6%)	10 (52.6%)	25 (27.2%)
4 or more	2 (4.4%)	6 (22.2%)	4 (21.1%)	12 (13.0%)
Total Respondents	46 (100%)	27 (100%)	19 (100%)	92 (100%)

Table 2.12. Number of Interactions with China, by Academic Rank, US, 2005.

[1] This column has the total number and percent of respondents for each level of interaction.
[2] Percent in parenthesis for first four rows in columns 2, 3 and 4 shows percent of assistant, associate, or full profs and their number of interactions. I deleted postdoctoral fellows and research associates from the data, yielding ninety-two cases. The results are statistically significant at the 0.01 level.
Source: Web-based survey of China-born academics in the US, 2005.

In 2008, I followed up these surveys with a focus group of China-born specialists that was arranged by the Chinese consulate in Vancouver. The most successful person in that focus group ran a lab at the University of British Columbia (UBC) that he said was one of the leading labs in the world on Alzheimer's.[164] He wanted to study psychology in the US, so he turned down a PhD fellowship at the Max Planck Institute funded by the Chinese government, for had he let the state sponsor him, it would have had significant control over his life. So, he accepted an offer from Purdue University for a PhD and went to Harvard on a three-year postdoc. He loved Vancouver, so in 2001, he joined UBC, which got him a grant of CDN 2 million to set up an Alzheimer's program, and found his wife, who is a research scientist, a job.

After China made him an NSFC "Overseas Specialist" (海外专家) and a Changjiang Scholar, he decided to do something for China. Relying on his many influential friends in China, including several academicians of the CAS, he set up a joint project in 2005 between the CIHR and NSFC, which gave fifteen to twenty awards each year to Chinese and Canadian principal investigators (PIs) who apply for local funds for the same proposal. PIs use their funds in their own country but fully collaborate. They had fifteen teams in 2005, seventeen teams in 2006, and twenty teams in 2007, where it was likely to remain. In 2007, with support from China's MOE and the CIHR, he also began the Canada-China Norman Bethune Fellowship Plan, under which thirty students per year from China got a PhD in Canada in life sciences.

As a Changjiang Scholar, he taught and did joint training for two to three months a year at Central Southern University (中南大学) in Changsha, Hunan Province, which has a National Key Laboratory on Medical Genetics. Another program between UBC and the MOE's China Scholarship Council (中国留学资金会) funded Chinese students to attend UBC. At that time, he had eighteen PRC students in his lab. One of his former students taught at Shandong University where they planned to hold the Sino-Canadian Symposium on Aging and Disease, to which he would bring senior Canadian specialists on Alzheimer's. This program, he hoped, would bring instant recognition to his student's program.

Academic Engagement around 2016

In 2016, I interviewed five Chinese academics in Toronto, including two directors of biomedical research labs, one astrophysicist, and one chemist, at the University of Toronto, and a mathematician who founded a research center at York University, called the Center for Disease Modeling (CDM), that tracked the spread of infectious diseases all around the world. Although the focus of this book is largely China's use of its American diaspora, I had easier access to scholars in Canada—I am Canadian—and technology transfer between Canada and China was, until very recently, a less sensitive issue than such exchanges between the US and China.

As we have seen, a significant segment of American and European analysts who look at these exchanges focus on the transfer of technologies with national security implications.[165] However, many China-born scientists in the diaspora use their knowledge to solve China's practical medical dilemmas. This was particularly true for this cohort in Toronto.

Dr. Wu Jianhong, the founding director of the CDM at York University in Toronto, applies mathematical modeling to discern the spread of infectious diseases in Canada and China. After a two-year postdoc (1988–1990) at the University of Alberta, he joined the University of Toronto in 1990 at age twenty-six. He established the center in 2010. As of 2023, he had over 33,558 citations! Among the professors in this center, four were born in China, of whom three were full professors.

One of his most important collaborative projects, funded by Canada's International Development Research Center (IDRC), builds capacity in China to manage HIV, tuberculosis, and hepatitis. This program was co-directed by the National Center for AIDS/STD Control and Prevention (Chinese Center for Disease Control and Prevention, China) and his CDM. The project's goals included: (1) developing, validating, and utilizing mathematical models for analyzing and predicting the dynamics of communicable diseases; (2) using these models to advise public health decision-makers; (3) training young scientists in these techniques; (4) organizing workshops, exchanges, and collaborations among Canadians and Chinese; (5) transferring these techniques to other countries; and (6) running a pilot study in 2013 in Liangshan County, Sichuan Province, where 10 percent of the population had HIV/AIDS, but where direct intervention under this joint program decreased the spread of AIDS by 26 percent.[166]

Papers from a conference were published in Chinese and English and led to the creation of a new journal. The project supported the writing of thirty PhD theses and seventy-six publications in top journals, including one of the world's leading medical journals, *Lancet*. The most important result was that the study found an underestimation of both new HIV infections and HIV/AIDS deaths in the Chinese national dataset, which affected how the Chinese government reported the prevalence of HIV.

Liu Mingyao directs the Institute for Medical Science (IMS) at the University of Toronto.[167] He had promoted exchanges with China from his previous post as director of international research relations from 2007 to 2010.

Approximately 350 (8 percent) of IMS's four thousand faculty members were born in China or of East Asian background. The IMS Summer Undergraduate

Research Program, begun in 2004, attracts one hundred undergraduate and graduate students from China each year. They started the program with students from Taiwan's Jiaotong University but then moved recruitment to the mainland.

IMS has eighty thousand students, of whom four thousand (five percent) are mainland Chinese. Liu himself had trained thirty to forty people, and twelve had gone back. Most of his visiting scholars are junior faculty from China who go overseas to get joint publications in good journals so that when they return to China, they will be promoted. While in Canada, they help him with his research.

Another specialist in biomedical sciences at the University of Toronto had a very active laboratory and research team.[168] After earning a Canadian PhD, he had a postdoc at Harvard. He had worked for fifteen years when I met him. He reported strong ties with friends back in his medical school in China, with whom he published good papers. Why? "I cannot lose my connection to China." He also trains postdocs from China—he had five in 2016, and five or six had already gone back. These mainland scholars work with him in Toronto to publish the papers needed for their promotion. He reported publishing about seven or eight articles with them in good Western journals, helping some to become associate professors back on the mainland. Although he engaged the mainland, he had little interest in returning. In his view, "China is unpredictable, things could be going well, then suddenly someone gets arrested for a minor offense. . . . The Chinese system is immature, not established, or stable, and very talented people are wasted." He also worries about their data, but "they know that if their data is not good, I cannot work with them. I insist on academic integrity." With so many downsides, why does he work with these postdocs? Because his home university in China gave him his preliminary medical training, so he wants to help that medical university. And although he did not articulate it, these visitors do a lot of the legwork that helps him get high-quality publications.

China's Interactions with World-Class China-Born Scholars Overseas, 2016

To further discern the quality of the people who stayed abroad and their level of interaction with China, Kang and I collected data on 121 of the top China-born scholars residing overseas at twenty-seven of the world's best universities (appendix, table A.3).[169] The distribution of fields was fifty-three engineers, twenty-three in medical schools, and forty-five in science. Their average age was forty-eight, and they had worked an average of 12.6 years (table 2.13). They published an average of 4.5 papers a year, while the total impact factor of the journals in which they published per year was 18.5, which is relatively high, depending on the field.[170]

Variables	Observations	Average	Minimum	Maximum
Gender (male)	121	79%	n/a	n/a
Current age[1]	93	48.7	35	60
Number of years working	93	12.6	6	31
Published papers per year	93	4.5	1	17
AAIF[2]	93	18.5	.66	87.9

Table 2.13. Background Information on 121 Top China-Born
Scholars Working Overseas, 2016.

Notes:

[1] Current age was estimated by the year they acquired their undergraduate degree.
[2] AAIF stands for the Average Annual Impact Factor of the journals in which they published.

Source: Data collected by Dr. Kang Siqin, 2017.

This group was rather engaged (table 2.14), with each person publishing, on average, 9.8 papers with colleagues in China, and 77.8 percent had coauthored at least one paper with a researcher there. These professors have trained, on average, 5.5 Chinese students, postdocs, or researchers who went to work with them overseas. Surprisingly, only 34 percent had given a talk in China, but the mean number of talks was 3.5, showing that some people gave lots of talks. Among this group, 5.8 percent directed a laboratory in China, allowing them to transfer much scientific knowledge. A similar percentage had joined the editorial board of a Chinese journal, which gave them the opportunity to improve the quality of research in China and uphold world standards in scholarship.

Types of Interactions	Average Number of Events
Lectures in China[1]	3.5
Percent of people who gave lectures in China	34.2%
Coauthored a paper with colleague in China	77.8%
Number of coauthored articles[2]	9.8
Sat on editorial board of PRC journal	5.8%
Held a joint position[3]	35.5%
Directed a lab in China	5.8%
Number of students/scholars trained from China[4]	5.5

Table 2.14. Top Overseas China-Born Professors'
Connections with China, 2016.

Notes:

[1] Includes the number of times they spoke at a conference or gave a visiting lecture.

[2] Includes both articles and book chapters.

[3] Joint positions include both academic and/or administrative positions.

[4] Includes PhD students, postdoctoral fellows, and laboratory researchers.

Source: Research by Dr. Kang Siqin, 2017.

The fact that 35.5 percent held joint positions is problematic, if these professors spent more than just their summers working in China, as doing so was what those running the CI under the Trump administration would call a "conflict of commitment." Yet this number also shows that China succeeded in getting many of the best Chinese researchers in the diaspora to engage with their former homeland and to work with colleagues in China.

I also analyzed this data statistically—through a multiple regression analysis— to see if the professors' gender, age, academic rank, and scientific discipline had an impact on any of the three ways professors might engage with China—lecturing, coauthoring, or holding an adjunct position in China (see appendix, table A.4). Most importantly, full professors, as compared to associate professors, were about 20 percent more likely to have joint positions in China. They were also much more likely to coauthor with researchers in China. Older faculty were more likely to have joint positions, as China sought out more mature scholars. Gender did not affect whether one got a joint position, suggesting that talent was more important than one's sex, though men, more than women, coauthored with scholars in China. Finally, engineers were far more likely to give lectures and hold joint positions compared to professors in the medical sciences, and they were more likely than professors in the sciences to hold a joint position. In sum, China was networking well with China-born senior engineers at the top universities in the world.

Part-Time Deans

Just as many people who were born in China but live abroad are willing to take part-time posts under these talent schemes, universities under the Ministry of Finance (MOF) introduced their own part-time program, relying on overseas talent to improve their ability to deliver high-quality education and research. To do this, several of these universities of finance and economics introduced a new phenomenon—"part-time deans" who maintain their overseas positions in the diaspora, even as they manage schools and improve the quality of China's universities. While their numbers remain few—as of 2016, there were approximately twenty part-time deans in China, and they worked mostly in universities under the MOF—most of those cases have been successful. Still, Xi Jinping could question a strategy that empowered foreign-trained academics.

In 2015 and 2016, I carried out interviews at the Shanghai University of Finance and Economics (SHUFE) and the Southwest University of Finance and Economics (SWUFE), and found that the part-time deans there effectively internationalized their schools, attracted more foreign trained faculty, and improved the global ranking of the school. Dr. Tian Guoqiang, who is the dean of the School of Economics at SHUFE, but maintained his post of professor of economics at Texas A&M University, is a case in point.

Tian worried that if he hired only one or two returnees a year, he would never transform the school. So, in 2005, his first year on the job, he recruited ten overseas faculty, who were evaluated by returnees only. And while he also hired two local PhDs, he let four locally trained professors leave. The following year, he hired nine returnees and two locals, and he let two locals go. In the following two years, he hired another nine returnees on an "overseas track"—where overseas-trained faculty had to meet higher standards for hiring and promotion but were paid double the salaries of locally trained faculty—and one person on the local track, and he let four local faculty leave. After 2009, foreign-trained faculty comprised 50 percent of the staff and dominated the school. The increased number of returnees created a richer academic and research environment, which included weekly in-house seminars and regular visits from top international scholars.

Despite moving in so many people from abroad, which could trigger serious opposition from locally trained faculty, Tian was not worried because if he kept his overseas post, the cost of such a confrontation would be low. As Tian commented, "[part-time deans] are not afraid of getting in trouble and losing our jobs, as we have a position overseas to which we can return."

To attract more overseas scholars, Tian also introduced the aforementioned "dual-track" hiring and promotion system, which demanded higher standards for hiring and promotion, but paid returnees double the salaries of locally trained faculty and gave them other benefits such as higher status, extra research funding, and a housing subsidy.

Another part-time dean at SHUFE is a Stanford PhD who holds a chair professorship at Columbia University. He supported part-time deans because by not making the dean return to China full-time, the university "relaxes the constraints on the position and increases the pool of candidates enormously. Because the deans then do not have to worry about getting in trouble, their quality is much higher." Why did he return to do this work?

I am absolutely attached to my homeland and academic research is my passion, but I want to do something different, give some value-added to students and junior scholars. Junior scholars with US PhDs but no overseas work experience, must overcome many high hurdles. They have a weak network in the US and in China. They need a big group of people to return with them which will keep continuity in their work environment. . . . Also, junior returnees feel more at ease if the person designing the evaluation system [for promotion] is a returnee who knows the system overseas.

He became a part-time dean at age thirty-five and quickly hired twenty-nine returnees in their early thirties to mid-forties. He felt that with fifty locals and twenty-nine returnees in the school, returnees in this school as well comprised "a critical mass."

These part-time deans have turned the university around. According to the 2016 Worldwide Economics Schools Research Ranking released by Tilburg University, for 2012 to 2015, SHUFE ranked first among all universities in greater China based on research contribution, second in Asia, and fifty-fourth worldwide.

Diaspora Policy under Xi

Every leader of the CCP since 1978 has addressed China's reverse brain drain and encouraged talent to return from abroad. Xi Jinping is no different. Writing in 2017, Wang Huiyao says Xi has stressed "talent" in his speeches at different venues more than a hundred times.[171] However, Xi has magnified the diaspora's responsibility to transfer Western knowledge back to China. In October 2013, one year after becoming general secretary of the CCP, Xi spoke at the one hundredth anniversary of Western Returned Scholars Association (WRSA—欧美同学会), emphasizing the role overseas scholars could play in China's development both by returning and helping from abroad.[172]

From November 1993 until October 2013, a twelve-character slogan had directed policy on overseas study. The phrase "Support studying overseas, encourage returnees to come home, grant the freedom to come and go" (支持留学, 鼓励回国, 来去自由) had been transformative in that it had allowed people who considered returning to feel comfortable that if they did return and were unhappy, the state would not block them from leaving again. However, in his 2013 speech at the hundredth anniversary of WRSA, Xi increased the twelve characters to sixteen by adding the phrase "play a useful role" (发挥作用) to the existing slogan, and that the CCP must ensure that "those who stayed abroad had a pathway for serving the state" (留在国外有报国之门).[173]

What did Xi mean by "playing a useful role?" Perhaps he wanted to shift emphasis from getting people to return to more effectively using those who had returned. Spear sees "playing a useful role" as encouraging those who stayed abroad to transfer technology back to China.[174] However, in this speech, Xi made no direct connection between serving the state and tech transfer, saying only that the party and government must make sure that those who stay abroad have "a channel to serve the country."

Nevertheless, while Xi emphasized that, "the Party and state respect the choice of overseas scholars," and that if people choose to stay abroad, the state would support their efforts "to serve the country from abroad in various ways,"[175] he wants the CCP to be actively involved in these efforts.

Speaking to a UFWD (统战部) meeting in 2015—the UFWD is the CCP's department working with non-CCP members within and outside of China—he stated that "overseas Chinese students are an important component of the ranks of talent (人才队伍)" and "also *a new focal point* of united front work" (也是统战工作新的着力点) (emphasis added), suggesting that the CCP would actively engage them even though they were living in other countries.[176]

In 2018, Xi spoke of an "efficient and flexible concept of talent" (效益意识和柔性引才理念) "that does not seek that they are here, only that they act" (不求所在但求所为).[177] Thus, China need not bring people back, but those remaining abroad should "act" on behalf of China, an issue that would be contentious among China's critics, particularly the US. He also wanted to "mobilize talents to engage in offshore innovation in foreign countries" (在国外调动人才离岸搞创新).[178] Such activity would mesh with the program to create "Offshore Innovation and Entrepreneurial Bases for Overseas Professionals" mentioned above.

In October 2018, Xi moved the work with overseas Chinese from the OCAO, which had been administered by the government's highest committee—the State Council—to the UFWD.[179] Reportedly, in 2016, the CCP's powerful Central Discipline Inspection Committee (中央纪律检查委员会) had criticized the OCAO because its work had been "softer" than that of the CCP's UFWD. So, the UFWD began to use the offices of the OCAO to do its work with overseas Chinese.[180]

This shift could affect how the CCP works with scientists, researchers, businesspeople, and their overseas organizations. Now the efforts to mobilize them to work with China fall to the Chinese Federation of Returned Overseas Chinese, which is directly controlled by UFWD and the CCP, and likely to be more assertive (and perhaps more secretive) than the OCAO.[181] Thus, Xi has tightened the ties between the CCP and China-born professionals in the diaspora to make sure that the latter advances the interests of China and the CCP.

During a visit to China in December 2023, I was told that discussion of talent programs had ceased because, since America's China Initiative, the CCP did not want to admit that they had been running so many programs. Overseas recruitment trips, once a hallmark of the CCP's efforts to attract returnees, had reportedly ceased too. Chinese colleagues, therefore, felt that the long list I had complied of talent programs (table 2.5), was particularly "sensitive" (铭感) as it highlighted the extent of China's efforts to get foreign technology. The sensitivity of my data was demonstrated to these Chinese intellectuals because, according to one source, the professor from Jiaotong University who had contributed to a widely cited paper in the prestigious magazine, *Science*, about the "Young Thousands Talent Plan,"[182] was investigated by the Ministry of State Security for revealing the number of participants in the program which, in the current environment in China, has become a state secret.

Conclusion

How do you get talented people to go study in a vastly richer, scientifically more advanced, Western world, replete with creature comforts, excellent schools for their children, and higher salaries; encourage them to integrate enough to gain the knowledge needed for your state's national self-strengthening; and then expect them to return? Was it too much? Was it a policy doomed to failure?

Perhaps.

As getting high-quality human talent to return is no easy task, the CCP, beginning in the mid-1990s, while still working hard to bring people home, adopted the diaspora option outlined by European researchers in 1997. Several of its key talent programs, initially targeted at getting people to return, offered China-born scholars a part-time option, where they could stay abroad, ensconced in the Western scientific ecosystem, but still be encouraged to work several months a year in China to "serve the nation from abroad." Such a strategy was necessary, as most talented, China-born scientists who earned PhDs in top Western universities refused to return home on a full-time basis.

Such a strategy was effective, in part, because many China-born scholars in the West felt strong affinity to their former homeland, where their family, friends, and former colleagues still lived and worked, and where many of them had received their initial college education; they truly wanted to contribute to China becoming scientifically more powerful. They wanted joint positions in the West and in China, and they sought to train students back in China or to bring those students, postdoctoral fellows, or junior faculty to their schools and laboratories in the West. They wanted to engage in collaborative research and utilize the scientific labor force in China to promote their own research and publish in world-class journals. In transferring technologies back to China, businesspeople saw excellent opportunities to make large profits, create their own companies, swap the technology for positions in hospitals, research institutes, or drug companies, or position themselves for returning full-time.

China's party/state had its own vision, which some overseas observers see as far less benign than collaborative research and transferring the tools to a developing country that wanted access to advanced Western science. These projects mobilized the overseas scientific community, and the organizations that Chinese had formed in the diaspora, to transfer their technology to special bases within high-tech zones in China, turning the fruits of their research into companies in China that could bring them good profits in the domestic market and improve China's global competitiveness by taking market share away from firms in the West.

In the eyes of some foreign governments, such strategies harmed their own economic security, which had become a component of their national security. Some of these transfers went to academic institutions with strong ties to the Chinese military, potentially turning this technology transfer from the diaspora into direct challenges to Western states' national security. And as Xi Jinping became more assertive in his rush to meet his "China dream," he transferred the work on overseas Chinese to the CCP, making the former a focal point of the Party's united front work, an act that unfortunately put many China-born scientists in the West, who were motivated by more benign goals of improving the quality of research in China, at risk of being accused of dual loyalty or even of being agents of the Chinese state.

Although these policies and the good intentions of China-born scholars overseas may fit the rubric of the diaspora option, the intensity of China's efforts to gain Western technology and know-how, particularly in recent years, and the scale of those transfers, can be perceived by OECD countries, whose technology is transferred, as a threat to their economic and national security. This outcome was not in the minds of the European advocates of the diaspora option, who were far more worried about improving the basic science of developing states to support their economic development. Add to that a strategic component, where that technology enhances the national power of a rising challenger to the Western order, and we reach the conditions of the mid-2010s, where our story continues.

3

The China Initiative

America Challenges China's Diaspora Strategy[1]

"Nontraditional collectors" are "exploiting the very open research and development environment that we have," making the risk "not just a whole of government threat but a whole of society threat."

> — FBI Director Christopher Wray, US Senate Select Committee on Intelligence, February 13, 2018

"They could have carried out the work without creating an 'initiative,' but the DOJ loves having initiatives as it gets big headlines, a big budget, and lots of attention."

> — Carole Lam, former US attorney for the Southern District of California, February 24, 2022

Introduction

Although President Clinton's Economic Espionage Act in 1996 did not focus on China, and although, under President Obama, egregious targeting of ethnic Chinese occurred, President Trump moved the attack on Chinese researchers working and living in America, particularly those born in the PRC, to a new level. In April 2018, even before his China Initiative (CI), the US government accused

China's Thousand Talents Plan (TTP—千人计划), and the technology transfer occurring under this program, of being a threat to US economic and national security. In a campaign reminiscent of McCarthyism in the 1950s and China's Maoist era, the Trump administration mobilized numerous government and semi-government agencies, as well as the DOJ and the FBI, to root out potential spies whom it accused of illegally transferring US technology to its emerging enemy, the PRC. China's project of engineering a large-scale reverse migration, and the effort to convince Chinese in the diaspora to abet the motherland's technological development by bringing their knowledge back home, became a fierce point of contention between the two countries that has greatly harmed Sino-American scientific collaboration and massively impacted the lives of Chinese who have come to the US to study and stay. An outline of the key events related to the CI is in Appendix C.

The Changing Global and American Environment

The Obama presidency welcomed research collaboration with China. During a visit to China, the head of the NIH, Dr. Francis Collins, heralded exchanges with China as "cancer research across borders," and the two countries signed an agreement in 2010 to end cancer worldwide.[2] And despite some cases of intellectual property (IP) theft by Chinese in the early 2010s,[3] the agreement was extended in 2015. Both sides contributed several million dollars. Still, while Cohen argued that "the space for multiple affiliations and associations that has been opened up outside and beyond the nation-state has also allowed a diasporic allegiance to become both more open and more acceptable,"[4] the US government was hostile to allegiances to China from within the ethnic Chinese scientific community.

Thus, in 2012, the Commerce Department's security unit, the Investigations and Threat Management Service (ITMS), investigated Dr. Sherry Chen, a US government employee, leading to her arrest and prosecution by the FBI and the DOJ for making false statements to government investigators and unlawfully downloading data from a restricted government database. All charges were dropped in 2015 but not before Dr. Chen was publicly arrested, sentenced to twenty-five years in prison, fined USD 1 million, and fired from her job. After a federal judge found Dr. Chen had been the victim of a "gross injustice," she received one of the largest settlements ever paid to an individual plaintiff in Commerce Department history.[5] Further justice came for Dr Chen when ITMS was officially disbanded in 2021,[6] following a Senate report detailing how the unit had become a "rogue, unaccountable police force" that operated outside the law and "opened frivolous investigations on a variety of employees without evidence suggesting wrongdoing."[7] Still, Chinese scientists were excluded from an international conference to limit their access to knowledge about production at US research sites.[8]

In September 2015, the FBI openly attacked the TTP, which was run by the Organization Department of the CCP, in a widely circulated memo.[9] Therein, the FBI counseled US researchers on how to protect their IP. The report emphasized the dilemma for the FBI because "associating with these talent programs is legal and breaks no laws."[10] During that period, the FBI charged a physicist at Temple University, Dr. Xi Xiaoxing, with sharing technology with China, but four months later, dropped the case. Still, as preliminary data suggested that China was benefiting enormously from its scientific cooperation with the US,[11] the Trump administration employed its intelligence agencies to challenge China's efforts to enhance its technology.[12]

The nature of the US's attack on China's talent programs brings two comparisons to mind: McCarthyism in the 1950s and an American version of a Maoist political campaign. McCarthy and his supporters, such as Patrick McCarran, argued that foreign enemies, linked to spies within the US, mobilized its internal agents in America to share information with the Soviet Union and used their positions within the US to threaten American security.[13] Fear ripped through the ranks of professionals, particularly journalists, academics, and filmmakers, in an "inquisition,"[14] where many universities did not protect their faculty, and in fact, turned against them.[15] New York University rooted out "spies."[16] Unlike the CI, where most cases went to court, Senators McCarthy and McCarran ran congressional hearings, where these "un-American" Americans were threatened, publicly interrogated, and fired.

The CI also reflects aspects of Chinese political campaigns in the 1950s and 1960s. Top leaders—in this case the US's president, attorney general, and FBI director—invoked an external security threat to mobilize the country to seek enemies within and without. Links, which were reportedly being kept secret, were found between the outside threat and actors in the country who allegedly were working for that enemy. The state established new organizations to manage the campaign and carry out investigations at the national level. Agents of the state received unofficial quotas as to the number of enemies that had to be discovered if that agent wanted to be promoted. As under a Chinese campaign, the FBI killed "chickens" to warn the "monkeys" not to engage in activities that were seen as a threat to the state. Andrew Lelling, the former US attorney for Massachusetts, explained the thinking behind this effort.

> Maybe next time an academic does not lie about his connections to a Chinese program. Or maybe next time an academic at an institution thinks twice or thinks a little bit harder about their collaboration with a Chinese institution and what the motivations of the Chinese institution might be.[17]

FBI field offices faced heavy pressure to find people to prosecute. And even if they could not prove guilt, they relied on "pretextual prosecutions,"[18] whereby the accused were pressured to plead guilty to a lesser charge so field offices could score points with headquarters in Washington, and FBI Director Wray could claim that his organization was opening a new case every ten hours.[19] According to Mike German, an FBI special agent from 1988 to 2004, by just interrogating an ethnic Chinese scientist at the airport, on their return from China, without discovering any illegal activity, an FBI agent could win kudos from his superiors.[20]

A climate of fear and intimidation swept the US, turning actions once deemed acceptable, if not virtuous, into duplicitous, if not traitorous, betrayal. As with Mao's campaigns, the excessively wide net caught mostly innocents whose careers were destroyed. Though this scenario sounds extreme, from 2018 to 2022, the Trump administration—and to a certain extent, the Biden administration—treated its Chinese scientists born in the PRC as foreign threats to be purged from within.

The US government, particularly the FBI, long suspected that ethnic Chinese willingly helped the CCP steal US technology.[21] In 1967, under J. Edgar Hoover, the FBI cited a confidential source who claimed that scientific secrets were passed to China through "networks operating among Chinese communities" in the US.[22] Director Hoover's office proposed compiling lists of ethnic Chinese researchers and students—including US citizens—and placing them under surveillance. The building of such lists of Chinese went on for decades.

Yet in December 2007, the Deemed Export Advisory Committee quoted the Office of the National Counterintelligence Executive report, entitled "Foreign Economic Collection and Industrial Espionage, 2005," stating that while many foreign students and academics working in the US are an "important funnel abroad for technologies," most foreign students and academics working in US research institutions were not technology thieves.[23] In the committee's view, almost all foreign nationals who attempted to steal technology neither came to the US with that intention nor were they directed to do so by a foreign agent. Rather, on finding that they had access to information that was in demand at home, they were driven by personal profit, the rewards of scientific or academic acclaim, or patriotism to acquire it.[24]

China's increasing hard power and Xi Jinping's more assertive foreign policy triggered concerns in America that "engagement"—the core principle of US policy toward China since the Nixon era—had failed.[25] The Clinton administration had joined in a "comprehensive engagement" with China to discuss bilateral and multilateral issues. In 2005, under Bush, these discussions culminated in the Strategic Economic Dialogue, which Obama relabeled as the Strategic and Economic Dialogue, which included discussions on security.

Yet by 2015, on the eve of the 2016 election, and as Trump made China policy a critical component of his presidential campaign, a renewed debate emerged about China policy.[26] Disappointment stemmed from Xi's tightening of domestic policy after 2012 and the CCP's leading role in the economy, despite calls for dramatic economic reform in the fall of 2013. But according to Harding, while the concerns about China's domestic policies were long-standing, intense concerns had emerged about China's external activities, including its stealing of intellectual property, cyber-spying, and the theft of technology. China was not becoming a "responsible stakeholder" in the existing international system, an aspiration expressed by Robert Zoellick in 2005; instead, it was seen to be "free riding" on the public goods provided by the US.[27] Many complained that China was undermining the US-led, rules-based global order by creating new institutions, such as the New Development Bank (also known as the BRICS Bank), the Asia Infrastructure Investment Bank, the Regional Comprehensive Economic Partnership for the Asia-Pacific Region, and the Belt and Road Initiative. Under "Made in China 2025," the state subsidized state-owned enterprises to buy foreign high-tech firms, and it invested several hundred billion dollars in increasing China's share of the value-added in advanced industrial products.[28] China had carried out major land reclamation efforts in the South China Sea, despite Xi's promise to Obama that he would not do it, and China was building a blue water navy to deny the US access to the region's sea lanes of communication. China had also created an expanded air-defense identification zone in the East China Sea, which challenged Japanese sovereignty over the Diaoyu/Senkaku Islands. And all these steps were occurring even though Americans saw no perceptible threat to China's national security.

Most observers and politicians demanded a tougher stand toward Beijing.[29] So Obama "rebalanced" toward East Asia, leading some analysts to believe that the US and China were nearing a "tipping point" where their relationship would assume a fundamentally competitive character, even turning into an outright strategic rivalry.[30] When the Trump administration came into office in January 2017, the stage was ready for a reset in America's China policy.

To galvanize support for an attack on PRC-born Chinese studying and working in America, FBI director Wray, on February 13, 2018, told the US Senate Intelligence Committee that all Chinese students in the US were potential spies.[31]

China's use of nontraditional collectors, especially in the academic setting, whether it is professors, scientists, students, we see in almost every field office that the FBI has around the country. It's not just in major cities. It's in small ones as well. It's across basically every discipline. . . . They're exploiting the very open research and development environment that we have [in our universities], . . . they're taking advantage of [this].

The idea that Chinese intelligence relies on individual Chinese who spy for the state was put forward by a former CIA analyst, Paul Moore, in 1996 and is known as the "thousand grains of sand" theory. Moore has since recanted this model.[32] Nevertheless, lacking reliable information of a CCP-led effort to steal US technology, the US government made those accusations to disrupt collaborative research with China and alienated large numbers of ethnic Chinese scientists who, after studying at the best schools in the US, chose to remain in the US. It also intensified the decoupling of US and Chinese scientific research, a situation that is bad for China, bad for the US, and bad for the world.

In March 2018, the Office of the US Trade Representative (USTR), acting under Section 301 of the Trade Act of 1974, concluded that China's practices are unreasonable and that "[a] range of tools may be appropriate to address these serious matters."[33] That same month, Trump imposed tariffs of 25 percent on some Chinese goods, starting his "trade war." The next month, the FBI pressed the NIH to investigate the CVs and publications of its China-born awardees, whereupon its program staff discovered affiliations in publications "where authors were listed as professors at universities in China when we had no record of this; grants were listed from the Natural Science Foundation of China (NSFC), but there was no mention of this in their grant applications to us, and we saw this repeated numerous times."[34]

Even before the CI began, the US Congress held hearings where some advocated denying research funding to all Chinese scholars in the US. At an April 2018 hearing titled "Scholars or Spies," which was organized by the US House of Representatives, Michael Wessell, director of the China Security and Economic Commission, advised Congress to cut federal grants, loans, or other assistance to participants of the TTP.[35] At that meeting, US Congressman Lamar Smith accused China of planting "sleeper agents" in US universities to steal scientific breakthroughs, a view very much in line with the "thousand grains of sand" theory. While the idea of consciously planting "sleeper cells" may seem over the top, we should remember that when China's leadership in 1988 discussed how to respond to its significant brain drain, the State Science and Technology Commission had asserted that scientists who stayed abroad longer could get access to US high-tech facilities, which would help China in the long run.[36]

The same month, the US National Intelligence Council described the TTP as part of a ten-part Chinese "toolkit for foreign technology acquisition."[37] According to that report, the TTP's unadvertised goal is "to facilitate the legal and illicit transfer of US technology, intellectual property and know-how" to China. They asserted that the pool of TTP "recruits" in the US was 2,629—close to my calculation of approximately three thousand—of whom 44 percent specialized in medicine, life, or health sciences; 22 percent in applied industrial technologies;

8 percent in computer science; and 6 percent each in aviation/aerospace and astronomy.[38] The Pentagon also argued that the Chinese were targeting top talent in American universities and private research labs, including defense contractors and the USG, threatening America's national security.[39]

The pressure for a major policy shift mounted in the summer of 2018. In June, the White House Office of Trade and Manufacturing Policy, under China hawk, Peter Navarro, issued a report entitled "How China's Economic Aggression Threatens the Technologies and Intellectual Property of the United States and the World," documenting "the two major strategies and various acts, policies, and practices Chinese industrial policy uses in seeking to acquire the intellectual property and technologies of the world and to capture the emerging high-technology industries that will drive future economic growth."[40] This report, and the trade war the USTR had launched against China, were concerned with China's program, named "Made in China 2025" and promulgated by the National Peoples' Congress in March 2015, which laid out a strategy by which China could leap forward by bringing foreign technology to the manufacturing sector. In August 2018, President Trump told senior US business executives that "almost every student that comes over to this country [from China] is a spy."[41] At a three-hour secret meeting in Houston at the Texas Medical Center, with approximately one hundred directors of hospitals, the FBI presented classified information to demonstrate the security threat from "foreign entities," as well as "inside threats" from employees of institutions.[42] This meeting on August 8, 2018, instigated broad community fear and concerns by whispering accusations against China-born scientists in the US.[43] Two months later, in October 2018, Stephen Miller, a senior aide to the president, tried to convince the president to prevent any Chinese citizen from studying in the US.[44]

In response to all this activity, in November 2018, the DOJ's attorney general, Jeff Sessions, announced a "China Initiative," whose "strategic priority" was to counter Chinese national security threats and reinforce the president's national security strategy.[45] The key goals included identifying priority trade secret theft cases, ensuring that investigations are adequately resourced, and bringing them to fruition in a timely manner and according to the facts and applicable law. It emphasized the need to deal with "non-traditional collectors (researchers in labs, universities, and the defense industrial base) that are being co-opted into transferring technology contrary to US interests." And administrators in the US would be educated in the art of detecting and reporting on their faculty. Blocking potentially thousands of Chinese who were reportedly collecting data for China without being active agents of Chinese intelligence creates a major dilemma because managing the flow of technology through the movement of people is extremely complex, as the role of human talent in transferring technology "doesn't involve the export of physical goods."[46] As we will see, some university administrators acceded to such pressures, while others strongly dissented from this entire effort.

This program meshed with the shift in the US government's perception of China. In the National Defense Strategy of 2018, the US government stated, "China is a strategic competitor using predatory economics to intimidate its neighbors while militarizing features in the South China Sea," and it "seeks Indo-Pacific regional hegemony in the near-term and displacement of the United States to achieve global pre-eminence in the future."[47]

According to the Pew Research Center, favorable views of China by Americans began to decline in 2017, while negative views increased dramatically after 2018 (Figure 3.1). As of 2023, unfavorable views reached 83 percent, leaving favorable views at only 14 percent.

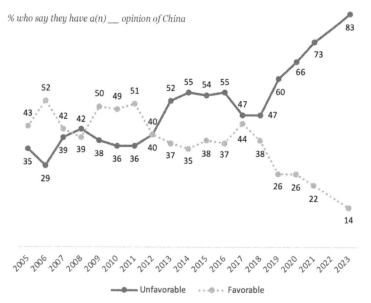

Figure 3.1. Negative Views of China Continue to Grow in US, 2005–2023.

Source: https://www.pewresearch.org/global/2023/04/12/americans-are-critical-of-chinas-global-role-as-well-as-its-relationship-with-russia/.

Note: "Don't know" responses are not shown.

Chinese scientists in the US were alarmed and could not understand the hostility targeted at them.[48] Even the Asia Society, whose writ is to enhance US-Asia understanding, joined the attack on China. Immediately after the announcement of the CI, the Working Group on China's Influence Activities in the United States, which combined scholars from the conservative Hoover Institution at Stanford University and the Asia Society's Center on US-China Relations, sharply criticized the PRC's efforts to influence American public opinion on China and the CCP, bringing many mainstream China scholars into the fray.[49] Motivated by the disparity in access between the US and China, where China has full access to an open US society and polity, while Americans face tight limitations on their ability to research Chinese society and have little or no access to Chinese technology, this report stated at the outset that it does not wish to impugn the reputation of Chinese Americans or ethnic Chinese who have established themselves in the US.[50] But it did emphasize that, through its "united front policy," the CCP tries to manipulate Chinese in the US, a view that largely supports the "thousand grains of sand" model. In the view of Diamond and Schell:

> the "united front" influenced bureaucracy in the PRC considers the whole worldwide Chinese diaspora as "overseas compatriots" (华侨同胞们), owing a measure of loyalty to "the Chinese Motherland" (中国祖国). Consequently, the Communist authorities treat people of Chinese ethnic origin as a special priority in the PRC's global influence-seeking activities.[51]

While we know from the last chapter that Xi Jinping saw the overseas Chinese students and scholars as a "focal point" of the united front strategy, the question was whether the overseas Chinese were willing to be played by the CCP.

The Campaign Unfolds

The first year of the CI was very busy. New organizations were established in the White House. On May 6, 2019, the White House's Office of Science and Technology Policy (OSTP) created the Joint Committee on the Research Environment (JCORE) to deal with China's scientific challenge, which was a cabinet-level office within the White House.[52] The foci of its four subcommittees included: research security, which was to balance "openness" with "security": rigor and integrity—that is, fostering rigorous research and freedom of inquiry but preventing inappropriate research practices; and the creation of a safe and inclusive research environment that is merit-based, safe, inclusive, equitable, and welcoming to all—even as institutions search aggressively for cheaters.[53] In June, the Department of Energy (DOE) announced that it would no longer employ anyone who joined a Chinese talent program. According to the Senate subcommittee report, five senior staffers at the DOE had previously joined the TTP.[54]

Director Wray intensified the climate of intimidation. Speaking to the Council on Foreign Relations, he repeated his view that everyone is in on it: China's intelligence services; its state-owned and what he called "ostensibly" private enterprises; and the 130,000 Chinese graduate students and researchers who work and study in the U.S. every year.[55] This idea, that Chinese intelligence uses Chinese scholars as "non-traditional collectors of information" and agents of the CCP, heralded accusations by the *Washington Post* that the CI had taken

America into "a land of fanciful enemy hunting."[56] Believing that U.S. universities were not taking Chinese technological threat seriously enough, the FBI searched for as many cases as possible to convince the academic community and university administrators that they needed to respond vigorously.[57]

On September 16, 2019, Director Drogemeier of OSTP, in a letter to the "United States Research Community," highlighted the problem of foreign talent recruitment programs.[58] New tasks for OSTP and JCORE included catching those who "abused" the open scientific environment in the US. These included "four lines of efforts:" (1) relay to federal agencies, academic research institutions, companies, nongovernmental organizations, researchers, and students "the nature and scope of the challenges America faces" and collect cases where foreigners exploited or compromised US research; (2) establish and coordinate disclosure requirements for participation in federally funded research; (3) develop best practices for academic research; and (4) develop methods to identify, assess, and manage risk in the research enterprise.

A widely cited US Senate report, published in November 2019 and entitled "Threats to the US Research Enterprise: China's Talent Recruitment Plans," presented misbehavior by TTP participants and argued that the TTP "incentivizes individuals engaged in research and development in the United States to transmit the knowledge and research they gain here to China in exchange for salaries, research funding, lab space, and other incentives."[59] But although the prestigious journal *Nature* called the report a "vivid depiction" of the problem, the findings are less than convincing in arguing that the TTP was a major source of technology theft.

Among three participants in DOE programs who were mentioned in the report, one was criticized for "disproportionate collaboration with Chinese institutions"—though what exactly that means is unclear—and for attempting "to initiate official sharing agreements between the laboratory and a Chinese organization." Moreover, that section of the report was titled "TTP Members *Likely* Stole Energy Research and Intellectual Property" (emphasis added), suggesting that the report's authors could not prove any IP theft.

Several accusations of China-born researchers involved in NIH-funded projects seemed problematic. "Individual 1" was accused of lying about affiliations because her name appeared on Peking University's website, despite her assertion that she had never taken up a position there. The NIH also told the Senate that the researcher had not reported a Natural Science Foundation of China (NSFC) grant, which violated NIH rules. Nevertheless, the US research institution allowed this ethnic Chinese researcher to keep her NIH project. In a second case, a Chinese scholar had appointments in both countries and two unreported NSFC grants. Still, the US institution allowed the principal investigator to keep his NIH grant. In a third case, the American university knew that the Chinese scholar had two half-time appointments, but it was the American university that had failed to inform the NIH of the "double-dipping."

In the end, no cases involved technology transfer or IP theft. Additionally, several reports by the American institutes revealed no overlap between the NSFC and NIH projects, despite investigations by the NIH.

Based on a conference in December 2019, OSTP published a report in June 2020 entitled "Enhancing the Security and Integrity of America's Research Enterprise," which laid out the Trump administration's case against China.[60] It defined "conflict of commitment" (COC) as a situation where an individual accepts conflicting obligations to several employers. Likewise, it included conflicting obligations to share information with, or withhold information from, an employer or funding agency. The report highlighted misbehavior by a researcher at MD Anderson, a world-leading cancer research institute, who reviewed grant applications to funding agencies but did not disclose her participation in a foreign talent program. She emailed grant applications to scientists in China and to some US-based persons, instructing one recipient to "keep it to yourself." She also emailed a grant application to a Chinese academic institution, offering, "Some methods you may learn from this proposal. Keep this confidential."[61] It published a contract between a TTP participant and the Chinese Academy of Sciences (CAS), in which the researcher was expected to transfer his US-based lab to China. He was given RMB 8 million for the lab and was to hire a research team, file two to three patents a year, and not tell his US home institution that he had agreed to such a contract.

In March 2020, the US National Science Foundation (NSF) created a new office composed of three people, called the Chief of Research Security and Policy (CRISP), whose job was to assess "capacity, overlap and duplication."[62] If they found a problem, they were to send the case to the Office of the Inspector General of the NSF, which is responsible for looking for "waste, fraud, or abuse." Seven institutions came forward, each with four to five cases, so by fall 2020, CRISP had over thirty-five cases.

According to Dr. Kaiser, who directed CRISP, these scholars signed contracts with institutes and universities that were "not the type of thing you would see in a normal western contract."[63] She told me that one faculty member in the US signed a contract with Shanghai University to spend three months a year there but did not tell his American university that he had signed a contract. The US university did not understand that the professor had agreed to set up a joint lab, and that he had obligations to fulfill responsibilities that he simply could not meet in three months, including getting graduate students, grants, and publishing articles in SSCI journals. "The US university has sanctioned the faculty member so he can't apply for grants for two years."[64]

In late-May 2020, Trump also imposed new restrictions on Chinese students or scholars who worked with any Chinese institution engaged in any way with China's program known as the "military-civil fusion strategy."[65] The proclamation defined this strategy as "actions by or at the behest of the PRC to acquire and divert foreign technologies, specifically critical and emerging technologies, to incorporate into and advance the PRC's military capabilities."[66] This policy affected about one percent of Chinese students in the US, but "experts have raised concerns about how broadly this could potentially be interpreted and how it will be perceived by Chinese students more broadly."[67] According to Dr Frank Wu, former chancellor and dean of the Hastings Law School in San Francisco, who is now president of Queens College in New York (CUNY), such proposals represent a continuum along a slippery slope.

> What's happened is the "Overton window" has moved way over to open discussion of excluding specific segments of a population defined by national origin . . . . We're one step away from it becoming politically acceptable again to talk about total exclusion.[68]

The FBI and the DOJ continued to attack Chinese technological policy at a conference in Washington at the Center for Strategic and International Studies in February 2021.[69] Attorney General Barr, FBI Director Wray, and DOJ Deputy Attorney General Demers, who ran the CI, all denounced the Chinese.[70] Their slides outlined ten methods China used to steal US technology, which included talent programs. Wray again claimed that the FBI was opening a new case every ten hours, with one slide of a graph showing exponential growth in the number of new cases that had no huge numbers, or any timeline, just an upward trend line.

Incentives to Cheat

The effort to block China from filling what I call "shortages" in its technological landscape was a key driver of the CI. By this I mean that technology transfer from the US to China around 2005 was largely middle-range technology that could earn large profits in China because it filled shortages in China's technological makeup, for which the Chinese marketplace would pay a premium.[71] But while the transfer of such middle-range technologies did not concern the US national security establishment, the high-quality technology that was being transferred to China around 2015 attracted the attention of the US government and its military and security agencies.

The Los Alamos Club, a 2022 study by the intelligence research company Strider Technologies, Inc., argues that the US government should worry about the flow of Chinese talent from Los Alamos to various research institutes and universities in China with ties to the PLA.[72] They said that they found numerous interconnections among former Los Alamos permanent staff of Chinese ethnicity and a bevy of twenty-five postdocs who came to Los Alamos and then went home after a few years in the program. While at Los Alamos, these postdoctoral fellows reportedly worked under senior Chinese scientists who recruited them and who themselves eventually moved back to China. Strider Technologies presents their findings in a manner that suggests a well-planned conspiracy with a history of over twenty years, even though the study reports that these research fellows never had access to the most sensitive research at Los Alamos.

The Importance of the US to the TTP and the TTP to the US

In the early 2000s, co-publication between scientists in the US and China intensified, and as of 2003, among its fourteen top research partners, almost one-third (32.6 percent) of the 49,346 Chinese co-publications were with the US, far ahead of China's co-publications with Japan at 14.7 percent (7,251 publications). According to the National Science Board's Science and Engineering Indicators, in 2016, 46.1 percent of China's internationally coauthored publications had a US coauthor, while China accounted for 22.9 percent of US internationally coauthored publications, followed by the United Kingdom (13.4 percent), Germany (11.2 percent), and Canada (10.2 percent).[73] Reports suggest that about 7 percent of these publications are between ethnic Chinese living in the US and Chinese in the PRC. Moreover, according to William Kerr of Harvard University, as of 2018, more than 10 percent of US inventions are made by scientists of ethnic Chinese origin (up from 5 percent in 2005).[74]

Data for 2017 show that Sino-American collaboration remained the most important scientific collaboration in the world, with a "collaboration score"—which sums the contribution to collaborative papers by both countries—of 2,673, compared to the second- and third-largest bilateral collaborations, that of Germany and the US, with a score of 1,880, and the US-UK score of 1,839.[75] China's second- and third-most collaborative bilateral relationships were also with the UK and Germany, with scores of 427 and 420, respectively, far below China's collaboration score with the US.

Data from 2018 also show that, except for US-Canada coauthorship (42.8 percent) and US-South Korean coauthorship (43.5 percent), Sino-US coauthorship outpaced US coauthorship with all other of America's partners by a large amount, as almost half of China's coauthorship happened with the US (43.7 percent).

The importance of the US to the TTP was quite significant. Among the 501 participants my research team found online in 2011, 55.9 percent had a PhD from the US, while 68.7 percent had worked in the US (table 3.1). Sixty non-US PhDs worked in the US before joining the program. In our 2013 sample, the share of TTP participants with American PhDs still comprised 53.9 percent of TTP participants.

Chinese students wanted to study and work in the US, and China sought to bring those students into the TTP. In fact, as mentioned by the US Congress, out of seven thousand TTP participants worldwide, over 35 percent were in the US.

Country/Region	PhD, 2013		PhD, 2011		Workplace, 2011	
	No.	Percent	No.	Percent	No.	Percent
US	383	53.9	274	55.9	334	68.7
China	96	13.5	59	11.8	N/A	N/A
Europe	67	9.4	52	10.6	36	7.4
UK	60	8.4	42	8.6	37	7.6
Japan	37	5.2	23	4.7	16	3.3
Canada	36	5.1	19	3.9	19	3.9
Hong Kong	nd	nd	2	0.4	16	3.3
Singapore	nd	nd	0	0	11	2.3
Others	32	4.5	18	5.9	17	3.1
Total	711	100	490	100	486	100

Table 3.1. Location of PhD and Last Residence of
Participants in the TTP, 2011 and 2013.

Note: PhDs from Hong Kong and Singapore were in "Others" for 2013. Half of the "Others" came from Australia. nd=no data. Source: Data collected online by my research team.

The data show that part-time participants in the TTP who have a US PhD are significantly better on all three of our quality measures than full-time returnees (Statistical Appendix, table A.5, row 1). However, when we compared those who had a US PhD and worked in the US to those who did not work in the US after getting their PhD there, we find that the key difference is work experience, where working in the US after graduating made them even better researchers. My findings show that only getting a PhD in the US, without working there, did not significantly enhance the quality of their research relative to China-born scholars with PhDs from other countries, such as the UK, Canada, or Germany. But receiving an American PhD *and* working in the US had a big impact on whether their work was cited, and on the influence of the journals in which they published (Statistical Appendix, table A.6).

While the TTP drew participants from the UK, Japan, the EU, Canada, and other countries, part-time participants in the TTP in the US were better than part-time participants in most other countries (Statistical Appendix, table A.6). Still, part-time participants in the UK were as well cited as those who stayed in the US, while part-time participants in Canada published in just as high-quality journals as the TTP participants in the US and were as widely cited.[76] The question for the US government, however, was whether it wanted part-time participants in the TTP to contribute to US scientific advancement if they also contributed to China's scientific advancement.

America's Key Funding Agencies

The federal government has long been the largest funder and provided 53 percent (USD 45 billion) of total research funds in the US in 2019.[77] And 90 percent of academic R&D in the US is funded by six agencies—the Department of Health and Human Services (which includes the NIH), the Department of Defense (DOD), the NSF, the DOE, NASA, and the US Department of Agriculture.

The US government institutions seen as most vulnerable to the TTP include the NIH, a major funder of biomedical research, the DOE, and the NSF. The NIH is the world's biggest public funder of biomedical research and wields immense power over America's health-research community. It allocates about USD 26 billion a year in federal grants, of which roughly USD 6 billion goes to cancer research.[78] The NSF gives out 27 percent of all federally funded, basic research grants at US universities and research institutes, with approximately USD 150 billion in research funds. The DOE is responsible for nuclear research and US nuclear weapons.[79]

Soon after FBI Director Wray testified to the Senate Intelligence Committee that universities and research institutions were enabling China to exploit US R&D activities, the NIH began a systematic search for collaborators with China who were using NIH-funded programs to advance China's interests. Reportedly the FBI gave the NIH the names of three thousand scientists (see Appendix 3, endnote 10). Institutions, such as the DOE, appear to have decided to stop funding research that might find its way to China.[80]

In March 2018, six months before the onset of the CI, NIH clarified its financial "conflict of interest" (COI) rules for the investigators it supported. These researchers were expected to report to their home institutions all personal income and research support from foreign universities and foreign educational institutions, and their home institutions in turn had to analyze this information to determine whether they imply COI or COC concerns. Then, in August 2018, before the inception of the CI, NIH Director Collins, who had heralded collaboration with China as a war on cancer, wrote to ten thousand US institutions to warn that foreign entities were mounting "systematic programs to influence NIH researchers and peer reviewers," leading to "unacceptable breaches of trust."[81]

A troublesome aspect of the CI was the shifting ground on collaboration with China, whereby once highly praised behavior became treasonous. NIH Director Collins, during his trip to Shanghai's Fudan University, was exultant about the possibility of Sino-American collaboration in finding a cure for cancer.[82] An internal NIH review had reported that between 2010 and 2019, joint projects funded by the NIH and the Chinese produced a number of high-impact papers on cancer.[83] But once the CI began, comments and reports about successful collaboration with China using NIH monies were removed from the NIH website.[84] At the same times, NIH officials said that *"excessive coauthorship with scholars in China is a sign of potential technological theft"* (emphasis added),[85] though it did not define what "excessive coauthorship" was. To the NIH, the organization was sharply criticized in several government reports at the outset of the CI for not diligently assessing the current emerging threat to national security.[86] Perhaps their fear that Congress might cut their budget led to their very tough response.

Unfortunately, this clarification by the NIH in March 2018 "moved the goalposts" in two ways. Involvement by US-based scientists with the TTP, which for many had begun in 2009 and 2010, and was not problematic then, became an act of betrayal by ethnic Chinese working in the US under the CI, and participation in the program cost some China-born professors their job. Second, the heightened level of scrutiny, whereby Chinese were accused of not reporting their participation in this program to the NIH, NSF, NASA, DOE, or other US government granting agencies, meant that actions in the past were being judged by the new standards of the day, which under the CI were much harsher.

In a Government Accountability Office (GAO) report in December 2020, which followed an extensive investigation of the five key government agencies funding university research,[87] an official admitted that the goalposts had been moved, suggesting that joining a foreign talent recruitment program might now be considered a financial conflict, even though, for many years, it was considered prestigious and an honor for American universities when their faculty members joined such foreign talent programs.[88]

The GAO report also found that, in light of recent concerns about foreign influence, "some universities added specific disclosure questions related to foreign affiliations, associations, and activities, although such disclosures were not required by government-wide guidance."[89] Administrators at one university told the GAO that in 2019, they added a question to their annual disclosures, asking faculty members if they had ever been a member of a foreign talent recruitment program. Administrators at another university said they had implemented a Global Activities Disclosure mechanism that mentions (but does not define) foreign talent recruitment programs. However, administrators from a third university had not updated their disclosure questions about foreign affiliations, associations, or activities as the emphasis had largely been on financial conflicts of interest, while nonfinancial conflicts, such as joining a talent program, had not been discussed.[90]

Despite moving the goalposts, and the comments of the GAO, universities did not grandfather in those who engaged in such behavior before the new rules were written. Yet, only in March of 2018 did the NIH issue NOTOD-18-160 which, for the first time, indicated that investigators were required to "disclose all financial interests received from a foreign institution of higher education or the government of another country."[91] Under the section about "Foreign Support," researchers were asked a new question: "Do you now or do you expect to receive in 2019 any financial or other support from a foreign governmental entity, a foreign academic institution, or a foreign research or healthcare organization associated with a foreign governmental entity or academic institution located either abroad or in the US?" The type of support included foreign academic or research grants; salary or other compensation from a foreign source; the ability to direct researchers who are supported by a foreign source; or foreign, in-kind research support, such as lab space or equipment.[92] A second notice in July of 2019, NOT-OD-19-114, further clarified the disclosure requirements relating to so-called "foreign components." The new disclosure covered external financial support for laboratory personnel and the provision of high-value materials that are not freely available (e.g., biologics, chemical, model systems, technology, etc.).[93] Academic institutions recognized this notice as setting forth new disclosure requirements for grant applicants and awardees. In 2020, this question was toughened as researchers were required to disclose honorary appointments, in-kind research support, including the selection to a foreign talent program, and "research collaboration that directly benefits your research endeavours, even if unrelated to the subject NIH grant."

Additional questions concerned many scientists and even a previous NIH administrator. Elias Zerhouni, former director of the NIH, wrote in *Science* in July 2019:

> We should remember that for years, scientific exchanges and collaborations with China were encouraged by US policy makers, including implicit support of China's Thousand Talents Program. Chinese-born, as well as American-born federally funded, scientists were publicly offered various positions in China over the years without opposition by relevant institutions. The "rules," now presented and enforced as severe violations of US ethics and intellectual property regulations, were not rigorously implemented by officials at many US institutions. The consternation, sense of targeted discrimination, and fear in the Chinese American scientific community are thus understandable.[94]

Similarly, according to Roger Wakimoto, vice chancellor for research at UCLA, "ways of working that have long been encouraged by the NIH and many research institutions, are now suspect."[95]

Writing in 2021, Lodish et al., professors at MIT, argued that federal guidelines and the enforcement of policies requiring US academics to report interactions with foreign universities and organizations had changed substantially. However, few universities communicated these changes to their faculty. Nor had university grant administrators been trained to respond to the changes. Furthermore, "if interactions with China were to be considered a special case, this should be made clear in federal guidelines as well, especially regarding collaborations and academic advising outside of federally supported programs."[96]

In August 2018, even before the CI began, the NIH reported that fifty-five institutions had conducted investigations in response to its inquiries, which targeted people who had NIH funding. In April 2019, 250 principal investigators had been flagged for suspicious behavior related to foreign ties, and as of September 2019, 180 were still under active investigation. According to Dr. Lauer, the NIH's staff responsible for vetting these scholars' activities spent an average of ten hours probing the publishing history of each of the 250 scientists it initially flagged.[97] This number included more than just PRC-born Chinese; some cases included Taiwanese, Singaporeans, and Hong Kong Chinese, triggering accusations of racism.

What really angered Dr. Lauer was the "double-dipping" on grants, because NIH funding was so competitive; yet here were Chinese who were taking NIH money away from top candidates when they also received NSFC money from China for what the NIH claimed was the same research work. He was also incensed that approximately 10 percent of the cases involved peer review violations. As mentioned, one scientist fired by MD Anderson used their position as a peer reviewer for NIH to share grant applications with Chinese colleagues, despite knowing that these actions violated NIH policy. "He'd send them off to China, often with commentary . . . and he would say this material is confidential."[98] The contracts were a huge issue too as they "can incentivize members to lie on [US] grant applications, set up 'shadow labs' in China . . . and, in some cases, transfer US scientists' hard-earned intellectual capital. Some of the contracts also contain nondisclosure provisions and require the Chinese government's permission to terminate the agreement."[99]

Still, Dr Lauer recognized that "individuals violating laws/policies represent a small proportion of scientists working in and with US institutions. We must not reject brilliant minds working honestly and collaboratively to provide hope and healing." Moreover, a study by the National Bureau of Economic Research in February 2023 showed that in areas that received significant NIH funding, and that had more Sino-US collaboration, the productivity of the research output declined after the NIH's "mini-China Initiative" began.[100] These scholars lost access to money, to research assistance from graduate students and postdocs from China, and to their Chinese colleagues, demonstrating that China-born scientists working in America often needed their Chinese collaborators to be successful scientists.

The data below show the characteristics of the 399 "scientists of possible concern" (table 3.2). Most importantly, in fifty-four cases (29 percent), the investigation had led the researcher to resign or had led the school to fire them, ending their career in the US. More examples, no doubt, followed, as we will see in case No. 2 in the next chapter with New York University. Of great concern to the NIH, and to Dr. Lauer, was that 133 foreign grants had not been reported to the NIH.

Finding	Number (%)
Undisclosed foreign grant	133 (70%)
Undisclosed talents award	102 (54%)
Undisclosed foreign company	17 (9%)
Undisclosed foreign patents	7 (4%)
Peer review violations	9 (5%)
Any NIH violation	154 (81%)
Violation of institutional rules	70 (37%)
Termination or resignation	54 (29%)
Institutional removal from NIH system	77 (41%)

Table 3.2. Violations Cited in the NIH Data, 2019.

Source: Michael Lauer, "ACD Working Group on Foreign Influences on Research Integrity Update," https://acd.od.nih.gov/documents/presentations/12132019ForeignInfluences.pdf.

In the summer of 2020, half a year after Dr. Lauer released this report, I interviewed him twice and exchanged emails, hoping to determine the scale of the problem. According to the NIH website, the total funds allocated to non-NIH institutions that are available for competitive grants is 80 percent of the USD 41.7 billion it allocates on an annual basis, equaling USD 33.6 billion. But if each grant lasts approximately five years, the total funds available for "cheaters, liars and thieves" annually would be USD 6.7 billion. According to Dr. Lauer, the total funds potentially used fraudulently equaled USD 164 million, which when divided by USD 6.7 billion, shows that 2.4 percent of NIH monies went to scientists whose morality he was questioning. In September 2020, Dr. Lauer accepted my numbers as appropriate.[101] Yet the implications were massive for researchers that Dr. Lauer targeted and for the scientific community of Chinese extraction in the US.

Dr. Lauer elaborated his views in an email:

We don't know the extent of the financial losses. Institutions often spend millions of dollars to build a faculty member's laboratory. If that faculty member shares their expertise, methods, data, documents, grants, and materials with outside entities without the permission of his/her employer, the institution loses a good part of its investment. . . . There is also a loss of trust, again hard to quantify. Scientists who lie to their institutions (and to NIH and the IRS) cannot be trusted to produce data or reports we can believe in.

He also worried that donors (no doubt the US Congress) might cut back NIH funding.

Dr. Lauer and Dr. Rebecca Kaiser, the head of the NSF's investigations group, also emphasized the opportunity costs when people hold two jobs concurrently or accept additional funding from China that is not reported to the US funding agency. This overcommitment made fulfilling their obligations to either their US funding agency or their American employer difficult, as they could not apply their full attention to the NIH or NSF grant they had received. But because the NIH only funds 20 percent of the applications, "honest scientists lose out."[102]

Because some China-born professors who reviewed grant applications for the NIH passed on the new research in these applications to colleagues in China or to Chinese colleagues in the US, the Office of Inspector General within the HHS, the NIH's parent body, suggested that the NIH pay "extra attention" to screening scientists "who would be reviewing grant applications with particularly sensitive subject matter or that have lucrative commercial applications."[103] It also recommended that the NIH, in consort with the HHS Office of National Security, develop a risk-based approach for identifying those peer-review nominees who warrant extra scrutiny.[104] As a result, many China-born scientists in the US were no longer allowed to act as reviewers.

Dr. Lauer's closing report came in December 2022.[105] Of the final 246 cases, 130 (53.1 percent) had not reported talent awards, 171 (69.8 percent) had "double-dipped" in terms of funding, 103 (41.9 percent) were terminated or resigned, and 156 (63 percent) scientists lost their grants, without which they could not do the necessary preliminary research for future applications. While in 2020, only nine people (5 percent) had been engaged in peer review violations, by 2022, 193 people (78.5 percent) could no longer serve as peer reviewers, reflecting the enormous loss of faith that the NIH had in China-born scientists. Quite troubling, too, is that, as of December 2022, 142 of the cases remained ongoing, even though most cases had been opened in 2018 and 2019, suggesting that 57.7 percent of these people were in limbo, uncertain whether they would be found guilty of some activity that might ruin their careers in the US.

The Role of Universities

As the institutions where many China-born researchers worked, where much of the scientific research in America occurs, where much government funding went, and where China-born graduate students and postdocs received training about the most recent American research, universities were deeply involved in efforts by the Trump and Biden administrations to stem the flow of US technology to China. According to Dr. Lauer's report, of the 399 "cases of possible concern," forty-four (11 percent) had been disclosed by the universities themselves.[106]

Once the NIH approached the universities with the names of "persons of interest" and threatened to cut off their NIH funding unless they terminated the tenured contracts of participants in the TTP who had not properly disclosed those affiliations, universities had two choices: (1) acquiesce to the demands of the funding agencies and delve into the foreign activities of their faculty; or (2) toughen their regulations on the disclosure of outside funding and activities, make the researchers revise their external activities file, but risk incurring the wrath of government funding institutions in defending their faculty who might be being treated improperly. According to a Senate report, after the NIH notified a university that a faculty member was a "person of interest," they had only thirty days to review the case and "confirm that this investigator and the [US institution that received the NIH funding] complied with [the NIH's] policies."[107]

Universities that wanted to protect their funding usually complied, and some went even further than the NIH in discovering and expelling their own faulty members.[108] The University of California at San Diego's (UCSD) handling of the accusations of Xiang-Dong Fu is a case in point, where the NIH was already satisfied when he was banned from applying for NIH grants for four years after it was discovered that he had received a monthly stipend from the TTP. But UCSD still went after him for breaking its own rules against a "conflict of interest."[109] A Moffitt internal report showed that the NIH was threatening US institutions: Do a better job vetting your researchers or risk that "failure to report and vet such collaborations causes NIH to question institutional competence to serve as a responsible steward of federal funding."[110] According to Dr. Epling-Burnette, who was fired from Moffitt for not disclosing that she took money from China, "these institutions live in absolute fear of NIH and worry that, if they don't go overboard in taking action, NIH might cut them off. But good people are being crushed in the process."[111]

When first told that "persons of interest" were among their faculty, many universities initially denied that their faculty could have engaged in the alleged misbehavior.[112] But when shown scientific publications bearing the names of their faculty as coauthors—but without listing their university and instead listing a Chinese university as their home institution—vice presidents for research and the professor's department heads could turn on them.

According to *Nature*, which interviewed vice presidents for research at ten US academic institutions, some universities were "changing their behavior" because they saw little choice but to respond to congressional oversight.[113] Administrators at Washington State University at Pullman, Oklahoma State University in Stillwater, and the University of North Texas in Denton began meeting regularly with local FBI liaisons but argued that they were helping their faculty by seeking "to familiarize the secretive agency (FBI) with university tenets of openness, and the need for foreign collaborations." The University of South Alabama even hired a former FBI agent who specialized in counterintelligence as its director of information technology and risk compliance. The University of North Texas also imposed restrictions on overseas travel to China or to what Vice President McLellan called "certain known foreign entities where technology may be compromised."[114]

In the case of Dr. Wu Xifeng, the director of the Center for Translational and Public Health Genomics at the University of Texas's MD Anderson Cancer Center in Houston, the center's head of compliance, Max Weber, found no record of her accepting any funds for taking up visiting professor posts at several Chinese universities.[115] Of the 540 papers which Dr. Xi had coauthored, only 16 percent were with PRC-born Chinese, so she was not so deeply engaged with sharing information with China. In fact, the only mistake Weber could find was that Dr. Wu had asked her staff to download NIH applications and edit her peer reviews of these proposals, perhaps to improve the English writing. This action, Weber concluded, violated MD Anderson's ethics policies and fell within the NIH's examples of misdeeds related to peer review. And because she preferred to answer his questions in writing rather than talk face-to-face, he was convinced that she had taken unreported funds from China.

In the end, the new president of MD Anderson protected its NIH funding, worth USD 148 million in 2018, instead of Dr. Wu. The cancer center, he argued, has a "social responsibility" to taxpayers and its donors to protect its intellectual property from any country trying "to take advantage of everything that is aspirational and outstanding in America." So, he hounded her out to protect the NIH grants, even though she was only guilty of a misdemeanor. Commenting on this case, Lynn Goldman, dean of the Milken School of Public Health at George Washington University, said that these kinds of compliance issues are universal among senior researchers. "Is it wrong? Probably. Is it a capital offence? Hardly."[116]

It was not so easy for the FBI to raise awareness within the universities because to do so, they needed to share information that had previously been treated as "secret." So, the FBI did not always apprise universities of potential threats in their research community, such as improper technology transfer, IP theft, and cyberattacks from foreign countries. As result, new intelligence legislation was necessary, which "include measures to promote increased information sharing across the interagency and with academia."[117] Among those measures was a requirement for a new unclassified report listing Chinese and Russian academic institutions that had a history of improper activities related to IP, or that worked with China's armed forces or intelligence agencies. Still, the FBI exercised an assertiveness in this search for internal enemies that bordered on zealotry, and when needed, they gave universities the spy tools to troll their own faculty's emails in order to determine if the Chinese scientists were lying about overseas affiliations.[118]

In 2020, the Trump administration, in a "scathing" report, concluded that top universities "massively underreported" funding they accepted from China, Russia, and other "foreign adversaries."[119] Education Secretary Betsy DeVos said her agency uncovered "pervasive noncompliance" from universities that had "significant foreign entanglement." According to DeVos, "For decades enforcement was lax, but not anymore. . . . We took action to make sure the public is afforded the transparency the law requires."[120]

Despite these threats to their funding, many research universities rallied around their Chinese faculty and resisted the pressures from the CI, including UC Berkeley, UC Davis, The University of Michigan, UCLA, Rice,[121] Stanford,[122] and others. MIT's president paid the legal defense of Professor Chen Gang, who was accused by the FBI of hiding his affiliations in China.[123] Baylor College of Medicine did not fire staff who had not followed NIH policies on disclosures because it felt that these actions were "not serious enough to merit disciplinary action."[124] The Permanent Subcommittee on Investigations' report gave an example of "Individual X," whose institution, after an investigation, asserted that the work in China did not overlap with any NIH grant, current or past, and therefore allowed the individual to remain the principal investigator on the NIH grant and only counseled this professor on the "importance of full and accurate disclosure."[125]

In an internal memo, the vice president for research at Texas Tech University warned his faculty that the US Congress was planning to introduce legislation targeting academics at American universities who associated with Chinese, Russian, and Iranian "talent programs."[126] Under that legislation, faculty who had participated in Chinese talent programs would be ineligible for grants from the US DOD, an important funding agency for a school such as Texas Tech. In his memo, he told the faculty of a case where a Chinese professor at Texas Tech was invited to join the TTP, but only if he helped establish relations between Texas Tech and a Chinese university, which turned out to have connections to the Chinese military. After consulting with the administration and the FBI, the professor declined the invitation.

In late 2019, nineteen research universities and associations urged the US government to "tread carefully."[127] The organizations acknowledged that "concern with the mounting global reach of Beijing's tech-enabled authoritarianism is valid," but they stressed that "calls to monitor individuals solely based on their country of origin violate norms of due process and should raise alarms in a democracy." In 2021, over 177 professors from Stanford University urged the US government to end the CI.[128] According to Peter Michelson, Stanford's senior associate dean for the natural sciences and an organizer of the letter, "I think what the FBI's done in most cases is to scare people—investigating people and interrogating them. And it's harmful to the country." Former US Energy Secretary and Nobel prize winner Steven Chu, a professor at Stanford, said that rather than protect US advantages in technology and understanding, the program risked undermining America's lead in science. "We were the brain gain for half a century," he told *Reuters*. "You really want to throw this away?"[129] Pressure, therefore, mounted on the DOJ to prove that the theft of US information related to commercial, scientific, and military technology was a large enough threat to US national security to warrant a crackdown on collaborative research and visa accessibility to the US for Chinese students and scholars.[130]

The scholarly community has long wanted to roll back intrusions by the national security agencies into the international circulation of scientific knowledge, preferring an open science model.[131] In the early 1980s, a National Academy of Sciences' panel concluded that, regarding exchanges with the Soviet bloc, "in comparison with other channels of technology transfer, open scientific communication involving the research community does not present a material danger from near-term military implications."[132] In 1999, a National Academy of Science's committee had insisted that if the US was to remain the world's technological leader, it must remain deeply engaged in international dialogue, despite the possibility of the illicit loss of information.[133] Therefore, Krige sees the outburst by the scientific community over the restrictions on Chinese nationals as anger at an "entrenched system of surveillance of the US research enterprise, including national laboratories, industry, and academia."[134]

The Foreign Thousand Talents Plan (FTTP)

The FTTP program, which began in 2012 with forty participants and expanded to 244 participants by 2015, was deeply troubling. Under it, China secretly paid large salaries, gave bonuses, and funded laboratories for leading foreign researchers who accepted large remunerations for transferring their knowledge to China.[135] And while such transfers are legal if the researcher reports the monies to the IRS, many significant transfers went under the radar. The issue is less problematic when American researchers move to China and work in a university or a research institute, as the Chinese side is paying their salaries, their affiliations are up front, and the new technology is developed in China with Chinese funding. But from the US perspective, much of the early research that is the scientific base of the technology that was transferred to China was funded by American taxpayers, and these "foreign talents" benefit financially from transferring this information to America's "strategic competitor." Cases in point were Professor Charles Lieber of Harvard[136] or the researchers at Moffitt in Orlando. The second case will be addressed in detail in the next chapter.[137]

The Situation in Life Sciences

The US is deeply concerned about the biomedical or life sciences field. Biological and biomedical sciences and engineering have driven the continual increase in academic science and engineering research. These two fields accounted for 60 percent of total research growth from 2007 to 2019.[138] No surprise then the NIH, as the major funder of biological or life sciences research in the US, embraced the CI.

Cancer research drives the medical industry in China, as 25 percent of cancer deaths globally occur in the PRC and one-fifth of all deaths in China are from cancer.[139] As a result, transferring the latest US cancer research has been a major part of the TTP. On December 20, 2019, in a conference call with the cancer center directors from all seventy-one National Cancer Institute-designated (NCI) cancer centers, NCI Director Dr. Ned Sharpless commended the compliance office of Moffitt for reporting their employees' and administrators' violations, calling for close coordination with NCI and the NIH.[140]

Of all participants in the TTP, 44 percent were engaged in life sciences, and as mentioned above, the NIH allocates roughly USD 6 billion, or 24 percent of the total USD 26 billion a year that it gives in federal grants, to nongovernmental institutions. Researchers in biotech and life sciences, where the US has a commanding but shrinking lead, are the largest group of TTP participants in the US after engineers. China also made life sciences one of its key priorities, and various research programs recruit US- and German-trained PhDs, or Chinese with local PhDs but with extensive overseas experience, to return to China.[141]

For more than a decade, cancer research has been a core sector of Sino-US collaboration. Between 2010 and 2019, the NIH offered about USD 5 million a year in grants for US-China collaborations, with 20 percent going to cancer research; a counterpart in China pitched in USD 3 million a year. An internal NIH review showed that joint projects have produced numerous high-impact papers on cancer. According to Waldman, international collaborations are intrinsic to the United States NCI's "Moonshot Program," the government's USD 1 billion blitz to double the pace of treatment discoveries by 2022. One of the program's tag lines was "Cancer knows no borders."[142]

The Problem of Racial Profiling

Attacking co-ethnic publications raises the possibility of "racial profiling," as approximately 10 percent of researchers on the American side who collaborate with the PRC were born in China. Thus, given America's long history of racial profiling, particularly vis-à-vis Asians, many Chinese in America denounced what they saw as racial profiling in the CI.[143] According to a March 2019 letter in *Science* composed by ethnic Chinese researchers:

> the recent political rhetoric and policies that single out students and scholars of Chinese descent working the United States as threats to U.S. national interests . . . have led to confusion, fear, and frustration among these highly dedicated professionals, who are in danger of being singled out for scapegoating, stereotyping, and racial profiling.[144]

Racial profiling has long been a problem within the US intelligence services.[145] FBI files from the 1970s show that unlike the program covering the USSR, which included monitoring potential non-Russian agents who might have been working with the Soviets, "in the case of the Chinese scientist program, subjects came under suspicion primarily because of their ethnicity."[146]

German argues that FBI leaders have propagated Chinese and other ethnic stereotypes since September 11 as part of their effort to focus more heavily on domestic counterintelligence.[147] FBI internal training materials viewed in 2011 under the Freedom of Information Act featured presentations on "the Chinese" that were full of generalizations about Confucian relationships ("authority and subordination is accepted") and saving face. According to German:

> The training is a form of othering, which is a dangerous thing to do to a national security workforce learning to identify the dangerous "them" they're supposed to protect "us" from. . . . Even the title, "The Chinese," imagines 1.4 billion people sharing the same characteristics. It seems more likely to implant bias than to educate agents about the complex behaviour of spies.[148]

German believes that racial profiling is ingrained into the FBI, because soon after being rebuked for seeing "Black Identity Extremists" as a security threat, FBI

Director Wray quickly stigmatized Chinese by asserting that the US faced a "whole of society threat," including from Chinese students in America who could easily be recruited to spy.[149]

A *Bloomberg News* analysis of more than twenty-six thousand security clearance decisions for federal contractors after 1996 demonstrates the US government's growing lack of faith in Americans with ties to China.[150] From 2000 to 2009, the Pentagon denied applications to people with connections to China at the same rate as applicants with links to all other countries: 44 percent. But from 2010 to October 31, 2019, the China-related denial rate jumped to 61 percent as the rate for all other countries fell to 34 percent. In other words, more than three-fifths of applicants who had ties to China were denied security clearances to work for US government contractors, while two-thirds of applicants with ties to other countries were approved. Even people with ties to Iran and Russia—whose denial rates of 64 percent and 52 percent, respectively, put them among the most rebuffed applicants in the early 2000s—saw their rejection rates fall after 2010 to 48 percent and 45 percent, respectively. Those declines compare with a seventeen-point jump in the rate of China-linked denials.

On May 21, 2015, twenty-two Chinese American members of the US Congress signed a letter to Attorney General Lynch requesting an investigation into whether federal employees were being racially targeted.[151] In November 2015, Congresswoman Grace Meng said:

> Nobody should live in fear of being persecuted for crimes they did not commit, solely based on their ethnicity. . . . We must fight against institutional biases where they exist, especially within the federal government. I . . . urg[e] the [DOJ] . . . [to] establish and enforce internal procedures against racial profiling so that we may prevent cases like these from happening in the future.[152]

On April 26, 2016, Representative Judy Chu said, "We cannot tolerate another case of Asian-Americans being wrongfully suspected of espionage. . . . The profiling must end."[153]

Andrew Kim's comprehensive study of racial profiling in December 2018 garnered much attention. In his paper entitled "Prosecuting Chinese 'Spies': An Empirical Analysis of the Economic Espionage Act," Kim analyzed a sample of cases under the Economic Espionage Act (EEA) from 1997 to 2015, before the Trump administration.[154] The author selected 136 cases involving 187 individual defendants using court documents from the Public Access to Court Electronic Records database.[155] These cases included Chinese and non-Chinese. Among these cases, Kim found that from 1997 to 2009, 17 percent of defendants indicted under the EEA had Chinese names, but from 2009 to 2015, that rate tripled to 52 percent.

Similarly, between 2009 and the end of 2014, when he looked at defendants charged under the EEA who were of "Asian heritage," he found that Chinese-named defendants were twice as likely to be wrongfully accused as compared to non-Chinese defendants.

Kim argued that when dealing with Chinese scientists, FBI agents were more likely to drop the charge of espionage, replacing it with lesser crimes in a process known as "pretextual prosecutions." This strategy is used when prosecutors, who believe but cannot prove that a defendant is guilty of a serious offense, seek conviction and punishment for a more minor one.[156] In fact, innocent defendants charged with espionage might plead guilty to such minor offenses to avoid harsher punishments.[157]

Kim also argued that federal agents and prosecutors assume ethnic Chinese scientists must be secretly working for China.[158] As a result, prosecutors are more likely to view ambiguous evidence of guilt as conclusive when it involves an Asian suspect because that evidence comports with their preexisting image of Asians as spies. The belief that certain racial groups disproportionately commit certain crimes can lead to charging and conviction rates that appear to confirm those stereotypes.[159]

Kim's data also suggest that Chinese defendants are treated more harshly than non-Chinese. Thus, 49 percent of defendants with Western names who were convicted of espionage received probation, as compared to 21 percent of convicted Chinese defendants and 22 percent of all Asian defendants.

An alternative explanation, however, is that particularly during the CI, these China-born scientists were targeted by the FBI, less because of an inherent "ethnic" bias within the FBI but more because they were returning from a country, China, that was seen as a strategic competitor of the US that had become the target of a widespread DOJ "campaign" and that had a record of engaging in illicit methods to get US technology. As a result, the FBI was quick to interrogate these researchers at the airport on their return to the US (as was the case with Dr. Chen Gang of MIT) or soon thereafter. During that process, the scientist may make false statements to the FBI agent, which is a federal crime. This description fits the case of Dr. Simon Ang of the University of Arkansas at Fayetteville, who was originally charged with fifty-nine felonies, fifty-eight of which were dropped. (See his case study in the next chapter.)

The DOJ was criticized for violating Asian and Asian American's civil liberties.[160] According to the ACLU, the initiative was accompanied by xenophobic, anti-China rhetoric from the Trump White House, as well as public statements by the FBI director that cast suspicion on virtually anyone with family or professional ties to China—including thousands of accomplished Asian American and immigrant scientists who have contributed to the US for years. These statements have encouraged racial profiling and discrimination, including within the FBI. The ACLU described singling out scientists based on their race, ethnicity, or national origin as "unconstitutional."[161]

How Did the TTP Turn Sour?

When and how did the TTP morph into a program that engaged in some IP theft and technology transfers that ignored the norms of scientific research and US national security? Why has the TTP, which incorporated many positive solutions in 2008, turned sour?[162] For me, the most important change was the replacement of Li Yuanchao by Zhao Leji, who had no overseas experience and no experience with education or R&D. The first year he headed the Organization Department, 2012, no officials from Beijing attended the Guangzhou Talent Fair; apparently, they feared being criticized for using public funds to travel.[163] Thereafter, transparency disappeared.

The rise of Xi Jinping in 2012 and his decision to promote "Made in China 2025," while ignoring a liberal reform program articulated at the Third Plenum of the Eighteenth Party Congress in October 2013, played a role. Under "Made in China 2025," China seeks overseas technology to improve its position within global manufacturing chains, and the CCP saw PRC-born Chinese in the diaspora as a source of, or channel to, that technology. Under Xi, the CCP has been pouring money into its diasporic community.[164] Likewise, the intensification of the CCP's united front strategy abroad could pull more China-born professors into China's orbit. As we saw in the previous chapter, in 2015, Xi made PRC-born Chinese in the diaspora a "focal point" of united front work.[165] Finally, Xi has "securitized" the national economy, putting great emphasis on China becoming independent of Western technology in AI, semiconductors, nanotechnology, and robotics, all of which are quite advanced in the US. In his view, independence could be advanced by China-born scientists who remain overseas.[166]

Part of the problem also lies with individuals who have a limited moral compass. The US Senate documented several egregious cases of "double-dipping," where Chinese scholars with jobs in the US concurrently held a full-time job in China under the TTP. Still, we lack systematic data on the extent of the problem except to say that, as we saw in the last chapter, 35 percent of the 121 China-born scholars in our sample held concurrent posts. Some researchers in the US are engaged in cutting-edge fields, such as biomedical products or procedures, that are in short supply in China, creating the opportunity for them to earn enormous profits because the market in China will pay a premium for these goods and services. These people have strong incentives to take the technology and run home![167] Chances to get rich are difficult to ignore, especially for those who helped create the product in the first place. To that extent, the "spies" who appeared in media headlines and courtrooms were more concerned with "trade secrets" through which to make money rather than trying to obtain nuclear launch codes.[168] According to Prasso, who collected fifty cases from the DOJ website that fit the time frame of the CI, most economic espionage cases listed on the CI website involved accusations of profiteering or career advancement by individuals rather than state-directed spying.[169]

No doubt, there was egregious behavior. Zhang Yiheng, a professor at Virginia Tech, used government research funds to set up a company in China and get grants for work already accomplished in China,[170] while in a second case which broke in 2018, a China-born General Electric engineer used technology he helped develop to establish a company in Nanjing. But there is no record of Chinese government involvement in the firm; moreover, GE knew about the company and did not force him to close it.[171] Another Chinese national, Zheng Zaosong, allegedly stole 21 vials of biological research from Beth Israel Deaconess Medical Center in Boston. He intended to bring them to a hospital in China and publish the results as if they were his own, when he was arrested.[172]

Nevertheless, we have many reasons to question the scale of any organized, state directed theft. In 2021, Truex argued that:

> At this point, we have a few well-cited cases of misconduct among Chinese citizens in university settings, but the actual incidence of wrongdoing among that population is unknown. Current estimates suggest there are 41,000 master's students, 36,000 doctoral students, and 38,000 postdoctoral/visiting scholars of Chinese citizenship currently in STEM fields at U.S. universities, about 115,000 in total. Based on current DOJ charges, this implies a criminality rate in this population of .0000869, less than 1/10,000.[173]

Third, the strategic context within which the CCP developed the TTP complicated this policy. While the diaspora option and state promotion of reverse migration are lauded worldwide, America's fear of China's rise, and the strategies China has used to speed up its scientific development, turned the technology flows under such initiatives into threats to America's national security. To shut down this technology flow, and as part of its overall "decoupling" strategy, the US government declared war on the TTP and built the narrative that China is engaged in an organized process of IP theft and spying that is a direct threat to the national security of the US.

Even co-ethnic publications, which are not directly articulated by the TTP, but which are key to the CCP's strategy to carry out collaborative research across the Pacific, and which were lauded in the "war on cancer," took on sharply negative connotations under the Trump administration. As mentioned above, the NIH saw the "frequent publishing with colleagues outside the United States" by American-based scientists as a warning of possible illegal behavior and technology transfer.[174]

Yet numerous studies show the importance of China to American science, as China is America's leading research partner based on first authorship and governmental funding (table 3.3). Their collaboration, measured by co-publications, is almost 2 times the co-publications between the US and the UK and more than US co-publications with Germany and the UK combined.

Country	1996	2000	2004	2008	2012	2016	2018	2020
China	3.8	4.6	7.0	11.2	16.5	22.8	25.7	26.3
United Kingdom	12.5	12.8	13.0	12.7	12.6	13.4	13.3	13.6
Germany	12.3	12.8	12.5	11.6	11.9	11.2	11.0	10.8
Canada	12.0	11.0	11.6	11.6	10.8	10.4	10.3	10.7
Japan	10.3	9.9	9.1	7.6	6.2	5.5	5.4	5.3
France	8.0	8.5	8.0	7.6	7.7	7.5	7.1	6.9
Italy	5.7	6.1	6.5	6.7	6.8	6.6	6.4	6.8
Switzerland	4.2	4.1	3.9	4.1	4.4	4.4	4.4	4.4
Australia	4.1	4.4	4.8	5.0	5.5	6.3	6.5	6.8
Netherlands	3.9	4.3	4.1	4.1	4.8	4.8	4.7	4.9
Sweden	3.1	3.2	3.0	2.8	3.0	3.3	3.3	3.2
South Korea	3.0	3.5	4.5	5.0	5.6	4.9	4.6	4.5
India	2.5	2.4	2.4	2.8	3.3	3.5	3.7	4.1
Brazil	2.1	2.6	2.6	3.0	3.2	3.9	4.0	4.3

Table 3.3. US Articles with Coauthors from Selected Countries, 1996–2020 (%).

Note: I do not know why each column totals more than 100 percent. Source: National Center for Science and Engineering Statistics; Science-Metrix; Elsevier, Scopus abstract and citation database, accessed May 2021.

A second study investigates Sino-American research collaboration by analyzing coauthorship over time.[175] The authors approached collaboration from three perspectives: (1) overall, (2) high-impact, and (3) high-technology research collaborations, using data from the Web of Science, Nature Index, and the Technology Alert List maintained by the US State Department. Again, the US is China's largest research collaborator, and China and the US are each other's primary collaborator much of the time in all three aspects. In terms of "high-impact collaboration," China historically has shared a higher percentage of its research with the US than vice versa. In terms of "high-technology research," the situation is reversed, with the US sharing more. The percentage of American high-technology research shared with China has been continuously increasing over the past ten years, while in China, the percentage has been relatively stable, allowing China to benefit more from working with US scientists.

A third study looked at joint grants between China and seventy-five countries from 2006 to 2016.[176] It examined collaboration partners in three aspects: overall collaboration activity, relative research effort, and the groups of countries that were collaborating. The US, with 53.3 percent of China's total NSFC grant collaborations in that period, ranked 45 percent ahead of the UK, which was China's number two research collaborator. The remaining fourteen countries accounted for 46.7 percent, less than America's total share.

Another finding showed that between 2013 and 2018, US research publications would have declined without coauthorship with China, whereas China's publication rate would have risen without the US.[177] Likewise, the top Chinese and US agencies are jointly funding research, creating a mutually beneficial situation rather than a zero-sum confrontation. China's financial contribution to joint projects shows that China is developing its science by partnering with the US.[178]

What Kang's data also suggest, however, is that joining the TTP part-time, while still working abroad, did not necessarily cause Chinese overseas to publish with colleagues in China. As he showed, collaboration increased significantly even when China-born scientists living abroad were affiliated with universities in China, whether or not they joined a talent program.[179] Affiliation with an institution in China itself, not joining the TTP, increases the proclivity for co-publication (and in the view of the NIH, increases the likelihood of illegal technology transfer). China's talent programs were not the real issue. But people who return to a university full-time are even more likely to publish with colleagues in China.

China Responds to the China Initiative

The Chinese government followed events in the US closely. According to the *Peoples' Daily*, the "China Action Plan" (the Chinese name for the CI) was a component of the "whole-of-government" strategy adopted by the Trump administration against China, whose purpose is to disrupt high-tech exchanges between China and the United States to slow China's development.[180] Moreover, the US government's false accusations against several Chinese American scientists had created widespread anti-China and anti-Chinese sentiment in society. "Some US media outlets have sensationalized these cases even before they reach a verdict, leading to the manipulation of public opinion," poisoning the environment for China-US technological and cultural exchanges. For China, this trend undermines "the normal exchange and cooperation between China and the US in the fields of science, technology, and humanities" and harms what are essentially interactions between individuals that should buffer bilateral relations. The foreign ministry spokesperson, Wang Wenbin, saw the CI as marking the resurgence of McCarthyism in the United States.[181]

Many views focused on what people saw as the continued anti-Chinese racism in America. Hu Wenli, a reporter for the *China Youth Daily*, the newspaper of the Young Communist League, portrayed the CI as another version of the infamous Chinese Exclusion Act of 1882, reflecting the deep-rooted mistrust of Asian Americans within white society in the US.[182] On December 15, 2021, a year into the Biden administration, Zhao Lijian, the Chinese Foreign Ministry's leading "wolf warrior," waxed eloquently on racism in America, a favorite Chinese topic in light of America's accusations that China discriminates against its Uighur and Tibetan populations.

> It is regrettable that discrimination against Chinese Americans in the United States has not been effectively corrected as the country has progressed economically and socially.... The hard work and contributions of Chinese Americans and other ethnic minorities in the United States have not been met with respect and protection but rather continuous discrimination and unfair treatment. This goes against the principles of "human rights" and "equality" that the United States claims to uphold, and it is a disgrace to American democracy. The US side should address its serious issues of racial discrimination and safeguard the legitimate rights and interests of ethnic minority groups, including the Chinese diaspora.[183]

In December 2021, a writer for *Xinhua News Agency* also raised the theme of racism in America, indirectly encouraging people to return.[184] That author quoted Peter Navarro, the former director of the Office of Trade and Manufacturing Policy at the US Department of State, who openly called China America's "first non-Caucasian competitor." He then quoted three scholars and politicians from the UK, Singapore, and Spain, who believed that the fear of China had activated the historical legacy of the "Yellow Peril" in the US, mutating into a malignant "political virus."[185] It quoted a former leader of the Liberal Democrats in the UK, who had pointed out that "for all researchers in the United States, any connection with China is a double-edged sword.... In the field of science, the threats faced by Asian experts further demonstrate the structural racial discrimination that exists in American society." It also cited Malcolm Cook, a research fellow at the Institute of Asian Studies at the National University of Singapore, who said that Americans should ask themselves, "How much of their reaction to China's rise is based on calm and rational analysis, and how much is deeply rooted in discomfort with the success of a non-white civilization?"

Zhao Lijian also saw the CI as another example of inappropriate behavior by US intelligence agencies to achieve political purposes. He quoted former Secretary of State Mike Pompeo's words, "We lie, we cheat, we steal," and then listed numerous efforts by the US intelligence services to manipulate the truth. He also highlighted challenges by scientists, civil rights organizations, and several US senators on February 1, 2021, to encourage the House Committee on Civil Rights and Civil Liberties to investigate the FBI's counterintelligence work and the actions of the NIH against Chinese or Asian American scientists for actions that harmed the work, reputation, life, and families of the relevant scientists.[186]

In response to this external scrutiny, the CCP ended all public discussion of the TTP, sending the program "underground." According to Mallapaty, a memo by the NSFC that circulated on social media instructed people interviewing potential applicants to avoid e-mail correspondence and not to mention the TTP when inviting candidates back to China. Another widely circulated message on social media, claiming to be from the human resources department of an institution that was not named, urged representatives of fellow HR departments to delete information on their websites related to the TTP, as "required by the Ministry of Education."[187] The director of a think tank in China received a phone call from the Cyberspace Administration of China, also known as the Internet Information Office, which is directly under the CCP's Central Committee, insisting that all reference to the TTP on their website be removed.[188] The *Financial Times* also reported that a "responsible official" at a top university in China had been directed by the Chinese government to remove all information about their school's professors involved in the program from the university website to "ensure that they remain free from suspicion."[189]

In fact, when I returned for a visit to China in December 2013, I was not allowed to present this current study in a public forum as no one in China was talking about these talent programs, particularly the TTP. Moreover, I was told that discussing the contribution of the former director of the Organization Department of the CCP, Li Yuanchao, to efforts to transform China's scientific environment, could place me in trouble, as I could be seen to be rummaging in China's factional struggles, since several of Li's colleagues had been arrested for corruption.

Officials in the Chinese consulate in New York raised what they called the "three unfairs."[190] One "unfair" was that Sino-US scientific cooperation had a history of over thirty years and that the Obama administration lauded collaborative biomedical research with China.[191] Now the Trump administration wanted to stop collaboration with China on research critical to the health of Chinese and Americans.

A second "unfair" was that many China-born scholars may have misunderstood the unclear rules of NIH grants and the impropriety of holding joint positions, mistakenly engaging in "double-dipping." Many American universities did a poor job of supervising grant applications from their faculty and did not clarify the rules, partly because they themselves were not that clear. The unfairness intensified because these minor offenses were criminalized, and their perpetrators fled the US or had to go to jail.

Some Chinese worried that participants in the TTP would lose all financial support from the US Department of Defense and other federal granting agencies (which, in fact, they did).[192] Chinese also foresaw problems for any TTP participant in the US because after they visit China, in line with their part-time responsibilities under the program, the US government "sets obstacles for them to return again to the US." Rao Yi, dean of the School of Life Sciences at Beida, had been denied visas to the US numerous times after moving from Washington University, in St. Louis, to Beijing. Still, despite loud calls not to discuss the program, recruitment ensued in December 2018.[193] Likewise, several provinces introduced new TTP-type programs in the summer of 2019, even as the national-level program was disappearing. Such actions would reinforce American concerns.[194]

A Chinese magazine, the *Intellectual* (知识分子), commenting on what it called a "disturbing" letter by NIH Director Collins, reminded readers that the original plan was to bring people back, not to steal IP or technology.[195] But because these people participated in the TTP from abroad, Collins suspects them of "eating America's lunch."

Several Chinese scientists told the *Intellectual* that China had no one to blame but itself for this problem because some Chinese scientists failed to follow the rules of scientific inquiry.[196] Chang Zengyi saw nothing "unreasonable" in the content of Collins' letter. "They're academic norms that should be abided by any honest scholar." Liu Haishen added that no one welcomed "fake part-timing," that China should manage part-time professors according to international standards for academic cooperation and it should set up a "reasonable system agreeable to all parties."

> Many scholars have been covertly taking money from both China and the US. This is "unethical." We must use this dispute as an opportunity to clean up our own act. If China wants to surpass its opponent at this critical moment, it must have a normative system. (author's translation)

These scientists worried about losing their American scientific connections and perhaps never catching up with the US because some Chinese scientists cheated. So, they favored greater regulation of participants in the TTP.

Finally, Dou Xiankang, CCP Secretary and Director of the NSFC, writing in mid-2023, decried the "trend of 'regionalization' of international cooperation," (this discussion is based on the author's translation) which he no doubt feels is being led by the US.[197] Worried that China will be cut out from future developments in international research, particularly basic research, he called for the creation of a "globally competitive open innovation ecosystem," and the "accelerated preparation of an international research funding department" which could promote global scientific research funds, deepen Sino-foreign joint research, build an international cooperative platform for basic research, and support talent from around the world "to carry out basic research *in China*" (italics added). Note that twice he refers to "basic research," which is where China's scientific endeavors fall short. He continued:

> Going forward we must plan and participate deeply in the governance of global science and technology, strive to create an open, trusting, and cooperative scientific research environment, to promote the optimal allocation of global innovation resources and, from a higher starting point, promote open cooperation.

The Case Against the China Initiative

The CI was highly problematic. DOJ "initiatives," just like Chinese political campaigns under Mao Zedong, bring their own baggage, particularly when the FBI sends out cues to its agents that felons must be found or when the White House, Congress, and the DOJ generate a climate of fear toward foreign powers. Did the problem facing America, in terms of the theft of IP, warrant the intense scrutiny it received? Was it necessary to disrupt or destroy the lives of China-born scientific researchers who had settled in America? What of the fact that almost none of those charged under the CI were found guilty of spying or the theft of IP but were only charged with not reporting multiple academic affiliations, "double-dipping" on grants, committing tax or wire fraud, or lying to the FBI? Was racial profiling a likely outcome of such a hunt for spies?

As I described above, Truex showed that the criminality rate in this population of Chinese working and studying in the US was miniscule,[198] while Prasso showed that the DOJ *never charged anyone for spying*.[199] Nevertheless, many of these indictments portray the thefts as being for the benefit of China, rather than by individual self-interest, what law professor Margaret Lewis calls "a conflation of individual motives with a country's policy goals."[200]

Between 2014 and 2019, the DOJ dropped theft charges against four Chinese American scientists,[201] but only after the scholars' reputations had been maligned. And even if there was theft—as there was in 2015, when the FBI arrested a Chinese student for stealing his American professor's IP—the report linked the felon to the TTP by citing his LinkedIn profile, which "indicated he held a position at Zhejiang University, which *has ties* to the Thousand Talent Program" (emphasis added).[202]

Nevertheless, the level of noncompliance—not reporting affiliations with foreign institutions or foreign funding—was significant. Of 130 individuals who had received NIH funding and who were suspected of misbehavior, fifty-one (39 percent) had undisclosed foreign affiliations. Still, the report did not state if these were all TTP participants. As demonstrated in the previous chapter, most members of the Changjiang Visitor's Plan (CJVP) who kept their jobs in the West did not post that affiliation on their, or their university's, websites.

A further problem was that the rules or guidelines on reporting were not that clear, forcing the NIH to amend its rules; but researchers who did not meet these guidelines were not given the time to amend their previous applications. In fact, while the CI was unwinding, the NIH shifted its target of attack from the faculty to the universities, saying that university administrators had not done their due diligence or explained to their faculty how to properly apply for NIH grants.[203]

Additionally, to root out a few bad eggs, the DOJ and the FBI had launched what former US District Attorney Carol Lam called an "initiative."[204] As in Maoist campaigns, leadership in this campaign came from the top, as President Trump, Attorney General Sessions and then Attorney General Barr at the DOJ, and FBI Director Wray threw out a wide net of potential felons that overshot the target. As with Maoist campaigns, where Chinese units were ordered to root out 5 percent of their members for alleged crimes, Deputy Attorney General Demers told *Politico* that the DOJ expected each of the ninety-four field offices to find one to two cases a year, a quota US federal agents had to fulfill to meet the demands of a politicized elite.[205] According to Lam, "they could have carried out the work without creating an 'initiative,' but the DOJ loves having initiatives as it gets big headlines, a big budget, and lots of attention."[206]

In Lam's view, initiatives undergo too little oversight at the top of the system, just pressure to bring cases to court. As a result, the DOJ was forced to dismiss or withdraw some cases prior to trial, or the judge threw them out of court because prosecutors, under enormous pressure to find criminal activity, had not done their research. According to Lam, "From a criminal prosecution perspective, the failure rate of the indictments was not acceptable, you simply cannot lose that many times" and still keep an initiative ongoing without harming the DOJ's reputation, so "the program had to be ended."[207] Lam could not understand how Lelling, director of the FBI's New England office, a year after the indictment of Dr. Chen Gang of MIT, could say that the case had "lost its way" when he was the one who initiated it and should have been guiding it on its path to conviction. According to Lam, FBI Director Wray does not understand the power of his own words, like saying that this was an "all-of-society" problem, especially in America, a country with a history of anti-China racism.[208]

National Security Presidential Memorandum-33

On the eve of leaving the White House, President Trump tried to tie the hands of the incoming Biden administration, as well as clarify and institutionalize the CI, by promulgating National Security Presidential Memorandum-33 (NSPM-33).[209] This document established new guidelines for managing America's open R&D environment that "underpins America's innovation, S&T leadership, economic competitiveness, and national security" and that facilitated China's access to America's technological advancements. The White House further argued that the PRC had not "demonstrated a reciprocal dedication to open scientific exchange" and had exploited the West's open research environment "to circumvent the costs and risks of conducting research, thereby increasing their economic and military competitiveness at the expense of the United States, its allies, and its partners." So, the US government had to ensure that participants in America's R&D enterprise fully disclosed information that could reveal potential COIs and COCs, a clear vote of support for the CI. This presidential memo was sent to twenty-seven agencies and departments.

Rather than target the theft of technology, NSPM-33 emphasized the problem of the lack of full disclosure on grant applications and the COI and COM that arose when China-born scientists had obligations on both sides of the Pacific. Administrators in America's R&D enterprise were ordered to (1) identify and manage risks to research security and integrity, including conflicts of interest and commitment; (2) work with law enforcement agencies to disclose activities that have potentially negative impacts on research funding, security, or integrity; (3) cooperate with their agency's inspector general and law enforcement in investigating suspected instances of failure to comply with disclosure requirements; and (4) ensure that violators of these disclosure policies are duly punished.

Some USG departments were given new tasks.[210] The Department of Homeland Security (DHS) became responsible to maintain a dataset of foreign students and researchers. The Department of State, through its consulates, was to supply the detailed data on all students or researchers coming to America, including their employment history, sources of financial support, education history, research advisor(s), R&D affiliations and projects, and any participation in foreign government-sponsored, talent programs. And the consequences for improper disclosures and engagement in "activities that threaten research security and integrity" were tough. They included termination of US government employment or contracts, termination of a grant or award, no participation in US government review panels, and suspension of eligibility for federal funding. Those who intentionally provided incomplete or incorrect information in their grant applications, or misappropriated trade secrets or exported controlled information, would face civil and criminal penalties.

Finally, all applications for USG grants had to include: (1) the applicant's organizational affiliations and employment; (2) any foreign and domestic support, including gifts provided with terms or conditions, financial support for laboratory personnel, and participation of students and visiting researchers supported by other sources of funding; (3) reports on participation in ongoing or pending participation in foreign government-sponsored talent recruitment programs; (4) disclosure of any contract(s) with foreign entities; (5) all domestic and foreign positions and appointments, any remuneration received, and whether the appointment was full-time, part-time, or voluntary.

On the other hand, drawing on twenty years as an FBI agent, German highlighted restrictions that needed to be imposed on USG agencies in light of NSPM-33.[211] All investigations had to be properly documented so cases could be audited. Individuals being investigated must receive notice of alleged violations, advice of rights, access to counsel, opportunity to correct their lack of disclosure, and a fair hearing before any administrative or civil penalty is imposed. Federal officials needed much better indicators that the subject has violated, is violating, or will violate a specific criminal law. Finally, hitting directly at President Trump and FBI Director Wray, he said that all government statements regarding the nature and scope of threats to national security and research integrity must be factual, supported by publicly available data, and must not promote, reinforce, or inflame racist or xenophobic sentiments within the government or among the public.

Brown University President Christina Paxson said that she was concerned that tighter federal government scrutiny of links between Chinese and US universities would hinder research and ultimately undermine the American economy.[212] "The message that we've been signaling out to the world is 'don't come'—especially if you're from China—and I think that's a huge, huge mistake."[213]

4

The Guilty, the "Not-So-Guilty," and the Innocent

Six Case Studies under the China Initiative

Some Chinese born in the PRC who came to America to study, do research, work, and settle in the US have engaged in theft that harmed the economic or national security of the United States. Some were academics, while others were research scientists, employees of US firms, or entrepreneurs who planned to open their own companies in China using the information they had stolen. Some Americans, too, engaged in illegal behavior, taking money secretly from China in return for services, information, or technology that should have stayed in the US. Finally, some PRC-born Chinese engaged in out-and-out spying, usually on behalf of the Chinese military, the Ministry of State Security, or for Chinese universities with military linkages.[1]

Yet inflammatory comments and widespread attacks on Chinese scholars in the US by the president, the attorney general, the director of the FBI, members of the US Congress, and officials in the DOJ and the NIH, accusing them of engaging in a conspiracy to illegally transfer American technology to China, enmeshed these researchers in a toxic environment of fear and intimidation that must have made them feel like they were back in Maoist China. These cases deserve detailed study, for as Schrecker argued, "the most useful scholarship" on McCarthyism was "the study of individual cases that reconstruct the processes through which the nation's public and private institutions collaborated with and contributed to the anti-Communist crusade."[2]

This chapter presents six case studies, three of people or organizations that the DOJ or the NIH found guilty of a crime or of behavior warranting dismissal from their academic posts, and three of academics whose cases were either dismissed or dropped once their innocence became clear.

The cases where people were exonerated highlight three points: (1) the importance of the support of colleagues and the university president in deflecting the charges; (2) how pressure on FBI field offices—from Director Wray—to open a new case "every ten hours" led them to lie and find guilty parties where none existed; and (3) how despite being innocent or guilty of only minor infractions, any scientist's engagement with China became toxic under the CI and could seriously harm, if not destroy, these people's careers.

Collecting detailed cases of scientists who were investigated under the CI is no easy task. The best dataset was compiled and published in the *MIT Technology Review*.[3] However, that dataset is not conducive to statistical analysis, nor does it have enough information about each case to discern clear patterns. Instead, I have chosen to use case studies to highlight the numerous problems in the CI. (In four cases, I interviewed the scientist.)

The Guilty

As I mentioned previously, there were clear cases of criminality. These involved individual activity, but in some cases, they included collective abuse by scientists and leaders in research institutions who took Chinese money that they did not report for secretive work in China.

Case One: Corruption in a Cancer Center

Established in 1981 by the Florida legislature, the Lee Moffitt Cancer Center and Research Institute ("Moffitt") in Tampa, Florida, is under the National Cancer Institute (NCI) Comprehensive Cancer Center and nationally ranked in various cancer specialties. In 2018, it received grants worth USD 36 million from the NIH and was therefore subject to its rules. Its partnership with the Tianjin Medical University Cancer Institute and Hospital (TMUCIH) had begun in 2008, when TMUCIH began paying Moffitt USD 500,000 a year for services, including training graduate students, postdoctoral fellows, physician-scientists, and research nurses from Tianjin who traveled to Moffitt for training. They also participated in "tumor boards," where they shared their opinions with TMUCIH on specific cases. They also carried out joint research.

In 2018 and early 2019, the Moffitt Compliance Office formally investigated this relationship, "based on the most recent national guidance by the NIH," to see if there was evidence of "predatory" activity by the Chinese.[4] After their initial report, the Compliance Committee recommended further investigation. What this further scrutiny revealed was that the relationship had become problematic when Dr. Sheng Wei—a graduate of Tianjin Medical University, who was an employee of Moffitt and the primary US collaborator with Moffitt's CEO, Dr. Alan List, and who had joined the TTP circa 2011—recruited three researchers around 2015, plus the CEO, to join the Foreign Thousand Talents Program. Dr. Wei had committed to such recruitment efforts when he joined the TTP.

His main success was to recruit Dr. List in 2015, which paved the way for the other three people to join. In his application, Dr List promised to work nine months a year for three years, and the Mandarin version of the contract listed his compensation as RMB 500,000 per year (USD 71,000). In the video he and Dr. Wei made for his application, he only promised "at least two months of effort" on behalf of TMUCIH, as he could not spend that much time in China. He also received other financial rewards, including another USD 70,000 when he successfully reapplied to the TTP in 2017, as well as USD 15,000 for joining an advisory committee, which he also did not report. Finally, he never told Moffitt that he had joined the TTP. However, in 2016, Dr. List signed a form that directed that his TTP award be assigned to TMUCIH. Because he was personally involved in these activities and they occurred on his watch, Dr. List was forced to resign.[5]

The other three participants promised to work in China for two months a year for three years in return for USD 70,000 a year.[6] Dr. Sellers, who joined in 2017, also reported receiving a monthly stipend of USD 7,000 while in China, despite being paid by Moffitt during these periods—a clear example of "double-dipping." During the initial questioning by Moffitt, he denied having joined the TTP. Interestingly, Dr. Sullivan, who went through the same process, reported his participation in the TTP to Moffitt in January 2019 before the investigation began, but after it became known that the NIH would be looking into how Moffitt's grants were being used. In February 2019, he disclosed to his financial advisor that he was being paid USD 70,000 a year for "research work." Finally, Dr. Epling-Burnette, who joined the TTP in 2015, said that her annual compensation of USD 70,000 was payment for supervising Tianjin students at Moffitt, but this work would fall into her responsibilities in the Moffitt-TMUCIH collaboration. She also claimed that she directed USD 85,000 to the TMUCIH hematology department.

These promises fall under the "conflict of commitment" (COC) concept used by the NIH and Moffitt, as these people were all full-time employees of Moffitt and—particularly without seeking approval from the board—would not be able to spend time working elsewhere. Moreover, the USD 70,000 they received was not reported on their Moffitt financial disclosure forms; it was also put in bank accounts in China, which were not reported to Moffitt or the IRS, breaking US law. The fact that they received undisclosed personal funds from TMUCIH, a unit with which Moffitt had a formal relationship, created a conflict of interest (COI). Nevertheless, the final report by the Compliance Committee stated that there was no evidence (to date) that intellectual property had been stolen or that research or patient care had been compromised, and Dr. Wei claimed that their time commitment was really an open "lie," necessary to apply for the TTP and to get their payments. In the end, much of the TTP monies put into their bank accounts in China by Dr. Wei was given to TMUCIH, which was a standard operating procedure, as the Chinese institutions who recruited these foreign participants did so in part to get monies from the CCP.[7]

Senator Marco Rubio of Florida, a sharp critic of China, tweeted that "China has undertaken a broad effort to exploit our openness and culture of scientific collaboration to steal valuable scientific research. . . . Sadly Moffitt Cancer Center, a fantastic institution in Florida was victimized."[8] Still, Timothy Adams, Moffitt's board chairman, defended the collaboration with China: "We started that relationship at a time when foreign policy was about bringing China into the fold of the rest of the world. . . . We looked at that as a great opportunity to collaborate." Quoting the view articulated by NIH Director Collins, he added, "Cancer knows no borders."[9]

The Not-So-Guilty

Case Two: Huang Chuanshu, the NIH, and the "Silent Purge"

Under the CI, cases investigated by the FBI and prosecuted by the DOJ were transparent, as charges were posted on the DOJ website. As the cases progressed from the initial arrest to a possible trial, researchers, academics, other China-born scientists in the US, lawyers, Asian American and civil rights NGOs, and journalists could follow them and shine a light on important aspects of the case. Still, after the initial posting, numerous cases went dark. In other cases, although the FBI harassed the academic under investigation, and although their university fired them, the case never went to trial, leaving the researcher in limbo. Such was the case of Qing Wang of the Cleveland Medical Clinic, who was charged, investigated by his school, and fired (perhaps for issues of "academic integrity"), only to have the government drop all charges on the eve of the trial.[10]

The NIH had enormous influence on this entire process and was empowered by the CI. Its Office of External Relations approached hundreds of universities with the names of faculty members who were "of possible concern," asking the schools to investigate and handle the cases internally. As so much of their research funding came from the NIH, most universities and research institutes followed dutifully. As Mervis notes, "in contrast to the very public criminal prosecutions of academic scientists under the China Initiative launched in 2018 by then-President Donald Trump to thwart Chinese espionage, NIH's version has been conducted behind closed doors."[11]

David Brenner, vice chancellor for health sciences at UCSD, told Jeffrey Mervis, "If NIH says there's a conflict, then there's a conflict, because NIH is always right." So, when UCSD received a letter in November 2018 from NIH's Dr. Michael Lauer asking it to investigate five medical school faculty members who were all born in China, "We were told we have a problem and that it was up to us to fix it." Robin Cyr, who was responsible for research compliance at the University of North Carolina at Chapel Hill (UNC), said that when the institution received its email in December 2018, "It came out of nowhere, and the accusations were pretty ugly." But "a Lauer letter meant that somebody at NIH thinks your faculty has wrongfully and willfully divulged intellectual property." Brian Strahl, chair of the UNC medical school's Department of Biochemistry and Biophysics, was under enormous pressure to fire the professor pinpointed by NIH. Strahl was told repeatedly that UNC's entire portfolio of NIH grants—approaching USD 1 billion—was at risk if a particular ethnic Chinese professor who had spent twenty-seven years on the faculty was not removed and that anything short of termination was not an option. Cyr felt that pressure.

> When you have Mike Lauer saying that certain individuals are not welcomed in the NIH ecosystem, that's a powerful message . . . . I get that Congress holds NIH accountable and that NIH felt it was in the hot seat. But in dealing with the problem, you shouldn't compromise human beings.

Faculty members might simply face disciplinary action and warnings to be more transparent in future applications, as several institutions, such as the Baylor College of Medicine, did. But at the peak of the CI, such (in)action risked the wrath of the NIH, which wanted to see those who did not report their China ties, and who "double-dipped" in their sources of funding, to be purged from the university entirely or, at best, forbidden to apply for NIH funding, ending that scholar's active research. Speaking in 2021, Dr. Lauer reported, "One way that we measure success . . . [is that] . . . there have been *over a hundred scientists who have been removed from the NIH ecosystem.*" (emphasis added).[12]

If the DOJ was not involved, there was little scrutiny about the alleged crimes, the university's institutional procedures, and the reason the school fired the Chinese professor. Thus, some of the over one hundred faculty members who were removed from the rolls of the NIH were fired by major research universities in cases that remain confidential.[13] As one senior NIH official told *ScienceInsider* in 2019, because of the NIH's effort, universities had fired more scientists—and refunded more grant money to the NIH—than was publicly known.[14]

Why do we know so little about these silent purges? According to Dr. Jeremy Wu, the director of APA Justice, there was enough work to be done to support those publicly accused by the DOJ, leaving little time or resources to pursue these secret cases.[15] Second, documentation in these cases remains private, as anyone involved in the case, and who has access to these documents, has signed a "nondisclosure agreement." Access would be possible only through a Freedom of Information filing. Third, those who lost their jobs, or whose careers were terribly disrupted, refuse to go public, even after returning to China, to protect their wives and children, who may remain in the US. Finally, the universities do not want to admit their own mismanagement or these secret purges. According to Lauer, "I can understand why [the universities] aren't talking about it. . . . No organization wants to discuss personnel actions in a public forum."[16]

The case of Dr. Huang Chuanshu sheds light on these internal investigations, though in this case, the information I present is sketchy because of my own nondisclosure agreement.[17] Dr. Huang worked at the New York University School of Medicine (NYUSoM) for many years, until he ran afoul of the NIH and its determination to punish people who had received NIH funding but who had not reported their involvement with the TTP or their affiliation with a China university to their university in the US or to the NIH. In this case, the NIH probably presented Dr. Huang to NYUSoM as a case "of possible concern," which would have triggered an internal investigation.

Dr. Huang's involvement with Wenzhou Medical University (WMU) began around 2011, three years after Li Yuanchao established the TTP. Then, a former schoolmate of Dr. Huang's, who was an administrator at WMU, asked Dr. Huang if he would be willing to apply for the newly created TTP, or if WMU could use his name in their application, as they needed the involvement of an overseas professor if the grant monies were to be forthcoming. Much was at stake for schools such as WMU because Li Yuanchao's campaign, which began in fall 2009 as a way to get cities and universities across China to seek top overseas talent, created enormous pressure for senior administrators to recruit a returnee under the TTP who would be affiliated with WMU. By recruiting an overseas professor, either in fact or fiction, the university administration would be displaying its loyalty and lining up with the Organization Department's program to recruit two thousand high-quality returnees. In hindsight, Dr. Huang knows that his big mistake was to say "yes," as WMU stated publicly that he had received the TTP award, had joined WMU, and was involved in collaborative research there.[18] While his involvement in the program may have been limited, coloring the truth in an application to the Organization Department's Thousand Talents Office involved low risk, as this office, hungry for success, was unlikely to question the university's application; but getting a TTP award was extremely important to leaders at WMU, and to Dr. Huang's friend.

A major accusation under the CI was that those who joined overseas talent programs had COIs or COCs. Dr. Huang denied that he had ever received any salary from WMU, or that had he used his NIH grants to travel to Wenzhou—hence, there was no COI.[19] He denied being actively involved in research at WMU—and, therefore, there was no COC—but as a recipient of the TTP award, his name had to appear as a coauthor on several publications; however, he did admit to advising them on how to design their research.

Dr. Huang benefited from his involvement in the TTP. In return for letting WMU use his name in their application, WMU and several affiliated medical schools in China sent researchers to work in his laboratory at NYUSoM for free, with the Chinese funding all the costs. For these researchers, a stint in a lab at NYU that was run by a world-class scholar was the chance of a lifetime. Dr. Huang, too, found this opportunity difficult to resist, as the research carried out with these researchers in his lab supplied data for his ongoing grant applications. In fact, Dr. Huang was reportedly one of the leading grant recipients in the NYUSoM system.

Problems arose for Dr. Huang when the NIH asked NYUSoM to investigate him. Activities that in the past were benign were now deemed harmful to American scientific security and indicated the betrayal of his home university. Affiliations with universities in China implied "shadow laboratories," where US-based Chinese recreated their research in China and gifted it to their Chinese colleagues. Copublications, once encouraged, now suggested the problematic transfer of technology, as did the training of researchers or postdoctoral fellows from China. And although NYUSoM must have known about the origin and terms of Huang's research team—the school had to approve their visa applications even though it did not pay them a salary—NYUSoM's support for his China involvement could be suspect as well. Schools had to be wary that the NIH did not deem them "uncooperative," which put great pressure on them to expunge these researchers from the NIH "ecosystem."[20] In the end, a closed hearing,[21] adjudicated by a panel of faculty from other schools in the university, recommended that Dr. Huang be terminated, whereupon he returned to China. When I contacted him by email, he told me he had no plans to continue his research but instead would care for his ailing mother in Anhui Province.

Case Three: Simon Saw-Teong Ang Pleads Guilty of Lying to the FBI [22]

Not all the Chinese charged under the CI were mainlanders. Dr. Simon Ang, an Asian American of Malaysian Chinese heritage, had been teaching at the University of Arkansas at Fayetteville (UAF) for 32 years, from 1988 until he was terminated in July 2020. His case is noteworthy in that he was accused of fifty-nine crimes, including wire fraud, falsifying a passport application, not disclosing on NASA grant applications his involvements in China, and lying to the FBI when he claimed he was a "courtesy" inventor, but not the "actual" inventor, of twenty-five Chinese patents registered in Beijing. As with the other cases, his alleged crimes did not include IP theft or illicit transfers of technology that initially lay at the heart of the CI. And it is not illegal to have patents in China. So had the FBI not asked about these patents, he would not have committed any federal offense.

The charge of passport fraud highlights the unprofessionalism of the FBI. As a Malaysian Chinese, Dr. Ang's name may be written in a multitude of romanization systems. Ang uses the PRC romanization system, called "pinyin," when dealing with the PRC. In America, however, Ang's Chinese name is different, as he uses the Malaysian romanization system that is on his Malaysian birth certificate. US passports only permit roman (English) characters. If Chinese characters were permitted, there would have been no confusion, and had the FBI asked anyone knowledgeable about Chinese living in Southeast Asia about the spelling of Chinese names, none of this would have happened.

As with Dr. Huang's case above, someone in China wrote the application on behalf of Dr. Ang, who does not write Chinese, to get a TTP grant for their Chinese institution. In Dr. Ang's case, a professor at Nanjing University of Aeronautics and Astronautics (南航大学), who had received his PhD in 1990 in Japan, and who was a specialist in advanced materials, applied on Dr. Ang's behalf for the foreign TTP award. In the application, the individual misrepresented Ang's curriculum vitae, attributing to Dr. Ang skills he did not have but that the real applicant possessed. Dr. Ang is a well-known researcher with the prestigious rank of "fellow" from four US and UK professional organizations, but these fellowships are in areas that are less strategically sensitive than the ones for which he received the TTP. As in other cases, many people living overseas, who let their colleagues in China use their names for these grant applications, did not realize that they needed to report these grants to their American university.[23] However, UAF had not required total disclosure on talent or academic grants or awards before the university revised its COI policy in 2021, more than a year after Dr. Ang's case.[24] Moreover, although Dr. Ang was accused of not telling his university of his involvement with the TTP, he says he did so in 2013, before he flew to China for the TTP interview. In fact, he informed his UAF supervisor, Dr. Juan Balda, when he received the award in 2014 and filed an outside employment request. He also told UAF about his involvement in an LED-lighting company in China, but because that topic was unrelated to Dr. Ang's funded research at UAF, this same supervisor declared that there was no COI and that, therefore, Dr. Ang need not report this work on any university form.

Dr. Ang's involvement with China and the TTP was driven by UAF's demand that he demonstrate "vision" and the capability to organize teams of researchers to produce game-changing breakthroughs. As it was stated in a memorandum written by the UAF's College of Engineering Honors and Award Committee on

November 15, 2011, such skills were a condition for him to be appointed as a UAF distinguished professor.[25] In fact, Dr. Balda had written to the College of Engineering's dean, Ashok Saxena, on October 28, 2011, reporting that one of Dr. Ang's most important external service activities for the university was being the honorary president and adjunct professor at Xi'an Aeronautical Polytechnic College in northwest China. "*Simon is an ambassador of our university*" (emphasis added), he wrote.[26] Clearly, Dr. Ang was not hiding his China activities from his department head, and his dean praised him for them.

Dr. Ang was criticized for his involvement with a Singapore-based, LED lightbulb company that was run by his brother. According to Dr. Ang's lawyer, he had served in an unpaid position as chief technology officer to help his brother's business, and "these patents were related to this company." So apparently Dr. Ang was not materially enriched "in any way" by this work and by these patents, which his brother's company used for dealing with China.[27]

Finally, although Dr. Ang did not disclose his involvement with Chinese entities in his grant application to NASA, an omission for which he was initially charged with a crime, these charges were dropped because NASA's guidelines for applying for the "Research and Opportunities in Space and Earth Sciences—2016" did not forbid collaboration with researchers in China on non-NASA-related projects, even if one had a NASA project.[28] In fact, NASA specifically allows international collaborations in China for projects unrelated to its own funding.[29] According to Dr. Ang, "The restriction on working in China only applies to NASA funds. It is acceptable as long as you keep your NASA projects and your PRC related projects separate, i.e., don't use any NASA funds for projects with the PRC and don't involve any scientists affiliated with an institution in the PRC in your NASA projects."[30]

UAF cooperated fully with the FBI once Dr. Ang fell under investigation.[31] Dr. John English, dean of engineering, recommended Dr. Ang's dismissal for "unethical conduct," claiming that Dr. Ang had profited from work done at UAF that he applied to his brother's LED company in China.[32] Mark Rushing, a spokesman for UAF, said that prior to Ang's termination,

> the University concluded that Dr. Ang violated multiple University policies . . . [and that] the plea agreement confirms that Dr. Ang had a role in multiple external entities (including multiple business enterprises), which were never disclosed according to the University's longstanding policies on conflict of interest, conflict of commitment, and outside employment.

Apparently these allegations were totally false. Dr. Ang denied profiting from his brother's company or that he had made any money from the patents he had registered in China. In fact, between 2016 and 2019, UAF flip-flopped on the IP-ownership assignment issue. Prior to 2016, patent ownership, resulting from independent work or permissible consulting activities without the use of facilities owned, operated, or controlled by UAF, stayed with the inventor.[33] From 2016 to 2019, all inventions were required to be assigned to UAF,[34] but the 2019 revision permitted employees to retain inventions that resulted from independent work or consulting activities that had been disclosed, approved, and authorized by UAF.[35]

In the end, Dr. Ang pled guilty to one count of lying to the FBI about the patents, and was sentenced to one year and one day in a minimum-security satellite camp at the Forrest City Federal Correctional Institution, Arkansas, and was fined USD 5,500.[36] He was released in early March 2023 after serving eight months under the First Step Act.[37] Dr. Ang decided to retire and spend time with his family, although he was unable to visit his elderly mother in Singapore until his ankle bracelet was removed nine months after his release from prison.

Three Problematic Case Studies under the CI: Guilty until Proven Innocent

The lives of the people involved in three cases were upended by the CI. Among these cases, one professor was exonerated before any trial was convened because of a forceful defense by his colleagues and his university; one was dropped under circumstances that were embarrassing to the FBI; and finally, one involved a non-Chinese who had his career severely disrupted when the DOD shut down his research, including work funded by the NSF, that it was funding after he visited an institute in his field of research at a university in China.

Case Four: MIT Rallies for One of its Own

Professor Chen Gang's (family name: Chen) problems began in January 2020, two years into the CI, when he was interrogated for three hours as he and his family were traveling through Logan Airport in Boston. The authorities took all his electronics. After Chen reported the incident to MIT, the university hired a lawyer and paid his legal fees. MIT also hired external lawyers to investigate the accusations against him, but they found no wrongdoing.

Despite the lack of evidence, Chen was arrested on January 14, 2021, and, according to the US Attorney's Office in Massachusetts, was charged with failing to disclose to the DOE contracts, appointments, and awards from entities in China.[38] He was also charged with wire fraud, failing to report a foreign bank account, and falsifying a tax return. They alleged that after 2012, Dr. Chen held appointments in China designed to promote its technological and scientific development by providing advice and expertise, often in exchange for financial compensation.

These activities included acting as an "overseas expert" for the PRC government at the request of the PRC Consulate Office in New York and serving as a member of at least two PRC talent programs. Since 2013, Chen allegedly received USD 29 million in foreign funding, including USD 19 million from the China Southern University of Science and Technology (中南科技大学—SUSTech) in Guangzhou. Professor Chen was then the ninth known academic to be dismissed or acquitted under the CI, but MIT was the only university to protect its faculty member. According to Chen, MIT's support was critical in keeping his spirits up and winning his case:

> What gave me hope and ultimately saved me is a lesson for all universities. MIT leadership, under President L. Rafael Reif, supported me morally and financially after I was detained at the airport, and the university made its support public soon after I was arrested.[39]

MIT President Reif criticized the Trump administration for creating "a toxic atmosphere of unfounded suspicion and fear" within the US scientific community, particularly as it related to ethnic Chinese.[40] While he admitted that "small numbers of researchers of Chinese background may indeed have acted in bad faith,"

> they are the exception and very far from the rule. Yet faculty members, postdocs, research staff, and students tell me that in their dealings with government agencies, they now feel unfairly scrutinized, stigmatized, and on edge because of their Chinese ethnicity alone.[41]

Immediately after Chen's arrest, President Reif clarified the relationship between SUSTech and MIT. The effort, he argued, which raised USD 25 million was faculty driven, but the funds did not go to any specific academic; instead, they supported the building of a new research center at MIT and collaborative research and graduate student training. Thus, the accusations that Professor Chen misappropriated funds belonging to MIT for his personal gain were unfounded. According to President Reif,

> MIT established a collaboration with SUSTech in 2018 to create the centers for Mechanical Engineering Research and Education, at MIT and SUSTech. While Professor Chen is its inaugural MIT faculty director, this is not an individual collaboration; it is a departmental one, supported by the Institute.[42]

In a letter, MIT's faculty challenged each allegation, calling on the MIT administration "to stand forthrightly, proudly, and energetically behind Professor Chen."[43] They pointed out that the accusations had nothing to do with protecting IP, which was supposedly at the heart of the CI. This case became a *cause célèbre* among China-born professors in the US, as few of them had paid much attention to the CI before this.

On January 20, 2022, when Rachel Rollins replaced US District Attorney Andrew Lelling, federal prosecutors, in a court filing in Boston,[44] said new information had emerged concerning Chen Gang's alleged omissions that undercut the wire fraud and other charges he faced, so the government could no longer "meet its burden of proof at trial."[45] Yet four months after the Justice Department dropped Chen's case, about sixty researchers at MIT were briefed by the FBI in a PowerPoint presentation about ongoing threats from foreign spies working in their labs.[46]

Dr. Chen was deeply upset that the DOJ never apologized for their actions. He wanted to sanction Lelling for what he called his unethical efforts to "generate greater publicity for this case" through a press conference and a press release.[47] Chen Gang's case occurred under the Biden administration—after the CI had failed numerous times but when US Attorney Lelling knew he was on the way out—so he seemed more interested in promoting the case than successfully prosecuting it.

During a February 2022 meeting of APA Justice, Dr. Chen shared his experience from two years under the CI.[48] He noted how the DOJ altered facts to turn normal scientific activity into a crime; used emails to which Professor Chen did not reply as evidence of a crime; portrayed even correct action as proof he was hiding something; rushed their case without interviewing critical witnesses; deliberately hid exculpatory evidence; and, despite knowing that they had made mistakes, never apologized, preferring to save face by offering an unacceptable agreement. Professor Chen hoped the judge would hold hearings so he could publicly chastise Lelling, but when that did not happen, he asked Congress to investigate all the misconduct.

Professor Chen offered five lessons from his experience: (1) We are all losers because the US is losing talent; (2) universities need to protect their faculty; (3) funding agencies must educate managers and defend researchers; (4) vulnerable people like us need to learn our rights; and (5) we need to speak up.

Case Five: Hu Anming: A Low Point for the FBI[49]

FBI Agent Sadiku was looking for a case he could investigate under the CI. After he read a translation of an article in Chinese saying that Dr. Hu Anming of the University of Tennessee, Knoxville (UTK) had participated in a short-term program beginning in 2012 to mentor Chinese students and lecture in China, Sadiku had found his target.[50] But Dr. Hu denied participating in any Chinese program, so Sadiku launched six or seven agents to monitor Dr. Hu and his college-age son for over a year and a half. He named the investigation "Operation Chelsea Dagger." They tracked their movements, searched for "evidence" in their household trash bins, and instructed customs to inspect Dr. Hu's phone, computer, and hard drive when he traveled to Japan for an international conference in November 2018.

Between June and September 2019, Sadiku met with leaders at UTK three times and presented several "material-rich" slides alleging that Hu might be a "Chinese spy," albeit without any evidence to support the accusation. In fact, at the trial, Sadiku admitted that, after a more than three-year-long "national security" investigation into Dr. Hu, he had found no evidence indicating that Dr. Hu had ever been a spy.

Dr. Hu was arrested on February 27, 2020, and went to trial on June 7, 2021. Federal prosecutors charged him with two felonies: wire fraud and lying to the FBI. Each felony included three allegations related to Dr. Hu's alleged failure for six years to disclose his part-time position at the Institute of Laser Engineering at Beijing University of Technology (北京科技大学—BJUT) to UTK and NASA. In addition, Hu had omitted his affiliation with BJUT from the CV he used when applying for tenure at UTK in 2018. That disclosure, too, would have made him ineligible for NASA grants. He engaged in these "fraudulent representations and omissions" because it was only if UTK verified that Hu did not have a job or research projects in China that the university could meet NASA's "Chinese Funding Restrictions." But according to Hu, a UTK official had told him that he could apply for the funds if he did not include a letter from a Chinese professor in China who was to be involved in the project, making the university complicit in this fraud. The charge of wire fraud involved transferring grant funds to participants in China from his NASA-funded project. Additionally, he was accused of using NASA funds to collaborate with Chinese universities, which violated a federal law passed in 2011. Yet the invitation letter to BJUT came from the head of UTK's Engineering Department, showing that the university was in the loop.

In his defense, Dr. Hu claimed to have submitted the necessary financial disclosure forms each year, but since he was not paid by BJUT, he did not need to report that activity. Also, NASA project applications did not require any history of collaboration; yet, Dr. Hu claimed to have mentioned his relationship with Chinese universities to the NASA project manager. Since then, he did not associate NASA projects with BJUT, nor did he include any Chinese visiting students in the NASA project team. Likewise, in this case, the judge has set a high definition for the crime of wire fraud: the judge said the defendant must have deceived the US government and intended to benefit from it for the charges to stand.

The importance of Dr. Hu's case lies in the fact that the FBI agent who arrested Dr. Hu admitted under oath that he fabricated data to make his case: "Based on my summary translations, my reports and my outline, no, Hu wasn't involved with the Chinese military."[51] So why did he continue the investigation and try to have

Dr. Hu found guilty? To meet the quota set by FBI Director Wray, as outlined in Deputy Attorney General Demer's *Politico* admission. According to Sadiku,

> I investigated him based on his association with the talent program that (the US government believed) benefits the Chinese military. . . . I opened it up as an economic espionage (case because the US government believes) the program is attempting to acquire technology and information from the United States.[52]

Sadly, based on Sadiku's falsification, UTK had fired Hu.

On page forty-two of the fifty-two-page not guilty verdict, Judge Varlan wrote:

> The government has failed to present sufficient evidence for any rational jury to find beyond a reasonable doubt that the defendant had a specific intent to defraud by concealing his affiliation with Chinese universities to obtain NASA funding. Even viewing all the evidence in the light most favorable to the government, no rational jury could conclude that "the defendant failed to disclose his affiliation with Chinese universities to deceive NASA."

One juror, shocked by the trial's outcome, believed that the FBI agent had pursued the investigation "out of ambition rather than an interest in justice."[53] She also believed that UTK administrators who had advised Hu on his grant applications hastily sacrificed their employee when they were questioned by federal agents. "This poor man just got sold down the river by his university and everyone else," she said. She felt strongly that the FBI owed Hu an apology. Given her and others' doubts, the jury could not reach a verdict, so the federal judge declared a mistrial.[54] The judge also chided the FBI for telling the university it was pursuing Hu as a spy, when it knew that this was not the case.[55]

On October 15, 2021, *Knoxville News* reported that UTK offered to reinstate Dr. Hu.[56] In a letter dated October 14, 2021, Provost John Zomchick detailed the offer. Hu was offered (1) a tenured faculty position in the Tickle College of Engineering; (2) back pay for the time he was suspended without pay but no payment for the time between his termination and his reinstatement; (3) an explanation of what the university was doing to support his work visa because as a naturalized Canadian, Hu needed a visa to work at the university; (4) payment for an immigration attorney; and (5) assistance helping him reestablish his research program, totaling USD 200,000 over three years. In the end, this dismissal played a major role in derailing the CI.

Case Six: A Caucasian Who Ran Afoul of the DOD

The CI also destroyed the career of a non-Chinese scientist (hereafter, Professor X), despite the absence of any wrongdoing whatsoever.[57] The perpetrator of injustice was the DOD, which feared that the results of Professor X's research, which they funded, might be transferred to China. As a result, he was denied the right to apply for DOD funding, despite being totally exonerated.

Unlike the Chinese professors facing the wrath of the CI, this non-Chinese professor was not fired after the charges surfaced. Nevertheless, his home university (hereafter, US University B) turned on him in a quick and arbitrary decision—denying him the right to carry on his research for a year—which it refused to amend, even after Professor X showed that their decision was erroneous. University administrators also ignored two grievances he filed, took away his NSF grant, forbade him from doing research for one year, never explained what he had done wrong—which was hard to do since he had done nothing wrong—and then enforced the DOD decision to shut him down and lock future access to their funds, potentially ending his career. Yet unlike Chinese professors who, after losing their jobs or choosing to leave the US, could be rewarded with a good position in China, he had no such option. Being close to sixty years old, he could try to resuscitate his research or simply retire. At the time of our last conversation, he was leaning toward the latter option.

The trouble began when Professor X returned from a three-month trip to China, where he spent eight weeks visiting a new research center at a major university in Beijing (hereafter, Chinese University C).[58] Professor X had been a postdoc in Boston, where he met another postdoc from China. When the timing was propitious, he decided to take a sabbatical trip to visit this friend at a new institute where his former colleague worked on common research. He drafted a program of activity and received a document from Chinese University C outlining the terms of his visiting scholar position. However, due to limited flights to China during COVID-19, he postponed his visit for two semesters. He shared this itinerary and the document from Chinese University C with his department head and the dean of sciences at US University B, who approved them; he also asked that that they get approval at the university level for his work plan. But the document was never checked by the Director of Outside Interests (DOI), whose job was to monitor such activities. His itinerary reported his plan to give two seminars about his research using information that was already published. At the dean's request, he filled out a COC form because he was giving these two lectures, which seemed quite unnecessary as he was on sabbatical.

The big problem for Professor X was that the original "visiting scholars agreement" with Chinese University C contravened various rules of US University

B, including accepting a monthly stipend while on sabbatical, when his university still paid his salary; establishing student exchanges on his own; registering at Chinese University C as a visiting scholar; agreeing to several speaking engagements; and promising to engage in collaborative research, and particularly that work done in China would belong to both universities. But because he changed his schedule, the visiting scholar's agreement was never signed or put into effect; still, during the investigation, the DOI at US University B constantly referred to that agreement and suggested that he had followed its guidelines, which was seen as one of his two major violations. The second alleged violation was what the DOI referred to as a "talent program," and Professor X's "willingness to help recommend and introduce excellent scientific talents in relevant disciplines" which he saw as an indicator that he had joined such a program.

When Professor X landed in the US, he was pulled aside (like Chen Gang of MIT), questioned, and his suitcase was searched. Eight days later, US University B asked him to clarify the dates of his China trip and submit another COC form. The DOI was copied on that email. Four days later, Professor X was informed that an official inquiry was being launched about his trip to China, so he had to stop all research. He was forbidden to talk to his students, and his grant monies were frozen. That email was copied to the vice president for research, the vice president of operations, the associate dean of the School of Sciences, and his department head. He was ordered to report what property belonging to US University B he had taken to China—they were probably considering searching his computer. He was also asked to respond to nineteen specific questions. He was told that this investigation would be completed in two weeks.

He immediately wrote a formal grievance, asking the vice president of operations to explain why his research, which was carried out on animals in his laboratory, had to stop while the DOI carried out an investigation. The dean of sciences rejected his complaint. Professor X also reported to the vice president of operations that he had asked the DOI if an external federal agency had been involved in the decision to shut down his operations. He also asked if the DOI and another administrator had read emails he wrote while in China, which he saw as an infringement on his privacy and, in his mind, illegal. In fact, they had read those emails but claimed they were the property of the university.

Five weeks after returning, Professor X received a memo from the DOI, and copied to senior administrators, which outlined a "Plan for Compliance." The terms were harsh. Professor X was to stop all research, regardless of the source of support, for at least twelve months: "These activities include the design, development, testing, evaluation, conduct reporting review and oversight of a program of scientific inquiry." This plan would be reviewed by the DOI, the department head, and even the provost. Professor X was to have no contact with any of his students, postdocs, or faculty involved in his research. The university would appoint a new principal investigator to run his lab and his NSF grant. He also had to report all the publications, collaborations, and presentations in which he had engaged for several years. (Clearly, they were looking for unreported collaboration with China.) He was switched to full-time teaching and was to teach five courses in the following academic year. Finally, he was to undergo COI training. When he asked his department head if he could go to his laboratory to work with one student, the department head told him that he had to be careful, as one option that they had considered was to fire him; but in the end, the DOI had decided not to recommend this option, though it was reportedly "a close call."

Professor X immediately emailed administrators at all university levels, from the department head to vice presidents, objecting to the inquiry's lack of due process and what he called "arbitrary and unwarranted damage."[59] His research was already being harmed by the original order to discontinue it, which cost his project upwards of USD 30,000. He also asked that all future communications be with him directly. Since no one responded to that email, Professor X filed another grievance with the vice president of operations, who supervised the DOI, concerning how the inquiry was being conducted and stating that the report contained factual inaccuracies regarding the visiting scholar agreement. He asked that the reference to that agreement be amended and complained that the "recommendations are inappropriate and disproportionate." However, the DOI refused to amend the recommendation and findings, despite what were clearly mistakes.

The following day, the DOI struck back. Professor X lost access to his laboratory, and he was warned that he might be fired and lose his NSF grant, that he could not apply for federally funded research indefinitely, and that grants currently under review were to be canceled. The department head said the sanctions should take effect immediately. He was prohibited from doing research for twelve months, prohibited from contacting his students or his collaborators on the grant who were working at a university in Florida, and he lost all his current funding. In the future, he would have to disclose all academic submissions and publications on a quarterly basis (perhaps so administrators could monitor his research). The department head reassigned his workload and ordered him to take COI training. All these decisions were made without consultation. From then on, Professor X decided to communicate with the administration solely through writing, so everything would be in the public record. The following day, after consulting with the administration, the department head reduced the prohibition on applications for research funding from indefinitely to twelve months, renewable on a year-to-year basis.

A new principal investigator, who had been working in the lab, took over all the work in the lab, as well as the supervision of Professor X's graduate students. However, in written communications with Professor X, this faculty member admitted that she lacked the technical expertise to supervise more than one graduate student; "this puts us in a bind," she told him, a point about which Professor X complained.

Other than agreeing to the nonbinding visiting scholars agreement, which was never executed or officially signed, and which was abandoned and expired before Professor X went to China, the DOI chastised him for not reporting the two additional seminars he gave in China, which was also at the heart of the matter. Professor X learned from an email from the NSF that he was deemed to have been "in noncompliance with the University's Conflict of Commitment Policy," including "the failure to disclose an outside commitment to an external entity, and failure to disclose a visiting scholar agreement with a foreign entity."[60] Professor X explained that he agreed to give these seminars after he got to China, so he could not disclose them before leaving the US. In response to the accusation that he had failed to report them within thirty days, which was the university's rule, Professor X claimed that he had reported them, albeit three to four weeks late. He also denied again that he was ever part of a "talent program."

In response to his assertion that the information he presented in his two additional lectures in China was already in the public realm, the DOI pointed out that one of the two speaking activities related to a paper that was supported by the Office of Naval Research, which was under the DOD, and listed the award number. This award was deemed to be "active," and it clearly was the award that the DOD wanted to shut down. However, according to Professor X, that Office of Naval Research grant was no longer active, and all paperwork had been submitted before Professor X had gone to China on the latest trip.

Two weeks later, the vice president of operations dismissed his grievance entirely, without providing any explanatory documentation. So he continued to ask why he had to stop his research during the DOI's inquiry. He was shocked that the university had accessed his emails without informing him, and he asked to see which of his emails had been accessed, but when he got no response, he again raised the issue of the involvement by a federal agency. The university never responded.

The concern that federal agencies were involved was reinforced by a visit to his home from two special agents, one from the FBI and another from the Naval Criminal Investigative Service, the primary law enforcement agency of the US Department of the Navy, who asked about his trip to China. They presented their visit as "educational" and that the goal was to make sure that he knew the evils of China. The agents denied that their visit was part of any investigation. When he asked if they had concerns, they said "no." But the FBI agent asked if he could return in two weeks with "someone more knowledgeable than him" to ask questions about what Professor X had learned in China. As he was "uncomfortable" with this request, he asked them to contact his lawyer, but he did not flat out say "no." The FBI agent never approached his lawyer, and although the agent called him several times, Professor X never responded.

Despite numerous requests, Professor X never saw the accusations against him. All he knew were the accusations in the university's letter to the NSF, which an administrator there had forwarded to him. When he asked the DOI to present him a final summary of the policies he allegedly violated, the DOI provided no such summary and refused to change her findings and recommendations. Instead, the vice president of research recommended he apply to the university's Public Records Request Office to see the case against him.

Six months after returning, Professor X accessed some records about his case and discovered that one month after he returned, the university's general counsel had convened a secret meeting among all relevant parties but before the DOI issued any findings or sanctions. One may assume that the university feared that there might be legal complications or challenges from the DOD if it did not act.

Professor X now mistrusts the university. Among documents he retrieved, one piece of evidence submitted by the DOI—a translation of the visiting scholar agreement—included his signature, though he had no record of this signed document. When he asked for clarification, he was told that this information was "withheld from disclosure in response to your request in the best interest of the state and due to attorney client privilege." Professor X writes: "To this day, I strongly suspect that the signature was applied by the DOI on a translation they made in-house, without my knowledge, essentially forging my signature."

Finally, more than a year after returning from his trip to China, Professor X received a memo canceling all sanctions and allowing him to return to his research and his NSF grant. He was, however, forbidden from ever applying for any DOD grant. But when he returned to his lab, he discovered that his staff was never paid and that his research was stopped. "My career is ruined as of today. I am trying to recover but may never be able to do it. I am close to retiring, so I may just do that," he told me.[61] Professor X also told me that he eventually "found out that the FBI was working with the university."

The letters from US University B's administrators suggest that they had lost confidence in the willingness of Professor X to follow university policy concerning the full disclosure of academic activity. More likely, the DOD had lost that faith due to his travels to China over the previous three to four years, and his willingness to give talks at Chinese University C on his research, even if all that information was in the public record. A letter from the provost to Professor X opined that he had previously taken three unauthorized trips to China, which he had not reported according to the rules of COC, yet he had followed the guidelines in reporting trips to other countries. "From the electronic record it appears that you have sustained a deep engagement with Universities in China, motivated by personal reasons, rather than to benefit the University of XXX, and have very deliberately sought to shield those relationships from the University of XXX by failing to request appropriate Travel Authorizations." In the provost's view, "This pattern of evidence raises a serious concern that you were actively working to specifically obscure your visits to China and to these particular Universities." The provost warned him that such behavior could lead to the termination of his contract. The provost also worried that, because Professor X was working on US government-funded research—in this case for the DOD—and had traveled to China, a country about which the US government "has made abundantly clear its concern over undue foreign influence on federally funded research, your failures to declare these travels to visit major Chinese universities have placed the University of XXX at risk with major federal research agencies."

Most likely, the DOD decided to put an end to his research program after it discovered that he was presenting findings, gained with DOD funding, at a major research university in China. While they had absolutely no proof that he was disclosing any secrets to China, or any findings other than what was in the public record, the DOD probably decided that the safest path was, in the words of Michael Lauer of the NIH, to "eradicate" him from the DOD's "ecosystem," which they did with US University B's active cooperation. In the end, this investigation and year-long suspension of research, due to only minor infractions, may have ended an excellent career.

Conclusion

With perhaps as many as three thousand scientists named as potential spies by the FBI or the NIH, why have so few been found guilty? Is it these agencies' poor work or is it because disrupting the lives and research of these scientists was an important goal, even if they were never found guilty?

According to Mike German, the FBI may not be perturbed that, in so many cases, people are accused but never go to trial or are exonerated for some technical issue, because an important goal of the FBI is to "disrupt" what they see as a spy network. The strategy of "disruptions" was applied in counterterrorism strategy, particularly against a supposed Muslim conspiracy that was threatening America in the wake of 9/11, but according to German, was also adopted for the anti-China effort.[62] This strategy meshed well with the CI by giving the FBI a green light to disrupt the research of these China-born scientists in America whom the FBI saw as passive, if not active, members of a CCP cabal to steal US technology, matching what Director Wray has called an "all society" strategy. Moreover, FBI agents generally saw the Chinese as guilty from the get-go because of their ethnic identity.

In the case of the ethnic Chinese scientists, these disruptions involved getting people fired, having them move back to China, "outing" them as spies, or undermining their working conditions in the US by getting their grants frozen or rescinded. According to German, FBI agents have strong incentives to arrest people for alleged crimes, even if they cannot prove a crime was committed, as one measure used to evaluate the agency's "accomplishments" after 9/11 was the number of actions they took to disrupt a spy network.[63] By creating difficulties for China-born academics, FBI agents proved their worthiness. These activities might involve searching academics at the airport when they come back, blocking their entry to the US at the border even though they have a visa, getting a warrant and searching their home, or other forms of disruptive behavior. The cost to these scientists' careers or their families was always deemed secondary and inconsequential.

5

Biden's Agenda and Continuing Changes in Sino-American Scientific and Academic Relations

After President Biden's inauguration, many observers anticipated a softer line from inside the Beltway toward China-born professors and researchers in the US and the end of the CI. However, these changes would have to take place within the context of an intensified confrontation between China and the US, as many of Biden's key foreign policy advisors were quite hawkish on China. Moreover, their strategy to limit China's military and technological modernization had direct consequences for Sino-US scientific cooperation, as it influenced how China-born scientists working in the US perceived their status in the US and determined whether they would continue to carry out significant levels of interaction with the PRC.

Changing policies often involve changing personnel, and the most important change was the appointment of a moderate attorney general, Merrick Garland, under whose leadership the DOJ tried hard to balance national security with equality and justice. Matt Olsen, who had a long history of working on issues related to civil rights, replaced John Demers as director of the DOJ's National Security Division (NSD), and is seen as much more sympathetic to concerns about racial profiling of Americans of Asian descent. On his watch, the CI was renamed, and its focus shifted to industrial espionage. But Olsen had previously expanded FBI powers after 9/11 and had recommended that President Obama keep the prisoners detained in Guantanamo under wraps.[1] According to Mervis, he was unlikely to be a panacea to a problematic policy.[2] John Yang, president of the advocacy group Asian Americans Advancing Justice (AAJC), said that the name change "recognizes that our concerns were legitimate. . . . But there is a lot more work to be done."[3]

Matt Olsen took over the NSD and the CI on November 1, 2021, so Demers ran the NSD and an unreformed CI for almost a year to the day that Biden won the presidential election. This slow transfer of authority explains why it took a year for major revisions to the CI, despite much clamoring for its repeal beginning in the early days of the Biden administration. A third important appointment sent a positive message to the Asian American community when Erika Moritsugu became deputy assistant to the president and senior liaison to Asian Americans and Pacific Islanders, a new cabinet-level position established by Biden in response to demands from several senators of minority extraction.[4]

While Demers was still running the CI, the DOJ, in July 2021, dropped its cases against five Chinese researchers accused of hiding ties to the Chinese military.[5] In his comments on the cases, DOJ spokesman Wyn Hornbuckle said that the department had reevaluated these prosecutions and determined that "it is now in the interest of justice to dismiss them." Apparently, a new report by FBI analysts questioned if the visa application question on "military service" was clear enough.

The Biden administration also proposed an amnesty program, where ethnic Chinese academics in the US could revise old applications to disclose past foreign funding without fear of punishment.[6] However, eight Republican senators, including Marco Rubio, Tom Cotton, and Rob Portman, wrote to the president, criticizing this plan because they had not been consulted, and they claimed that amnesty ran against policies articulated in various Defense Authorization Acts.[7] They also accused the DOJ of not consulting the inspector generals of the NSF and the NIH, who, according to the letter, "are on the frontlines of combatting grant fraud by corrupt researchers." The letter asked that the DOJ provide a brief, outlining the department's plans. Not surprisingly, their efforts killed the idea of an amnesty program.

Nevertheless, pushback against the CI intensified. In July 2021, nearly one hundred members of Congress urged Attorney General Garland to investigate the DOJ's alleged racial profiling of Asians.[8] In October 2021, Representative Ted Lieu (D-California), pressed Garland in a congressional hearing, perhaps triggering the DOJ review of the CI one month later.[9] Judy Chu (D-California), the first Chinese American woman elected to Congress, complained that, "They have turned the China Initiative into an instrument for racial profiling . . . to terrorize Chinese scientists and engineers. Something has gone dramatically wrong."[10] In March 2022, a bicameral coalition led by Representative Lieu delivered a letter to Attorney General Garland that stated, "Over the years, multiple people who happened to be of Asian descent have been falsely accused by the Department of Justice of espionage, which turned innocent lives upside down." In his view, both

Democratic and Republican administrations were "making the same mistakes over and over again."[11]

Organizations representing Asian Americans attacked the CI. The Hu Anming case sparked widespread anger among US congressmen, the academic community, Asian American groups, and civil organizations. Many individuals and organizations jointly wrote letters to Judge Thomas A. Varlan, urging him to dismiss the case and exonerate Dr. Hu. In April 2021, AAJC delivered a petition to the new US president with over thirty thousand signatures calling for the CI's end.[12] APA Justice held monthly meetings, inviting members of Congress, scientists investigated under the CI, lawyers, and academics to inform the public about the CI. And in October 2021, the Committee of 100, an organization of elite members of the Chinese community in the US, released a survey (cited later in this chapter), showing that the fear within the Chinese academic community was causing many to consider returning to China.[13]

The arrest and investigation of Professor Chen Gang of MIT was a wake-up call for many China-born academics living in the US leading them to set aside their political passivity. A cohort of senior China-born scientists formed the Asian American Scholars Forum "to promote academic belonging, openness, freedom, and equality for all."[14] On many campuses across the US, new Associations of Chinese Professors (ACPs) sprung up, some of which carried out surveys of their Chinese faculty. Rongwei Yang of the State University of New York at Albany's ACP organized a letter signed by two thousand Chinese academics calling on Biden to rescind the CI. All these efforts were abetted by anti-Asian violence that rose 71 percent between 2019 and 2020.[15]

In March 2022, APA Justice put forward a series of recommendations that responded to problems with the CI.[16] Primary was the idea that, for any projects with implications for national and economic security, the funding agencies must clearly define the disclosure requirements to the institutions and the scientists. Therefore, nondisclosure would not be an innocent act of omission but would be a clear sign that the scientist was trying to hide something. They recommended that the vice president of research and development at universities be responsible for reviewing all proposals for compliance so that institutions could not turn on their own faculty by claiming the administration was unaware of the situation. All such cases should be brought to the attention of the relevant federal department's inspector general, such as the DOJ or HHS. Investigations should follow clearly defined and publicized guidelines and procedures (i.e., greater transparency). Finally, if neither national nor economic security was breached, the scientist should be allowed a grace period to correct the incomplete or inaccurate information even for earlier cases, without legal punishment, reestablishing trust between the federal government and Asian scientists.

Some professors became active in opposing the CI. One of the earliest victims of the FBI's overzealous search for enemies within the Chinese scientific community, Dr. Xi Xiaoxing, lectured across the US, telling how the aggressive arrest by the FBI terrified his family and ruined his career. For his efforts, he was awarded the Andrei Sakharov Prize.[17] Suo Zhigang, a Chinese-born Harvard academic, told the *Guardian* in February 2022 that for most of the thirty years he has lived in the US, he was uninterested in politics. But the arrest of his best friend, MIT's Chen Gang, turned him into a political activist.[18] "Before [the CI], you were innocent until proven guilty. Now, you are guilty until you prove you are innocent."[19]

Members of America's legal community defended the Chinese, driven by their sense of injustice. Peter R. Zeidenberg, attorney for several professors under attack, said he'd like to see the DOJ refocus the CI "on cases that involve the improper transfer of intellectual property or technology to China, which when the China Initiative was announced was supposed to be the focus."[20]

> My belief and speculation is that when they started doing these cases and investigating these cases, they didn't find the kind of misconduct that they were hoping to find. . . . But they had a directive to bring cases involving Chinese American scientists, so they are left with bringing these cases, which look suspicious on the front end because there are undisclosed relationships. But when they dig in deeper, there is no improper transfer. Rather than move on, they're taking these cases and they're prosecuting them.[21]

Beth Margolis, a lawyer in New York City, and several of her colleagues, defended Dr Huang Chuanshu for free, and several others unjustly accused of crimes under the CI, while Drew Ledbetter defended Dr Simon Ang.

Even federal judges weighed in.[22] In January 2023, US District Court Senior Judge Julie Robinson, while sentencing Franklin Tao, a chemical engineer formerly at the University of Kansas, lectured the DOJ and the FBI about academic activities, including the search for jobs, the need for research funds and laboratories, and the importance of families as a deterrent to China-born professors returning to China. According to Mervis, "Although Robinson was only speaking about Tao, her comments also raise questions about how the government has prosecuted some two dozen US scientists." She saw that what was first titled as a case of espionage, or even a conflict of interest, fell far below the threshold needed to prosecute those crimes; instead, it was the crime of omission. Judge Robinson felt that prosecuting Dr. Tao had a deep impact on the scientific community, as they were "terrified it could happen to them." So, she sentenced him as lightly as possible: time served, no fines, and two years of probation, despite the DOJ's request that he spend thirty months in jail and pay a fine of $100,000.[23]

The End of the China Initiative

On February 23, 2022, thirteen months after the Biden administration came to office, the DOJ ended the CI. Speaking at George Mason University, Assistant AG for National Security Matt Olsen emphasized the DOJ's commitment to judicial equality for all foreign nationals, even as the DOJ continued to pursue ongoing Chinese government efforts to gain US technology illegally.[24] He replaced the CI with a broader policy, called the "Strategy for Countering Nation-State Threats," which included Russia, Iran, and North Korea. And while Olsen said that China's threat "stands apart," FBI Director Wray in a speech at this time did not mention the PRC's use of "nontraditional" agents and its efforts to engage US-based former mainlanders in illicit efforts to transfer US technology to China.[25] According to Olsen, the DOJ had listened to concerns that the initiative had "fueled a narrative of intolerance and bias," that had led to "a chilling atmosphere for scientists and scholars that damages the scientific enterprise in this country," and had created an "erosion of trust" among the very same Chinese community that the PRC was "targeting."[26]

> We are focused on the actions of the PRC government, the Chinese Communist Party, and their agents—not the Chinese people or those of Chinese descent. As we talk about the threats that the PRC government poses to the United States, we must never lose sight of that fundamental distinction.[27]

He did, however, state that "These cases were brought by real, sincere, serious concern about national security. . . . I have not seen any indication of bias or prejudice in any of the decision making I've seen by the Department of Justice. Full stop."

Still, in December 2022, speaking to students and professors at The University of Michigan, which had conducted an important survey on the CI among its faculty, and is one of the very top centers for China studies in the US, FBI Director Wray said the agency remains concerned about Chinese government "talent programs" that pay American professors secretly.[28] And while the FBI does "not base our cases on race, ethnicity or national origin," he argued that the CCP is engaged in an international talent war "to leverage and steal intellectual property and sensitive research and data from countries all over the world." So, the FBI must work with universities to try to protect that information by divulging hidden relationships US-based academics and researchers have with Chinese universities, especially if the academics are conducting research funded by American taxpayers. "I think it's appropriate for universities and the US government . . . to understand what kind of relationships exist between the scholar and the Chinese government," which has "a very different objective in the way it sees the world, including suppression of human rights, including theft of intellectual property, including military dominance."

When asked to defend his statement that the Chinese government is engaged in a "whole of society" effort to steal from the US, Wray noted that he had only used that phrase once, and early in his tenure. Still, argued one Chinese American professor, since the FBI wants to mobilize an "all of society" response to China, and Chinese Americans are part of American society, "what advice do you have for Chinese Americans like myself, who hope to be able to bridge the differences between our two countries, but instead find themselves caught in the middle, subject to accusations of disloyalty?" As for the many FBI cases against China-born professors that floundered due to a lack of evidence, Wray said that the Justice Department's losses in court are a testament to the US justice system.

> I respect the decisions of juries and judges that have found against us, just as I trust others to respect the juries and judges that have found for us in those cases where it's gone the other way. . . . The fact that we sometimes lose cases actually speaks volumes about the integrity and independence of our justice system. . . . I'd be willing to bet you that our counterparts over in China don't lose very many cases, and it ain't because they're better than we are.[29]

To that end, NSD would apply the DOJ's Justice Manual, whereby "merely because [the probable cause] requirement can be met in a given case does not automatically warrant prosecution; further investigation may instead be warranted."[30] The NSD would henceforth "take an active supervisory role" in investigations and prosecutions of cases of academic integrity and research security, imposing a layer of oversight that may slow some investigations and prevent other investigations from ever getting off the ground. Likewise, errors of omission were no longer punishable, as the FBI would have to prove "intent" and that the case really was a threat to national or economic security. In line with the idea of amnesty, which had been rejected in early 2021, Olsen said, "Where individuals voluntarily correct prior material omissions and resolve related administrative inquiries, this will counsel against a criminal prosecution under longstanding department principles of prosecutorial discretion."[31]

Still, in a sharp critique of this new DOJ strategy, George Pense emphasized that "there is good reason to believe DOJ will continue to pursue many of the goals of the China Initiative, and often by the same means—namely, criminal prosecution."[32] It also did not reject former President Trump's NPSM-33, and Olsen never apologized for the wrongs done under the CI. Still, in Pense's view, Olsen's remarks suggest that the NSD may exercise greater care in initiating criminal cases, focus on cases with a demonstrable nexus to the Chinese government or the CCP, and consider remedies other than criminal charges for alleged misconduct.[33]

In fact, the FBI has continued to go to American campuses, such as MIT, warning faculty members that rogue nations such as China, Russia, and even India were sending secret agents to steal intellectual property from university labs and asked them to take steps to stop it, including vetting their staff.[34] According to Boston public radio station WGBH, campus administrators at MIT are following new national security guidelines, first announced under Trump and enacted by the Biden administration, that are supposed to protect research labs from international espionage. At MIT, that has meant not only on-campus briefings by the FBI but a new requirement asking professors who receive federal funding to sign a disclosure form certifying that their students are not participating in suspicious activities.[35] Such actions at MIT are particularly sensitive given the DOJ's arrest of Professor Chen Gang in 2021, only to have all charges dropped for lack of evidence.

Under the Chips and Science Act, signed into law by President Biden in August 2023, starting in the summer of 2024, research universities that receive any federal funding will be required to certify that none of their researchers or students are participating in "a malign foreign talent recruitment program." This policy means that professors must "interrogate" their students by asking questions that will alienate them. Such efforts may have a chilling effect on postdoctoral fellows, graduate students, and even professors who were born in China but have made the US their home. As Keith Nelson, an MIT physical chemistry professor commented:

> As soon as I'm the one who has to sit down with my student from China and ask those questions, it can't help but somehow poison the relationship. . . . After all, I'm not asking that of my American citizen students.[36]

One big problem in this entire tale of the CI is Executive Order (EO) 12333 (1981) and Section 702 (S702) of the Foreign Intelligence Surveillance Act. According to Gallagher and Moltke, National Security Agency (NSA) documents show that under EO 21333, US intelligence agencies were collecting 1.8 billion emails a month, most of which went from one country to another, but are accessible to the NSA because they pass through servers in the US.[37] Some of these communications, however, are with US citizens or permanent residents, which allows US intelligence agencies "to perform warrantless 'backdoor' searches on Americans if they can make the case that an investigation is reasonably likely to return foreign intelligence or evidence of a crime," which they can easily do.[38] Thus, in 2022, under Section 702, the US government conducted over two hundred thousand searches of American citizens' and permanent residents' communications, more than 500 warrantless searches of American's communications every day. While S702 prohibited targeting American citizens and residents directly, the FBI frequently used it to monitor communications of scientists in China with China-born scientists in the US, who could then be investigated "without judicial oversight. In other words, the FBI has a treasure trove of information it can use to prosecute citizens, even if it has never made a case before a judge."[39]

The mistaken arrest of Dr. Xi Xiaogxing occurred under these circumstances, as the FBI totally misunderstood the technology that Xi was exchanging with China, which was discovered through this backdoor channel. And yet, they subjected him and his family to arrest at gunpoint.[40] Little wonder China-born scientists in the US now worry about collaborating (or even communicating) with colleagues in China, as this transnational collaboration could bring them into the firing line of the FBI. Similarly, China-based scientists are worried about communicating with their China-born colleagues in the US, as under Section 702, they could trigger investigations into their joint research and harm their colleagues and their families.

Revising Section 702 became a *cause célèbre* among Asian American human rights groups when it came up for renewal in the fall of 2023. In a letter to Congress, fifty-two Asian American groups (see Appendix A) demanded comprehensive reform of this legislation considering "the perils of unchecked national security programs and the historical discrimination our community has endured."[41]

As the climate toward prosecuting ethnic Chinese professors in the US changed, the NIH shifted responsibility for the lack of full disclosure onto the academic and research institutions that failed to inform scientists about the importance of full disclosure on their NIH grant applications. A US government survey of 773 institutions who received NIH funding for fiscal year 2020, done in late 2020 and early 2021, showed that 23 percent of the institutions receiving NIH grants (140 out of 609) had not required their investigators to complete all of the NIH-required training, and over half of those institutions (81 out of 140) did not require or offer any other training regarding the disclosure of foreign financial interests.[42] They also found that "many grantees could strengthen their oversight practices to better ensure that all materials submitted to NIH are complete and accurate."[43] Thus, much of the blame thrown at the Chinese scholars for not fully reporting their China ties on their NIH applications was deemed the fault of the very same universities and institutions that abetted the FBI and the NIH in investigating and prosecuting the researchers, and then quickly fired them in order to cover their tracks.

Despite the formal end of the program, some Asian Americans worried about the emergence of CI policies without the CI. In his speech on closing the initiative, Assistant DA Olsen announced that all ongoing investigations would be resolved quickly if the cases did not have "evidence of intent and materiality." Yet NIH cases were not being resolved in this manner. As we saw in chapter 3, as of December 2022, almost a year after the CI ended, 142 of the cases remained ongoing, leaving 57.7 percent of the people investigated by the NIH uncertain about their future in America.[44]

In March 2023, the House of Representatives attempted to resuscitate the China Initiative when it put forward a draft bill, called the CCP Initiative Program, which received its first reading in May 2024. The bill uses language identical to the declaration of the China Initiative, including raising concerns about "non-traditional collectors" who are "being coopted into transferring technology" by China.[45] As of the summer of 2023, China-born scholars in the US, such as Hu Anming, Chen Gang, and Xi Xiaoxing, were still telling *Nature* that they were afraid to apply for grants due to the lingering impact of the China Initiative.[46]

On the bright side, the NSF set an excellent example on how to handle the secrecy surrounding cases when its Office of the Inspector General (OIG) began publicly airing the closure of their investigations.[47] A link on the OIG website supplied information on all the cases that had been completed.[48] Previously, these investigations had remained unresolved, leaving the professors in limbo for months, if not years.

Impacts of the CI: Student Flows, Reverse Migration, and Scientific Decoupling

The CI dealt blows to the US. It undermined scientific and biomedical collaboration with China. The Chinese student population in American schools shrank, taking away graduate students who helped American scientific research and decreasing the number of full-tuition undergraduates whose monies supported universities and the communities surrounding these schools. The CI increased the flow of high-level talent away from the US. Finally, the CI created massive disillusionment among China-born scientists and professors who had studied in the US, had become naturalized citizens, and had raised their families in America. On a personal level, the CI disrupted their lives, even though many had not broken any US law.

The combination of the CI and COVID-19 led to a leveling off of the flow of Chinese students to the US between 2018 and 2020, and then to a significant decline in those numbers between 2020 and 2022, of 22 percent (table 5.1). In 2023, the inflow was almost the same as in 2022. However, the number of international students in the US bounced back in 2023. Since the flow of Indian students to the US picked up in 2022 and in 2023, while the flow from China declined, the decline must have had something to do with US policy toward Chinese, rather than other foreign, students. And while this decline may have delighted the Trump administration for its impact on technology transfer, fewer graduate students shrinks the pool of Chinese researchers on which American science had come to rely. The Center for Security and Emerging Technology at Georgetown University, which sharply criticizes most CCP activities, recognized that the US needs Chinese students to enhance its competitiveness with China,[49] while Graham Allison and Eric Schmidt believe that the US needs one million immigrants from China to compete with China.[50] If STEM students, blocked from studying in the US, are educated in Europe or Japan, they are more likely to go back to China afterwards rather than wind up in the US working for American companies or universities.[51] In line with these views, Professor Rao Yi, the dean of the School of Life Sciences at Peking University, reported a surge in the quality and quantity of applicants to his life sciences program.[52]

The decline in undergraduate students harmed the US economy as well. Chinese students spend billions of dollars on tuition and in colleges' neighboring communities. In 2018 alone, foreign students supported approximately 450,000 jobs,[53] with Chinese accounting for at least 35 percent of foreigners studying in the US.[54] During the 2019–2020 academic year, Chinese students contributed USD 15.9 billion in economic value (i.e., one-third of a total of USD 45 billion in total from foreign students) to the US economy.[55]

	2013	2014	2016	2018	2019	2020	2021	2022	2023
Chinese Students	235,597	274,439	328,547	363,341	369,548	372,532	317,299	290,086	289,526
Annual Increase		16.6%	7.9%	3.7%	0.95%	0.81%	-8.5%	-8.5%	-0.02%
Indian Students	96,754	102,673	165,918	196,271	202,014	193,124	167,582	199,182	268,923
Annual Increase		6.3%	25%	5.4%	3.0%	- 4.4%	-13.5%	19.2%	35%
Total Foreign Students in the US	819,644	886,052	1,043,839	1,094,792	1,095,299	1,075,496	914,095	948,519	1,057,188
Annual Increase		8.2%	7.4%	1.5%	0%	-1.8%	-15.0%	3.7%	11.4%

Table 5.1. Changes in the Number of Chinese and Indian Students in the US, 2013–2023.

Source: Project Atlas, Institute for International Education,
https://www.iie.org/Research-and-Insights/Project-Atlas/Explore-Data.

Moreover, between 2019 and 2022, Chinese students going abroad decreased worldwide by 4.7 percent but the number going to the US shrunk by 24.1 percent, which must have dealt a major blow to the US economy, to US colleges, and to the research of American professors. Instead, the students went to the UK (up 37.6 percent), Canada (up 9.4 percent), Japan (up 9.3 percent), Germany (up 8.1 percent) and Russia (up 33.3 percent). As a percent of total students going to the nine countries documented in table 5.2, America's share from 2017 to 2022, declined by 8.4 percent, from 40 percent in 2017 to only 31.6 percent in 2022. The largest increase in this period went to the UK (up over 5 percent) and Australia, up 3.6 percent.[56] Given that the COVID scare in the US was long gone by 2022, the outbreak of anti-Asian violence that persisted after COVID, and the hostility towards Chinese students demonstrated by the CI, must have played a major role in the significant shift away from studying in America.

Country	2017	2019	2021	2022	Change, 2019–2022	% of Total in 2017	% of total in 2022
US	350,755	369,548	317,299	290,086	-21.4%	40.0%	31.6%
Australia	114,006	153,822	140,111	152,715	-.01%	13.0%	16.6%
UK	97,850	109,180	158,335	150,720	37.6%	11.2%	16.4%
Canada	90,700	96,195	80,370	105,265	9.4%	10.3%	11.5%
Japan	75,262	86,439	85,762	94,063	9.3%	8.6%	10.2%
Germany	32,268	36,915	40,055	40,122	8.1%	3.7%	4.3%
France	25,388	30,072	27,479	27,950	-6.7%	2.9%	3.0%
Russia	22,529	29,950	37,5153	39,939	33.3%	2.6%	4.3%
South Korea[1]	68,184	50,600	26,949	16,968	-66.5%	7.7%	1.9%
Total[2]	876,942	962,721	886,102	917,828	-4.7%	100%	100%

Table 5.2. Chinese Students Studying Abroad, by Country, 2017–2022.

Source: Project Atlas, Institute for International Education, https://www.iie.org/Research-and-Insights/Project-Atlas/Explore-Data.

Notes:

[1] The data for Korea for 2017 come from the National Statistical Bureau. The data for 2019, 2021, and 2022 are from a reliable Korean source which, unfortunately, I cannot cite. The number for 2023 was down further, to 15,857.

[2] Total is only for countries in this table.

No one should be surprised that the number of PRC students going to America declined. The USG made it particularly difficult for Chinese students to get visas. In May 2018, the time Chinese graduate students could spend in the US was cut from five years to one year.[57] In 2019, nine Chinese students were unable to attend Arizona State University, despite having all the paperwork.[58] In the first half of 2022, the US issued 31,055 F-1 visas to Chinese nationals, down from 64,261 for the same period in 2019, a decrease of over 50 percent compared with pre-COVID levels.[59] According to Hua, the US was "losing ground as the most-coveted place for Chinese students to pursue higher education abroad."[60] As one Chinese student commented in 2019, "What's the point in going to the US if I might be shut out of a research lab just because I am Chinese?"[61]

Reverse Migration Picks Up

The story has come full circle. While the opening of the US to Chinese students created the legal and educational environment for China's massive "brain drain," the Trump administration's CI helped China in its effort to orchestrate a "reverse brain drain" of high-quality talent. As of February 2017, about 90 percent of Chinese nationals and 87 percent of Indian nationals who earned STEM PhDs between 2000 and 2015 were still living in the US five years after graduation, compared to just 66 percent of graduates from other countries.[62] Still, the number of returned Chinese with a PhD in STEM from the US—both fresh PhDs and senior scholars—grew after 2010, increased throughout the decade, and then jumped after the CI (table 5.3).[63]

	Engineering and Computer Science	Mathematics and Physical Science	Life Science	Social Science	Total
2000	3	18	6	0	27
2002	6	19	10	1	36
2004	18	44	37	2	101
2006	30	74	51	6	161
2008	36	111	81	11	239
2010	77	149	131	13	370
2012	85	193	192	20	490
2014	138	239	280	34	691
2016	168	319	348	40	875
2018	196	416	393	57	1062
2019	202	468	430	73	1173
2020	244	495	423	53	1215
2021	298	639	478	75	1490

Table 5.3. Number of US-Based Chinese Scientists Who Replaced US Affiliations for China Affiliations, Selected Years, 2000–2021.

Source: Yu Xie, Xihong Lin, Ju Li, Qian He, and Junming Huang, "Caught in the Crossfire: Fears of Chinese-American Scientists," *PNAS*, vol. 120, no. 27 (June 27, 2023), https://doi.org/10.1073/pnas.2216248120.

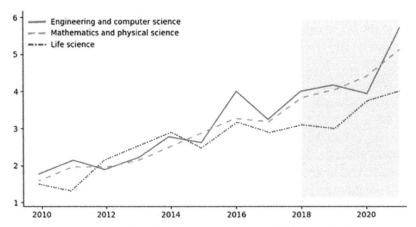

Figure 5.1. Number of Experienced US-Based Chinese Authors Moving to China, 2010–2021.

Note: The y-axis represents the ratio of the number of returning scientists each year relative to the baseline of 2005–2010, by corresponding fields.

Source: Yu Xie, Xihong Lin, Ju Li, Qian He, Junming Huang, "Caught in the Crossfire."

Xie et al. differentiated by field, but more importantly between more junior and what they call "more experienced" scholars, which indicated that China-born scientists, who were well ensconced in some of America's top academic institutions, such as Harvard, MIT, and the University of Chicago, were leaving the US and returning to China (figure 5.1).[64]

In the words of *ProPublica*, "The government's investigations and prosecutions of scientists for nondisclosure—a violation previously handled within universities and often regarded as minor . . . is unwittingly helping China achieve a long-frustrated goal of luring back top scientific talent."[65] *ProPublica* cited the example of Tan Weihong, a former senior researcher at the University of Florida who left for China abruptly in 2019 when, triggered by the NIH, the university investigated his alleged failure to report academic appointments and funding in China. After moving full-time to Hunan University, where he had been a part-time professor, he led a three-hundred-person research project that developed a rapid COVID-19 test.[66]

Since 2021, Xie et. al. carried out three surveys, each using a different methodology to build their sample, and discovered the depth of fear flowing through the US-based, ethnic Chinese academics who were staying in the US. Their key findings were that the CI had created "fear and anxiety" among the scientists, so that more than four in ten were considering leaving the US.[67] Many said that they would stop applying for research grants, given that grants were the source of the problem for most academics investigated under the CI. According to Xie et al., the decision not to seek research funding, even as they remained *in situ* in the US, meant the underutilization of an immense pool of talent whose publications and research should be helping to maintain America's lead in global science.[68]

Still, the public records of NIH awardees from 2014-2024, show that the number of China-born scholars receiving NIH funding rose from 3,052 in 2014 to 3,888 in 2019, and continued to rise to 4,582 by 2023. The funding for Chinese, as a share of total NIH funding, rose from 5.97 percent of the total NIH monies allocated in 2014, to 8.81 percent in 2024, though the growth rate of new awardees decreased slightly after 2019, but picked up after COVID-19. And their numbers have been growing.

Another study by He and Xie shows that the intensification of Sino-US hostility, and the perception of China as a threat, made many Americans, particularly in counties that voted for Donald Trump in 2020, view Chinese as untrustworthy and less moral.[70] This finding can only reinforce the anxiety of China-born scientists working in America.

A study by the University of Arizona and the Committee of 100 found similar feelings of fear in the hearts of many China-born scientists and professors working in the US. This survey, which was carried out in late 2021 and which had 1,949 valid responses, found that:[71]

1. 50.7 percent of Chinese-descent professors/researchers in the US felt considerable fear and/or anxiety that they were being surveyed by the USG, as compared to 11.7 percent of non-Chinese-descent professors/researchers.

2. Among the non-US citizens in the sample, 42.1 percent of Chinese-descent professors/researchers indicated that FBI investigations and/or the CI affected their plans to stay in the US.

3. 42.2 percent of scientists of Chinese descent feel racially profiled by the USG, while only 8.6 percent of scientists of non-Chinese descent feel so.

One associate professor of chemistry articulated why he might leave the US:

As a Chinese professor who is trained and has been working in the US for nearly twenty years, these investigations and restrictions against Chinese scholars make me feel unwelcome and somewhat discriminated and I sometimes feel my Chinese identity may be the limiting factor for my career advancement in the US. In the past few years, I felt for the first time since I have been in the US that Chinese scientists are not valued as much as before and politics is intervening [*sic*] academic freedom. This makes me seriously consider moving to China if the current trend continues or even worsens.[72]

A third study, which received responses from 123 faculty members at The University of Michigan (U of M), found that 17.8 percent of them had been questioned about their research collaborations with China.[73] In fifteen cases, interviewers were university officials, nine cases were federal law enforcement agents, and five were from a federal funding agency. Some faculty faced scrutiny from more than one source. Only 20 percent of the Chinese faculty who were investigated by U of M officials said the interviewers informed them of their "rights and responsibilities," compared with 33 percent of those queried by law enforcement and 70 percent of those contacted by a funding agency. Clearly, The University of Michigan was actively investigating its own faculty under the CI.

Finally, an OECD study similar to that of Xie et al., finds that the US is losing the race for scientific talent to China and other countries, which, according to the Cato Institute, showed that China's strategy to recruit scientific researchers to work at China-affiliated universities was working (figure 5.2). In 2021, the US lost published research scientists to other countries, while China gained more than 2,408 scientific authors. This was a remarkable turnaround from 2017, when the US picked up 4,292 scientists and China picked up just 116.

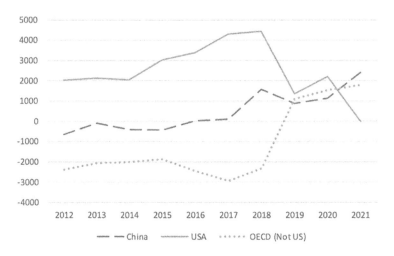

Figure 5.2 Other Countries Surpass US in Attracting Published Scientists: Net inflows of scientific authors, 2012–2021.

Source: OECD Science, Technology, and Industry Scoreboard, OECD Publishing, Paris, https://www.oecd.org/sti/scoreboard.htm, cited in David J. Bier, "Abandoning the US, More Scientists Go to China," CATO Institute, April 11, 2023, https://www.Cato.Org/Blog/Abandoning-US-More-Scientists-Go-China.

The CI had a terrible impact on the lives of the people it investigated, as well as on their ability to carry out research. Chen Gang was suspended from doing research while the investigation ensued, and his lab was closed. In case study number six in chapter 4, because the professor was forbidden to do research or talk with his students, all graduate students and postdocs left his research group. When the ban was lifted one year later, his research had been so devastated that he had to decide between trying to resuscitate it or simply retire, despite only being in his late fifties. Hu Anming estimated that he lost two years of his life.

For the accused who were facing a trial, mounting a defense was very costly. As their universities were often involved in prosecuting them, professors could expect little financial help from them. Particularly if they were fired or suspended, they lost their salary, which could have helped cover their costs. Fortunately, lawyers who took on these cases often reduced their fees, seeing the case as an abuse of the professors' civil rights.

Hong Peng, the wife of Franklin Tao, one of the earliest targets of the CI, said that uncertainty continued to weigh on her husband and their family. "Our lives will never be the same as before [his arrest]. . . . It's hard to find the words to describe what we have been through." So, she set up the Franklin Tao Legal Defense Fund and mounted a GoFundMe campaign, which, as of 2019, had raised USD 750,000 toward the goal of USD 1.9 million to help defray his legal fees.[74] Though the vast majority gave funds anonymously, Chen Gang of MIT, who contributed USD 10,000, and Suo Zhigang of Harvard, were unconcerned about going public with their donations. While Tao was found guilty of one charge, and sentenced for time served by a very sympathetic judge, his appeal overturned the verdict in July 2024.[75]

Collaboration or Decoupling?

Many politicians believe that the US should decouple from China to protect its technological advantage. But even if China is benefiting substantially from scientific collaboration, some recent research suggests that close research collaboration between the US and China will hurt US scientific scholarship more than China.[76] In fact, collaborative research has long benefited the US, particularly in terms of published research articles. But as of mid-2024, the jury was still out as to whether the CI succeeded in decoupling US-China scientific cooperation or at least led to a slowdown in line with the goals of the CI. The capital to finance such business interactions had dried up as early as 2019.[77] And in July 2021, the

US House of Representatives passed a bill that would bar scientists and academics from participating in US-funded research projects if they were also receiving support from Beijing.[78]

Politics was influencing collaboration. When China offered access to its five-hundred-meter Aperture Spherical Radio Telescope, the world's most sensitive single-dish radio telescope, some Americans hesitated from using it, due in part to China's human rights record.[79] Other scientists in the US and Canada thought that cooperating would be good, invoking US-Soviet collaboration during the Cold War. Still, the US government had passed a law in 2011, banning NASA, and perhaps researchers with NASA funding, from using its funds to cooperate with China.

Brown University President Paxson worried about decoupling, especially because after the CI began, most major US universities had instituted new guidelines to strengthen disclosure rules and prevent technology transfer from occurring under the radar. In her view, collaboration should continue. "We can't have overly restrictive policies that will end up actually hurting the research that is going on to drive cures for diseases, economic development, things like that."[80]

Contrary to assumptions that political rhetoric, scientific nationalism, and policy proposals to decrease joint publications and collaborative research would succeed, Lee and Haupt, using SCOPUS bibliometric data, found that COVID-19 had increased Sino-US collaboration. From January to May 2020, papers with authors from multiple countries made up 32 percent of the science and engineering literature on COVID-19 published in that period, compared to 26 percent of the general science and engineering literature published over the previous five years.[81] And despite Sino-US geopolitical tensions, the highest number of coauthored COVID-19 articles between any two countries involved the US and China.[82]

Much of this collaboration went on despite the Trump administration. In April 2020, Li Jian of the University of Florida coauthored a paper with researchers from the Institute of Acoustics, Beijing, in *IEEE Transactions on Aerospace and Electronic Systems* on better ways for sonar operators to estimate the number and location of enemy jamming machines.[83] Sponsors of Li's laboratory included the US Air Force, Army, and Navy; NASA; the Defense Advanced Research Projects Agency; and arms contractors Lockheed Martin and General Electric—all this despite close ties between the Institute of Acoustics and the People's Liberation Army. Still, one must doubt that Li would ever get new funding for such collaboration. Pan Jianwei, father of the world's first quantum satellite, who works at the Chinese University of Science and Technology in Hefei, Anhui Province, and Marlan O. Scullya, a leading quantum theorist at Texas A&M and Princeton, coauthored a paper in *Physical Review Letters* in October 2020. Such long-established ties were most likely to be resilient, but the worry is that younger researchers on both sides of the Pacific will eschew collaboration. New projects were also initiated. In August 2022, for example, Nanjing University and the American Chemical Society signed a memorandum of understanding to collaborate on a new open access journal, *Chemical & Biomedical Imaging*.[84]

The ethnic Chinese and non-Chinese surveyed by the Committee of 100 and the University of Arizona in 2021 supported continuing collaboration between the two countries.[85] According to the survey, 92.2 percent of Chinese scientists, and 82.3 percent of the non-Chinese scientists, believe that the US should build stronger research collaboration with China. Moreover, 85.8 percent of the ethnic Chinese who were surveyed, and 76.1 percent of non-Chinese, reported that collaboration with Chinese scientists was important for their scholarly research. When asked about the impact of limiting collaboration with China, most ethnic Chinese and non-Chinese scientists indicated that limiting collaboration would negatively impact academia (95.9 percent and 92.2 percent, respectively), their academic discipline (95.7 percent and 91.4 percent, respectively), and their research projects (95.9 percent and 90.6 percent, respectively). Furthermore, between 2018 and 2021, 50.9 percent of Chinese and 35.6 percent of non-Chinese scientists had conducted international collaborative research involving China.

Still, this survey discovered serious reservations about collaboration, suggesting that it might decline over time.[86] According to a Chinese assistant professor of computer science in the US: "There are no clear rules about what kind of collaboration is allowed and not allowed. To be safe, I limited my connection with my Chinese collaborators. However, it impacts my research progress as funding and student support are very limited in the US."

A Chinese assistant professor of biology shared that view. "To avoid any potential administrative trouble, I have to minimize the collaboration, even though that hurts my project." A Chinese American professor of genetics voiced the greatest concerns.

> [The] China Initiative has a significant impact on my research and personal life. I assume all my electronic communications are potentially monitored by the US government. I decided not to collaborate with researchers in China and other foreign countries due to perceived conflict of interests. I even decline outside research consulting activities in the US. In summary, [the] China Initiative has a great negative impact on my research productivity.

Finally, one non-Asian professor of genetics interviewed by Xie et al. was particularly worried because much of his funding came from the NIH. "I am funded by NIH and must be very careful not to violate rules regarding collaboration with Chinese scientists on NIH funded projects."[87] So he avoided collaborations entirely, "even if the collaborations are not directly related to my NIH funded research and are funded by Chinese agencies, such as the Chinese Academy of Sciences (CAS), as they might threaten my NIH funding or create personal career risks."[88]

China worries about scientific decoupling. A report by a think tank at Peking University argued that China had more to lose from decoupling than the US, especially in the fields of high-end semiconductors, operating systems and software, and aerospace—all areas where the US is far ahead.[89] The report was soon removed from the website of Peking University. Another team of researchers in China argued that while Sino-American joint applications for international patents comprised 40 to 48 percent of all of China's applications under its Twelfth Five-Year Plan, which ran from 2012 to 2016, that number decreased to 37.3 percent of all of China's patent applications during the Thirteenth Five-Year Plan (2016–2020). The actual number declined from 1,265, under the Twelfth Five-Year Plan, to 997 applications, a decline of 21 percent, leaving the country vulnerable to further cuts in collaborative research and suggesting that China would suffer much more from decoupling than the US.[90] According to Zhang, after the attacks on China during COVID, Chinese scientists are extremely hesitant to work with the West, assuming that they will be subject to lectures on the weaknesses of their system.[91] Still, Li, Cao, Wang, and Zhou see a win-win scenario when both countries collaborated, but they see a lose-lose scenario from decoupling with far-reaching adverse impacts beyond bilateral territories.[92] Thus, despite pressing for more domestic innovation and self-reliance in scientific development, Xi Jinping, speaking to the United Nations in September 2021, called for continued Sino-US scientific cooperation.[93]

New Chinese government policies could harm cooperation, even in the face of the risks of decoupling. In the early days of the pandemic, China wanted to control the narrative. In March 2020, the CAS indicated that any COVID-19-related research publications must be evaluated by the government for "academic value" and "timing" prior to public release.[94] Only after gaining approval could the scholars publish their work. In other cases, a university committee had to give approval.

China also announced research-evaluation reform during the pandemic. Rather than basing researcher performance and tenure decisions on publication counts in SSCI journals, China would measure quality based on its domestic priorities, including publishing in domestic journals. This move could decrease papers by Chinese researchers in international journals and limit Chinese researchers from reaching out for collaborators.

The fear described above led many Chinese, other Asians, and even non-Asians to curtail collaboration with the PRC. Xie et al. found that 42 percent of China-born scholars had been so intimidated by the CI, and Section 702, that

that they were afraid to collaborate with China, "lest it trigger an investigation of their scientific activity and potentially result in a moratorium on their work."[95] The Committee of 100/University of Arizona survey found that 23.6 percent of US-based Chinese scientists reported ending collaborations with China in the previous three years and canceled most planned projects.[96] That share was four times larger than the 5.8 percent of non-Chinese scientists who reported taking such steps. Among the US-based professors and researchers who collaborated with China over the previous three years, 23.6 percent of Chinese-descent professors/researchers decided not to involve China in future projects, as compared to 5.8 percent of non-Chinese-descent professor/researchers. Among non-Chinese Asian faculty, who would also raise their antennae on this issue, 14 percent reported terminating their collaborations with researchers in China. The survey showed that 19.5 percent of Chinese researchers in the US "prematurely or unexpectedly had to end/suspend all research collaborations with scientists in China over the past three years, and among that cohort, 78.5 percent did so due to the CI, compared to 27.3 percent of scientists of non-Chinese descent." Lee and Haupt had similar findings.[97]

Thus, Wagner and Cai found a decline in US-China collaboration in the years preceding January 2022, but they saw no such decline in China-EU collaboration, suggesting that the politicization of US-China ties caused this decoupling more than the pandemic.[98] And while the pandemic hurt China's overall international collaborations in 2021, the most notable decline was with the US. Still, bio-scientists from the UK, the US, and China have established a dialogue, called the BioGovernance Commons, to establish mutual support, devise strategies of conflict resolution, and manage experimentation, so that if ties between China and the West improve, community rebuilding will be possible.[99]

In the summer of 2023, even as the Biden administration tried to improve ties with China by sending its top administration officials there, who uniformly declared that the US was not decoupling, President Biden decided to prevent Americans and US permanent residents from any interactions with China that might improve China's micro-processing, AI, surveillance, and cyber capabilities. On August 9, 2023, Biden tightened the constraints on China's access to Western (i.e., US) technology—which had begun with the Chips Bill—when, in a Presidential Executive Order, he forbade US investment in Chinese firms producing advanced semiconductors and quantum computers.[100] In a step that might directly affect China-born researchers in the US, President Biden also barred US citizens and permanent residents from taking part in any of these prohibited deals. Since most China-born scholars of any scientific standing in the US would be permanent residents, if not citizens, this order effectively froze them out from helping China's technological strengthening.

As the deadline for extending the US-China Science and Technology Cooperation Agreement (USCSTA) neared, a strenuous debate emerged within the US Congress.[101] Congressional critics argued that China has been an unreliable partner and that, as it has developed greater competencies, it has sought to restrict US researchers' access in certain areas.[102] Mike Gallagher (R–Wisconsin), former chair of the Select Committee on China in the US House of Representatives, was one of ten Republicans who wrote Secretary of State Antony Blinken, whose department is responsible for establishing science and technology agreements (STAs), urging him to let the agreement lapse. In their view, "even fundamental research discoveries can help China gain an advantage over the US." Their letter turned quiet negotiations "into a front-burner political issue."

Supporters argue that it guided US science and technology work with China without mandating activity and the USCSTA provided access to large pools of research subjects for longitudinal health studies. We can see this in a collaborative project between Bob Li of the Memorial Sloan Kettering Cancer Center in New York and the Chinese Thoracic Oncology Group in Guangzhou. Because China has so many people with subtypes of cancer who are easily recruited, "trials that typically take 10–15 years can be sped up to 2 to 3 years with China's participation," allowing for the approval of many new cancer drugs by the US Food and Drug Administration.[103] But even ardent supporters, such as Denis Simon of Duke University, admit that the USCSTA needs improvement, especially to ensure that there is a free flow of information.[104] At the time of writing, the Biden administration demonstrated a commitment to continued scientific cooperation when it approved a six-month extension, during which time it must negotiate many sensitive issues with China.

CONCLUSION

WHY THE WAR?

Most developing states confront a brain drain, where a generation of university students, having been trained abroad, settle in OEDC countries that can pay premium salaries and supply a quality of life for them and their families with which developing countries cannot compete. In other cases, such as India, fully trained PhDs or junior faculty move abroad in search of greener pastures.[1] China has suffered such an outflow of talent, though as shown in chapter 1 (table 1.1), China's loss has been less catastrophic relative to India or the Philippines, which lost over eight hundred thousand and four hundred thousand more men with some college education to the US, respectively, than China did. On a scale of zero to ten, with ten reflecting the greatest impact of lost brainpower on economic development, Indonesia (6.0), India (5.2), Mexico (4.6), and Malaysia (4.4) all suffered more than China at 3.5.[2] Nevertheless, since the mid-1990s, China's leaders introduced a series of incentives to attract these talented people back.

For two decades, governments worldwide have adopted programs similar to the Chinese to bring back talented expatriates who settled abroad. Canada Research Chairs, funded by Canada's foreign ministry, gives higher salaries and extra research funds to Canadian academics who return full-time. Taiwan and South Korea developed similar programs, as have some state governments in India.[3] The US, as the largest repository of such talent, is the major target of these programs.

For various reasons, China's effort to trigger a reverse wave of high-quality academics and scientists has floundered on the shores of the OECD, despite deep engagement by the CCP from 2003 onward.[4] For many PRC-born Chinese living abroad, and particularly the most talented of that cohort, the rewards of overseas life have outweighed the benefits proffered by academic or research institutions, by Chinese companies, by the central and/or local governments, or by China's market. The work environment's thick social relations, often referred to as "the complicated nature of interpersonal relations" (人际关系太复杂), administrative hierarchies, bureaucratic obstructionism, and other complications are widely cited as major impediments to returning. Cabals of earlier returnees undermined any large-scale reverse migration of top talent that would threaten their power bases within those institutions.[5]

Jiang Zemin, who touted various programs to attract overseas talent, such as the CAS' One Hundred Talents Plan (百人计划) in 1996 or the Changjiang Scholars Plan (长江学者计划), begun by the Ministry of Education in 1998, preferred full-time returnees. Li Yuanchao and the CCP Organization Department shared that preference. But hunger for international technology, cutting-edge research, global knowledge, and management skills convinced these leaders to offer overseas scholars rewards that could be attained without returning full-time. As of 2011, most participants in the Thousand Talent Plan (千人计划) opted for the "diaspora option"—that is, part-time positions and awards given out under Jiang's policy in 2001 called "serving China from abroad" (为国服务).

China's adoption of this "diaspora option," which was lauded by European academics as a positive strategy to ameliorate the pain of the brain drain, created enormous opportunities for China-born talent living abroad.[6] Those who stayed abroad could employ cheap but talented graduate students to work for them overseas or in China; they could receive large research grants from China, especially if they linked with local scholars, that supplemented awards received in their new homeland; they could coauthor world-class papers with colleagues in China, some of whom they had trained in their own laboratories abroad; they could attract excellent postdocs and assistant professors from China to work in their labs in the West; they could summer in China, perhaps near their aging parents, and work as adjunct professors at universities that sought their services; and they could get awards and titles that enhanced their status in their former homeland. Little wonder thousands took up these opportunities and helped drive Sino-US collaboration and the transfer of US technology to China.

However, the European scholars who saw a nation's diaspora as a partial solution to long-term economic and scientific backwardness failed to realize that the target of that "option," the OECD countries, and particularly the US, may be quite displeased to see a concerted, state-directed effort by a large developing country (i.e., China) to get its hands on technological innovations designed and funded in the West and to use that science to challenge the OECD countries for global leadership and threaten their economic and national security.

And even if the process is not led by the CCP, in the current climate of Sino-US strategic competition, how should states in the OECD, particularly the US, respond when increasing numbers of China-born professors living and working in their midst, who are leaders in fields such as artificial intelligence or quantum computing, use Western funding to develop these cutting-edge technologies replete with national security implications to advance their research, all the while being willing to transfer those innovations and scientific discoveries to the People's Republic?

The example of Zhu Songchun is a case in point.[7] Zhu, who worked for UCLA for eighteen years, established a major research center there on AI, and received significant funding from the DOD and the NSF, returned to China, whereupon he set up several key research centers on AI and worked closely with several universities that are categorized by American intelligence as being closely linked to the Chinese military. According to some reports, he had begun to build these centers when he was still working in the US. Moreover, his work is "now at the forefront of China's race to develop the most advanced artificial intelligence—which he compared to the atomic bomb due to its military importance."

China's party/state has been quite aggressive in trying to access Western technology and know-how, much of which was in the hands or minds of these PRC-born Chinese living abroad. In the late 1980s, the Ministry of Science and Technology reportedly recognized the function China's former nationals could play. Xi Jinping, who seeks to fulfill his "China dream" and lead the resuscitation of the Chinese nation that can compete technologically and militarily with the West, has pushed the CCP to intensify these efforts. Agents of the state, such as the PLA and intelligence bureaus, also engaged in illicit efforts to gain that knowledge.

Chinese institutions, such as universities, are driven by incentives proffered by the party/state under programs such as the "985 Plan" (九八五计划) or the CJSP to bring back talent, even if only part-time. As adjunct professors, these overseas scholars can contribute much to the university. Beginning in 2009, under intense pressure from Li Yuanchao, the director of the CCP Organization Department, cities all around China demanded that their universities hook up with PRC-born Chinese living abroad, pulling them into the TTP, as portrayed in two of my case studies under the CI. High-tech zones—such as one in Chengdu, Sichuan Province, described in chapter 3—or companies encouraged overseas entrepreneurs in the West to bring them their innovations, which they would commercialize.[8] And China's entire biotechnical sector, including hospitals, drug companies, and research labs, sought the latest medical advances in the West that could enhance their market positions in the struggle targeted at diseases such as cancer.

Individual scientists, too, for many years have been sharing information with former units back home out of a sense of obligation, cultural affinity, or in anticipation of resettling in China. In our interviews with academics in the US in the early 1990s, Chen Changgui and I found that 24.7 percent of our sample of academics had regular interactions with their home unit.[9] Saxenian's data showed that this trend was strong in 2001, especially among those I have categorized as "servers," while I have argued elsewhere that in the mid-2000s, the opportunities available from bringing back technology that was in short supply in China stimulated reverse migration by entrepreneurs.[10] And as the data from 2016 about the actions of 121 of the world's top China-born scientists working abroad show, an astonishing 35.5 percent of them held part-time appointments in China, while 77.8 percent of them engaged in some form of collaborative research that brings knowledge from the West eastward. Particularly those running research centers overseas, such as the China-born professors I interviewed in Toronto in 2016, were deeply engaged in this transfer of knowledge.

Contrary to the opinion that most PRC-born Chinese living in America were part of a systemic effort to steal America's lunch,[11] I have argued here that for many of these researchers—perhaps the majority of them—their main goal was to build a better research ecosystem in China, pay back the country for their own education, and help China overcome its backwardness and the loss of an entire generation of scientists through the Cultural Revolution.[12] Many of them were apolitical, leaving them vulnerable to blandishments from the Chinese state and its institutions. Many loved the high status endowed on them by the Chinese system because of their Western-based knowledge and their willingness to support China's self-strengthening. And some, no doubt, saw golden opportunities to enrich themselves by bringing the bacon back to China.

Ironically, though, aggressive efforts by the CCP, the state, and Chinese institutions to access Western technology, sometimes by questionable means, put China-born individuals working and living in the West at risk. Just looking at the type of contracts they were encouraged to sign in order to join the TTP, government and CCP officials should have realized that if those contracts were discovered, these scientists could find themselves facing the US legal system. The CCP-led state should have been sensitive to the danger it created for PRC-born Chinese working in America—a country with a long history of racial animus against Asians, and particularly against Chinese—when it encouraged them to help a foreign government, a rising communist power that could easily be presented as an external threat to American freedom and prosperity. Under these conditions, when the US declared war on such transfers and launched the DOJ's CI, these professors, scientists, and some employees of American companies got caught between the worsening relationship between the US and China, and the US' efforts to slow China's rapid rise and maintain its own hegemony in science and technology and the dominance of global norms and institutions it established at the end of World War II.

As an observer looking in, I believe that Americans just don't get it, having never suffered a brain drain of their own. America has never spent billions in government funds or taxpayer dollars to create a talented cohort of young people and prepare them for careers in science or engineering in the hopes that they will help their country compete globally, only to see those people leave and go work in another country. But much of the world—including countries in the OECD such as Canada, the UK, and the EU—has experienced this loss of brain power and investment in human capital and may be more sympathetic to China's diaspora option and its efforts to generate a reverse brain drain, especially since they too employ such strategies and programs.

In fact, America has only benefited from these flows of human talent. So many students and talented people from so many countries come to study or work in America, helping the US maintain its lead in science and innovation as graduate students and lab technicians ultimately choose to stay in the US and enhance its global dominance. The stay rate of American-trained PhDs, particularly from countries or continents such as China, India, Europe, and Canada, are shockingly high. Little wonder, then, that Americans and their government have little sympathy for states that try to minimize their brain drain and trigger the reverse migration of talent.

Thus, the US, under President Trump, declared war on China's strategy to use the diaspora to promote its national interest—particularly on the TTP that was administered by the CCP—and the Biden administration was slow to end a program that turned many minor offenses into treasonous behavior and sent some very talented people trained in the US back home.

While Indian entrepreneurs in Silicon Valley used The Indus Entrepreneurs (TIE) platform to transfer a great deal of technology they created in the US to India, which could undermine America's global competitiveness, the US and India are not strategic rivals, so Americans have voiced few complaints over this technology transfer. In the case of China, however, a policy that moves knowledge from the US to China, even if its focus is to cure cancer, led the US government to accuse China of a strategically motivated, organized conspiracy to steal US technology with the goal of replacing the US as the dominant power in the world.

For Mike German, the irony is rich.[13] During the Cold War, the openness of America's scientific environment was one of America's great strengths that attracted foreigners to the US to study, work, and settle down. America's scientists fought hard to maintain that scientific model. But now, America's security establishment has countered that an excessively open scientific system has allowed China to rip off America's scientific accomplishments and bring that technology back to China, empowering America's strategic rival.

Could this dilemma have evolved differently? The CCP could have been more open with the US government and American academic/research institutions about the content of its agreements with China-born scientists working in the US. It also could have eschewed demands that participants sign secretive contracts committing them to questionable behavior. The Hong Kong University of Science and Technology (HKUST) and Sun Yat-sen University in Guangzhou struck a deal, where HKUST deferred the salary of one of its faculty members who worked in Guangzhou each summer under a TTP award. Or Chinese scholars in the US could have been more transparent about their academic affiliations and the financing they received from China for their research and could have been more sensitive to the dangers they were creating for themselves in agreeing to such terms of engagement. Many of these talented Chinese who stayed in America after their US education kept their distance from the TTP, aware of the dangers inherent in working with the CCP. Funding agencies, such as the NIH, the NSF, or departments in the US government such as NASA, should have put out clearer guidelines for reporting outside funding. Universities could have grandfathered those who failed to report their "double-dipping" and allowed them to revise their grant applications. And the NIH itself could have been less aggressive in "cleansing its ecosystem" of those who broke its rules. On the other hand, like the FBI, which, according to Mike German, may not care so much about finding foreign scientists guilty of crimes but instead investigates an entire category of researchers to "disrupt" their networks, the NIH investigations have definitely had a disruptive effect on Sino-US scientific collaboration, as many China-born researchers in the US have reported in surveys that they will no longer work with colleagues on the mainland.[14]

Still, the goals of China's talent programs were public, even if their tactics were not; rather, it was individual Chinese, and even some non-Chinese, academics, albeit with some strong incentives, who chose to engage in "double-dipping" by drawing two full-time salaries or by requesting funding from the two countries for the same, or very similar, projects without reporting their actions to US funding agencies, some of whom proved vindictive over these conflicts of commitment and interest.[15]

Going forward, China-born scholars in America—as well as Taiwanese and Hong Kongers—will feel watched, and they will avoid publishing many papers with colleagues in China for fear of triggering an FBI investigation under Section 702 (which was reconfirmed by the US Congress in April 2024). They will also be deeply uncertain about the future of their children in an America that has become anti-Chinese, and therefore look more favorably on blandishments from China. According to McKinney from the Association of American Medical Colleges, "the effects [the CI] will have on long-term, trusting relationships are hard for us to face."[16] All this is unfortunate, as co-ethnic publications and Sino-US collaborations have benefited both countries. Closing down cooperation in the biomedical field is a global problem, as findings from these collaborations have improved human health.[17] Perhaps the transfer of some IP back to China is the price the US must pay for retaining this cohort of world-class Chinese talent that came to America to study, work, and contribute.

However, if ethnic Chinese in the US work more transparently when moving technology from the US to China, cooperation between these two scientific academies may persist. According to the JASON group of elite scientists, research integrity requires full disclosure of all affiliations and personal commitments— such as ties to foreign military or security organizations.[18] "A failure to make the proper disclosure must then be treated as a violation of research integrity and should be investigated and adjudicated," like plagiarism or the falsification of data.[19] Increased clarity and explicitness regarding the boundaries of the permissible sharing of unpublished research information is also needed. JASON agrees that actual theft or espionage is of course punishable by law. But as a general principle, foreign scientists who emigrate to the US should be treated like any other citizen and "should be judged on their personal actions and not by profiling, based on the actions of the government and political institutions of their home country."[20]

Still, without moderating its strategy underlying its diaspora option, China could lose its ability to draw on the talent of its overseas scientists living in the US, as the Biden administration seems to be following in the footsteps of Trump, despite promises of greater sensitivity espoused by the deputy attorney general running the replacement of the CI. According to Krige, the only reasonable security policy is to protect the most sensitive knowledge by building "high walls around small fields," as the Augustine committee proposed, rather than to try to build "nominal walls around large fields."[21] Thus, in 2020, President Trump banned graduate students from China with any ties to the military, while President Biden imposed restrictions on the transfer of some sensitive items such as AI capabilities.

On the other hand, without changes to the US perception of China's national talent programs, and the end of indiscriminate attacks on Chinese working in America, the US will only help the PRC promote a reverse brain drain of exceptional Chinese talent currently residing in the US, a goal that, for decades, China could not accomplish on its own.

NOTES

Preface

[1] The direct translation would be "sea turtle faction."

[2] David Zweig, Chung Siu-Fung, and Han Donglin, "Redefining the 'Brain Drain': China's Diaspora Option," *Science, Technology, and Society* 13, no. 1 (2008): 1–33, https://doi.org/10.1177/097172180701300101.

[3] David Zweig and Siqin Kang, "America Challenges China's National Talent Programs," Center for Strategic and International Studies, no. 4 (May 2020), https://www.csis.org/analysis/america-challenges-chinas-national-talent-programs.

[4] National Institute of Allergy and Infectious Diseases, "US-China Collaborative Biomedical Research Program," https://www.niaid.nih.gov/research/us-china-collaborative-biomedical-research-program.

[5] David Zweig, Siqin Kang, and Henry Wang Huiyao, "'The Best Are Yet to Come': State Programs, Domestic Resistance, and Reverse Migration of High-Level Talent to China," *Journal of Contemporary China* 29, no. 125 (September 2020): 776–791.

[6] David Zweig and Changgui Chen, *China's Brain Drain to the United States: Views of Overseas Chinese Students and Scholars in the 1990s*, with the assistance of Stan Rosen. New York: Routledge, 2013.

[7] See, for example, *Brain Drain and Brain Gain (III), Sending Students Abroad and Attracting Them Back*, March–April 2003. Armonk, NY: M. E. Sharpe, 2003.

[8] David Zweig, Kellee Tsai, and A. Didar Singh, "Reverse Entrepreneurial Migration in China and India: The Role of the State," *World Development* 138 (2021), doi: 10.1016/j.worlddev.2020.105192.

[9] Miao Danguo, ed., 出国留学六十年 (Sixty Years of Study Abroad). Beijing: 中央文选出版, 2010.

[10] David Zweig and Huiyao Wang, "Can China Bring Back the Best? The Communist Party Organizes China's Search for Talent," *China Quarterly* no. 215 (September 2013): 590–615.

Chapter 1

[1] Samia El-Saati, "Egyptian Brain Drain: Its Size, Dynamics, and Dimensions," in *Brain Drain: Proceedings from the Second Euro-Arab Social Research Group Conference*, edited by Mourad Wahba, 39–64. Cairo: Ain Shams University Press, 1980.

[2] Wei-chiao Huang, "An Empirical Analysis of Foreign Student Brain Drain to the United States," *Economics of Education Review* 7, no. 2 (1988): 231–243.

[3] P. G. Altbach, "Servitude of the Mind? Education, Dependency, and Neo-Colonialism," *Teachers College Record* no. 79 (December 1977): 187, https://journals.sagepub.com/doi/10.1177/016146817707900201.

[4] W. A. Glaser, *The Brain Drain: Emigration and Return.* Oxford: Pergamon Press, 1978.

[5] Gutta Lacksmana Rao, *Brain Drain and Foreign Students: A Study of the Attitudes and Intentions of Foreign Students in Australia, the USA, Canada, and France.* Queensland, Australia: University of Queensland Press, 1979.

[6] Cong Cao, "China's Approaches to Attract and Nurture Young Biomedical Researchers," a report for the Next Generational Researcher Initiative, US National Academies of Sciences, Engineering, and Medicine (March 2018), http://sites.nationalacademies.org/cs/groups/pgasite/documents/webpage/pga_184821.pdf; and Li Xiaoxuan, 中国科学院出国留学效益研究 (A Study by the Chinese Academy of Sciences on the Efficiency of Study Abroad), 出国留学工作研究 (Research on Work Concerning Overseas Studies), no. 1 (2003): 25–35, in *Chinese Education and Society,* 37, no. 2 (March–April 2004): 61–87.

[7] Stanley Rosen and David Zweig, "Transnational Capital: Valuing Academics in a Globalizing China," in *Bridging Minds across the Pacific: US-China Educational Exchanges, 1978–2003*, edited by Cheng Li, 111–132. Lanham, MD: Lexington Books, 2005.

[8] Cheng Li, "The Status and Characteristics of Foreign-Educated Returnees in the Chinese Leadership," *China Leadership Monitor*, no. 16 (2005).

[9] Jan Henrik Gruenhagen, Per Davidsson, and Sukanlaya Sawang, "Returnee Entrepreneurs: A Systematic Literature Review, Thematic Analysis, and Research Agenda," *Foundations and Trends in Entrepreneurship* 16, no. 4 (2020): 310–392. doi: 10.1561/0300000096.

[10] Mark. R. Rosenzweig, "Consequences of Migration for Developing Countries," paper presented at the United Nation Expert Group Meeting on International Migration and Development, New York, July 2005, cited in *Harnessing the Resources of Overseas Professionals*, edited by C. Wescott and J. Brinkerhoff, viii. Manila: Asian Development Bank, 2006.

[11] S. Y. Bang, "Reverse Brain Drain in South Korea State Led Model," *Studies in Comparative International Development* 27, no. 1 (1992): 4–26.

[12] Nan M. Sussman, *Return Migration and Identity: A Global Phenomenon, A Hong Kong Case.* Hong Kong: Hong Kong University Press, 2010.

[13] S. L. Chang, "Causes of the Brain Drain and Solutions: The Taiwan Experience," *Studies in Comparative International Development* 7, no. 1 (1992): 27–43.

[14] Vivek Wadhwa, Sonali Jain, AnnaLee Saxenian, Gary Gereffi, and Huiyao Wang, *The Grass Is Indeed Greener in India and China for Returnee Entrepreneurs—America's New Immigrant Entrepreneurs, Part VI*. Kansas City, MO: Ewing Marion Kauffman Foundation, April 2011.

[15] AnnaLee Saxenian, *Silicon Valley's New Immigrant Entrepreneurs*. San Francisco: Public Policy Institute of California, 1999.

[16] Hélène Pellerin and Beverley Mullings, "The 'Diaspora Option,' Migration, and the Changing Political Economy of Development," *Review of International Political Economy* 20, no. 1 (2013): 89–120, http://dx.doi.org/10.1080/09692290.2011.649294.

[17] Jacques Gaillard and Anne Marie Gaillard, "Introduction: The International Mobility of Brains: Exodus or Circulation?" *Science, Technology, and Society* 2, no. 2 (1997): 195–228.

[18] Gaillard and Gaillard, "Introduction," 218.

[19] "Human Flight and Brain Drain—Country Rankings," https://www.theglobaleconomy.com/rankings/human_flight_brain_drain_index/.

[20] IAB—Institute for Employment Research, https://knowledge4policy.ec.europa.eu/migration-demography_en.

[21] https://data.oecd.org/rd/researchers.htm.

[22] World Bank, "Researchers in R&D (per million people)", https://data.worldbank.org/indicator/SP.POP.SCIE.RD. 6.

[23] Jacques Gaillard and Anne Marie Gaillard, "Can the Scientific Diaspora Save African Science?" *SciDev.Net*, May 22, 2003, www.SciDev.Net/Opinions/index.cfm.

[24] David Dickson, "Mitigating the Brain Drain Is a Moral Necessity," *SciDev.Net*, May 29, 2003, www.scidevnet/editorials/index.cfm?fuseaction.

[25] Pellerin and Mullings, "The 'Diaspora Option,' Migration, and the Changing Political Economy of Development."

[26] Charlie Mitchell, "How Can Africa Make the Most of Its Huge Diaspora?" *African Business*, October 21, 2022, https://african.business/2022/10/trade-investment/how-can-africa-make-the-most-of-its-huge-diaspora.

[27] Joseph E. Stiglitz, "Towards a New Paradigm for Development," United Nations Conference on Trade and Development, Geneva, October 19, 1998, https://unctad.org/system/files/official-document/prebisch9th.en.pdf.

[28] Kathleen Newland and Carylanna Taylor, *Heritage Tourism and Nostalgia Trade*. Washington: Migration Policy Institute, September 2010, https://pdf.usaid.gov/pdf_docs/pnaeb990.pdf.

[29] Aaron Terrazas, *Diaspora Investment in Developing and Emerging Country Capital Markets*. Washington: Migration Policy Institute, August 2010, https://www.migrationpolicy.org/research/diaspora-investment-developing-and-emerging-country-capital-markets-patterns-and-prospects.

[30] Terrazas, *Diaspora Investments*, 3.

[31] Gabriela Tejada, Vitalie Varzari, and Sergiu Porcescu, "Scientific Diasporas, Transnationalism and Home-Country Development: Evidence from a Study of Skilled Moldovans Abroad," *Southeast European and Black Sea Studies* 13, no. 2 (2013): 157–173, doi:10.1080/14683857.2013.789674.

[32] Jean-Baptiste Meyer and Jean-Paul Wattiaux, "Diaspora Knowledge Networks: Vanishing Doubts and Increasing Evidence," *International Journal on Multicultural Societies* 8, no. 1 (2006): 4–24, https://unesdoc.unesco.org/ark:/48223/pf0000149125.

[33] Koen Jonkers, "Transnational Research Collaboration: An Approach to the Study of Co-publications Between Overseas Chinese Scientists and their Mainland Colleagues," in *Diaspora and Transnationalism: Concepts, Theories, and Methods*, edited by Rainer Bauböck and Thomas Faist, 227-244. Amsterdam, NL: Amsterdam University Press, 2010.

[34] M. Boyle and R. Kitchin, "Diaspora-Centred Development: Current Practice, Critical Commentaries, and Research Priorities," in *Global Diasporas and Development: Socioeconomic, Cultural, and Policy Perspectives*, edited by S. Sahoo and B. K. Pattanaik, 18. New Delhi: Springer India, 2014.

[35] Meyer and Wattiaux, "Diaspora Knowledge Networks."

[36] The TOKTEN program was introduced in Turkey in 1977. It is currently in twenty-five developing countries. See http://www.tokten-vn.org.vn/introduction.htm.

[37] Meyer, et al., "Turning Brain Drain into Brain Gain."

[38] Meyer and Wattiaux, "Diaspora Knowledge Networks," 5.

[39] Thomas Faist, "Transnational Social Spaces out of International Migration: Evolution, Significance and Future Prospects," *European Journal of Sociology* 39, no. 2 (1997): 213–247. https://doi.org/10.1017/S0003975600007621

[40] Interview with directors of TIE in Silicon Valley, April 2018.

[41] AnnaLee Saxenian, *The New Argonauts: Regional Advantage in a Global Economy*. Cambridge: Harvard University Press, 2006.

[42] David Zweig, Kellee Tsai, and A. Didar Singh, "Reverse Entrepreneurial Migration in China and India: The Role of the State," *World Development* 138 (2021), doi:10.1016/j.worlddev.2020.105192.

[43] A. Didar Singh and I interviewed Indian entrepreneurs in Silicon Valley, March 2017.

[44] Rachel Brown, "What Can India and China Learn from Each Other about Diaspora Policy?" *Diplomat*, February 2, 2017, https://thediplomat.com/2017/02/what-can-india-and-china-learn-from-each-other-about-diaspora-policy.

[45] Brown, "What Can India and China Learn from Each Other about Diaspora Policy?"

Chapter 2

[1] Deng Xiaoping, "Why China Has Opened Its Doors," *Foreign Broadcast Information Service, Daily Report: China*, February 12, 1980, LI–5.

[2] Paul Englesberg, "Reversing China's Brain Drain: The Study Abroad Policy, 1978–1993," in *Great Policies: Strategic Innovations in Asia and the Pacific Basin*, edited by John D. Montgomery and Dennis A. Rondinelli, 99–122. Westport, CT: Praeger, 1995.

[3] Englesberg, "Reversing China's Brain Drain," 102.

[4] David Zweig, *Internationalizing China: Domestic Interests and Global Linkages*. Ithaca, NY: Cornell Series in Political Economy, Cornell University Press, 2002.

[5] Leo A. Orleans, *Chinese Students in America: Policies, Issues, and Numbers*. Washington, DC: National Academy Press, 1988.

[6] See Lisong Liu, *Chinese Student Migration and Selective Citizenship: Mobility, Community, and Identity between China and the United States*. New York: Routledge, 2016, 52.

[7] Hans de Wit and Nannette Ripmeester, "Increasing the Stay Rate of International Students," *University World News*, Global Edition, Issue 259, February 16, 2013.

[8] Ruth Hayhoe, *China's Universities and the Open Door*. Armonk, NY: M. E. Sharpe, 1989.

[9] The data draw on David M. Lampton, *A Relationship Restored: Trends in US-China Educational Exchanges, 1978–1984*. Washington, DC: National Academy Press, 1986, 48–49, and Leo Orleans, *Chinese Students in America: Policies, Issues, and Numbers*. Washington, DC: National Academy Press, 1988, 91.

[10] 陈薛飞，（Chen Xuefei）et al., 留学教育的成本与效益: 我国改革开放以来公派留学效益研究 (Costs and Returns: A Study of the Efficiency of Government-Sponsored Overseas Education since 1978). Beijing: 教育科学出版社, 2003.

[11] Committee on Scholarly Communication with the PRC, Issue Paper, "Student Funding," May 1987. The CSCPRC in Washington, DC, gave me this file.

[12] Chen, et. al., *Costs and Returns*.

[13] This category was expanded in the late 1980s to help units in China maintain closer links with employees who had gone abroad. Under this category, the employee and their family received many benefits from the unit, such as housing, health care, and education.

[14] Data supplied by Professor Chen Changgui, my collaborator for more than a decade.

[15] Fox Butterfield, "China Plans to Let Fewer Students Go Abroad, Especially to the US," *New York Times*, March 24, 1988, 1.

[16] Interview with a former official in the State Education Commission (formerly called the Ministry of Education), Cambridge, MA, November 1989.

[17] The numbers were based on a table in Liu Shengli, "Research and Analysis Concerning Non-Returning Mainland Scholars Who Came to the United States," 中国大陆研究 (Research on Mainland China) 33, no. 8 (1991): 59.

[18] Lecture by Xu Lin at the Fairbank Center, Harvard University, December 1989.

[19] Miao, *Sixty Years of Overseas Study*. Miao published an eight-hundred-page compilation of policies, speeches, documents, and data about China's efforts to manage the outbound flow and encourage an inbound flow. He kindly gave me a copy.

[20] Donglin Han and Dingding Chen, "Who Supports Democracy? Evidence from a Survey of Chinese Students and Scholars in the United States," *Democratization*, June 4, 2015, doi: 10.1080/13510347.2015.1017566.

[21] Michael Finn, *Stay Rates of Foreign Doctorate Recipients from US Universities, 2013*, Oak Ridge Institute for Science and Education, January 2014.

[22] Jack Corrigan, James Dunham, and Remco Zwetsloot, "The Long-Term Stay Rates of International STEM PhD Graduates," Center for Strategic and Emerging Technology, *CSET Issue Brief*, April 2022, https://cset.georgetown.edu/wp-content/uploads/CSET-The-Long-Term-Stay-Rates-of-International-STEM-PhD-Graduates.pdf.

[23] Remco Zwetsloot, Roxanne Heston, and Zachary Arnold, *Strengthening the US AI Workforce*. Center for Security and Emerging Technology, Georgetown University, Washington, DC, September 2019, https://cset.georgetown.edu/strengthening-the-u-s-ai-workforce/.

[24] Xiang Biao, *Promoting Knowledge Exchange through Diaspora Networks (The Case of People's Republic of China)*, ESRC Centre on Migration, Policy, and Society, University of Oxford, a report written for the Asian Development Bank, March 2005, 18.

[25] Zou Shuo, "Chinese Students Studying Abroad Up 8.83%," *China Daily*, March 28, 2019, http://www.chinadaily.com.cn/a/201903/28/WS5c9c355da3104842260b30eb.html.

[26] Personal communication with the author, September 12, 2018.

[27] "As Attitudes to the West Sour, China's Students Turn Home," *Economist*, January 21, 2021, https://www.economist.com/special-report/2021/01/21/as-attitudes-to-the-west-sour-chinas-students-turn-home.

[28] 教育部留学服务中心 (Ministry of Education, Service Center for Overseas Study), 中国留学回国就业蓝皮书2015情况介绍 (Introduction to the 2015 Bluebook on Employment of Returned Overseas Students), March 25, 2016, http://news.xinhuanet.com/english/2017-09/12/c_136604325.htm.

[29] https://research.com/scientists-rankings/materials-science/us.

[30] Qingnan Xie and Richard B. Freeman, "The Contribution of Chinese Diaspora Researchers to Scientific Publications and China's 'Great Leap Forward' in Global Science," National Bureau of Economic Research, Working Paper 27169, http://www.nber.org/papers/w27169.

[31] Corrigan, Dunham, and Zwetsloot, "The Long-Term Stay Rates of International STEM PhD Graduates."

[32] 鞠峰 (Ju Feng), "中美人才之争，美国正 '搬起石头砸自己的脚'" (In the Competition for Talent between China and the United States, the US Is Picking Up a Stone to Smash Its Own Foot), 观察者网 (Observers Network), http://news.cyol.com/gb/articles/2021-07/04/content_J4ZKASZBO.html.

33 https://industrialhistoryhk.org/red-capitalist-the-life-and-ventures-of-k-c-wong-%E7%8E%8B%E5%AF%AC%E8%AA%A01907-1986/.

34 Chen Shujin, 对我普美留学人员的状况分析和政策建议 (Analysis and Suggested Policies on the Conditions of Chinese Students Studying Abroad), 科技导报 (Science and Technology Review), no. 11 (1992): 54–55.

35 Miao, *Sixty Years of Overseas Study*, 446.

36 Editorial Board, 扩宽报国之路 (Expand the Road for Repaying the Nation,) 神州学人电子版 (China Scholars Abroad Electronic Board), November 25, 2003, http://www.chisa.edu.cn/service/chunhui13.htm.

37 赵峰, 苗丹国, 魏祖钰, 程希 (Zhao Feng, Miao Danguo, Wei Zuyu, Cheng Xi), eds., 留学大事概览, 1949–2009 (An Overview of Overseas Study, 1949–2009). 北京: 现代出版社, 2010, 86.

38 In Chinese, the document was entitled 知乎海外留学人员短期回国工作专项经费实施办法, in Feng, et. al., *An Overview of Overseas Study*, 86.

39 韦钰 (Wei Yu), 实施'春晖计划'讲求为国服务的实效 (Implement the "Spring Light Program," Pay Attention to the Effectiveness of "Serving the Country"), 出国留学工作研究 (Research on the Work on Studying Overseas), no. 3, 2000, republished in 全国出国留学工作研究会成立十周年纪念文集 (Collected Works on the Tenth Anniversary of the All-China Meeting on Research on the Work on Overseas Study). 北京: 北京大学出版社 Beijing: Beijing University Publishing House, April 2002, 9–11.

40 The Chinese was 睡眼寸草心, 难报三春晖 . Thanks to David Cowhig for the translation.

41 Wei, "Implement the 'Spring Light Program,'" 9–11.

42 Zi Hui, "The Ministry of Education Set Up a Project under the 'Light of Spring' Program for Overseas Student Talent to Come Back and Work in China During Their Sabbatical Leave," in *Chinese Education and Society* 36, no. 2 (March/April 2003): 40–43.

43 Zi, "The Ministry of Education Set Up a Project."

44 Miao, *Sixty Years of Overseas Study*, 477.

45 Lin Qitan, "利用海外华人'智力库,' 国健上海人才资源新结构 (Tap the Intellectual Resources in Shanghai by Using the Think Tank of Overseas Chinese), 科技导报 (Science and Technology Review), no. 5 (1996): 15–17.

46 Jiang Zemin's Report to the Fifteenth National Congress of the Communist Party of China, http://www.fas.org/news/china/1997/970912-prc.htm.

47 Wang Xi, 开发利用中国留美学生资源 (上下) (Develop and Utilize the Resources of Chinese Students in the United States, Parts 1 and 2), 内部参考 [Internal reference materials], no. 25 (June 30, 1999) and no. 26 (July 7, 1999): 17–20, translated in *Chinese Education and Society* 33 (September/October 2000): 21–30.

48 The author attended as the guest of Peking University.

49 In Mandarin Chinese, "Cheung Kong" is pronounced "Changjiang."

[50] Information gained by the author at a meeting with SAFEA and the Ministry of Personnel and Social Security.

[51] 刘 彬, 乔黎黎, 张 依 (Liu Bin, Qiao Lili and Zhang Yi), 生命科学领域国家杰出青年科学基金 项目资助状况及影响力分析 (Analysis of the Funding Status and Achievement Impact of National Science Fund for Distinguished Young Scholars in Life Sciences), 中国科学基金 (*China Science Fund*), 第 2 期 (issue no. 2) (2016), 122–131.

[52] Miao, *Sixty Years of Overseas Study*, 889.

[53] 出国留学工作研究 (A Brief Discussion of the Work of Sending People Overseas), 神州学人 (*Chinese Scholars Abroad*), http://www.chisa.edu.cn/newchisa/web/3/2003-05-23/news_46.asp. As of 2001, the number was reportedly three thousand, suggesting that another four thousand had visited in two and a half years. See http://www.why.com.cn/abroad_3/weiguofuwu/10_1/2.htm.

[54] Wei, "Implement the 'Spring Light Program,'" 9–11.

[55] For a list of how organizations in China encouraged overseas Chinese to "serve the country," see "Expand the Road for Serving the Nation."

[56] Thanks to Dr. Bai Lian, who introduced me to the Chinese consulate in Vancouver, which arranged the focus group in the fall of 2008.

[57] Matt Richtel, "Brain Drain in Technology Found Useful for Both Sides," *New York Times*, April 19, 2002.

[58] See 人事部, 教育部, 科技部, 公安部, 财政部关于印发关于鼓励留学人员以多种形式为国服务的若干意见的通知 (A Number of Opinions on Encouraging Overseas Students to Provide China with Many Different Forms of Service), May 14, 2001, 人发 (*Renfa*), no. 49, 2001, in *Chinese Education and Society*, 36, no. 2 (March/April 2003): 6–11.

[59] Boyle and Kitchin, "Diaspora-Centered Development," 18.

[60] See Jean-Baptiste Meyer, et al., "Turning Brain Drain into Brain Gain: The Colombian Experience of the Diaspora Option," *Science, Technology, and Society* 2, no. 2 (1997): 285; and David Zweig, Chung Siu Fung, and Han Donglin, "Redefining the 'Brain Drain': China's Diaspora Option," *Science, Technology, and Society* 13, no.1 (2008): 1–33.

[61] This is called the "dumbbell" model because individuals have a foot in two worlds.

[62] "A Number of Opinions," 7-8.

[63] "A Number of Opinions," 9.

[64] Miao, *Sixty Years of Overseas Study*, 449.

[65] Pal Nyiri, "Expatriating Is Patriotic? The Discourse on 'New Migrants' in the People's Republic of China and Identity Construction among Recent Migrants from the PRC," *Journal of Ethnic and Migration Studies* 27, no. 4 (October 2001): 635–653.

[66] Interview WXELA-2004.

[67] Chen, et al., *Costs and Returns*, 84.

[68] UPDATE—From CSA and Chinese American Professors/Scholars Network, January 8, 2002.

[69] Chen Changgui and Liu Chengming, 人才: 回归钰于用 (Human Talent: Its Return and Use). Guangzhou: Guangdong People's Publishing House, 2003, 191.

[70] Interview with a leader of a Chinese student organization in Toronto, August 2003.

[71] Xinhua News Service, "China Welcomes Students Studying Abroad to Develop Careers at Home," January 5, 2003, http://www.chinatopnews.com.

[72] Chen et al, *Costs and Returns*, 85.

[73] Xiang, *Promoting Knowledge Exchange through Diaspora Networks*, 22.

[74] Zweig and Chen, *China's Brain Drain to the United States*, 71.

[75] www.gov.cn/jrzg/2010-06/06/content_1621777.htm.

[76] https://news.southcn.com/node_54a44f01a2/f984fabf2a.shtml.

[77] I attended the Ninth Conference in December 2016 as guest of the director of the association and interviewed the director and several participants. Thanks to Dr Wang Huiyao who introduced me to the director.

[78] Wenhong Chen and Barry Wellman, *Doing Business at Home and Away: Policy Implications of Chinese-Canadian Entrepreneurship,* Asia Pacific Foundation, April 2007, https://www.asiapacific.ca/sites/default/files/cia_doing_business.pdf, 10.

[79] Chen and Wellman, *Doing Business at Home and Away*, 16.

[80] Interviewee Number 46, Chen and Wellman, *Doing Business at Home and Away*, 15.

[81] Brendan J. Lyons, "GE Engineer's Attorney: 'This Is Not Espionage,'" *Times Union*, August 7, 2018, https://www.timesunion.com/7dayarchive/article/GE-engineer-to-be-released-on-100K-bond-13127249.

[82] I am deeply grateful to Dr. Saxenian, whose work was funded by the Public Policy Institute of California, for sharing her dataset. The 386 China-born entrepreneurs who responded to her survey comprised my dataset.

[83] The four questions were: (1) Have you helped arrange business contracts in China? (2) Have you ever served as an advisor or consultant for companies from China? (3) Have you invested your own money in start-ups or venture funds in China? (4) Do you regularly exchange information with friends, classmates, or business associates about technology? For this latter question, where the choices were "never," "sometimes," and "regularly," I included only people who said "regularly." "Sometimes" could reflect casual conversations, while "regularly" suggests that some significant transfer was underway. All four questions reflected ways people helped others do business, not how they promoted their own business.

[84] While such activity was widespread in 2015 and 2016, Chinese investment dried up in 2017 and 2018 as the US government toughened its position on Chinese firms buying American technology firms.

[85] Interview in Silicon Valley, April 2018.

[86] Interview no. 2 in Silicon Valley, April 2018.

[87] 教育部, 高等学校学科创新引智基地管理办法, 教技 (2006) 4号, 2006-08-30 (Ministry of Education, Method for Managing the Innovation Bases in the Fields of Universities, Teaching Skills, no. 4, 2006), http://web.archive.org/web/20200120224929/http://www.moe.gov.cn/srcsite/A16/s7062/200608/t20060830_82287.html), found at Wayback.

[88] For a detailed description of the Chunhui Cup (春晖杯), see Andrew Spear, "Serve the Motherland While Working Overseas," *China's Quest for Foreign Technology*, edited by Hannas and Tatlow, 31.

[89] Spear, "Serve the Motherland," 31-32.

[90] This section draws on Hongxing Cai, "Deploying the Chinese Knowledge Diaspora: A Case Study of Peking University," *Asia Pacific Journal of Education* 32, no. 3 (2012): 367–79, https://doi.org/10.1080/02188791.2012.711242.

[91] Cai, "Deploying the Chinese Knowledge Diaspora," 377.

[92] Spear, "Serve the Motherland," 31.

[93] Alex Joske, "'Picking flowers, making honey," *Australian Strategic Policy Institute* (ASPI), 30 October 2018, https://www.aspi.org.au/report/picking-flowers-making-honey.

[94] An English version of this document was published at https://cset.georgetown.edu/wp-content/uploads/t0425_foreign_experts_EN.pdf.

[95] Spear, "Serve the Motherland," 27.

[96] Spear, "Serve the Motherland," 28.

[97] "Flexibility Central to Attracting International Talent," *China Daily*, October 27, 2016, 19, www.chinadaily.com.cn/regional/2016-10/27/conteny_27191223.htm.

[98] Spear, "Serve the Motherland," 28.

[99] Thanks to Chen Siru, my former student at HKUST, for research assistance on this project.

[100] 赤子计划, 全国留学生心思服务网 (Newborn Plan: National Overseas Student Information Service Network), https://www.cscss.com.cn/CZ.

[101] 浓浓尺子亲, 回应中国梦, 2017 (Strong Love for Children, Reflecting the China Dream, 2017), http://www.mohrss.gov.cn/zyjsrygls/ZYJSRYGLSgongzuodongtai/201706/t20170622_272945.html.

[102] 年 汇聚青年海智 弘扬丝路精神 主题论坛在宁召开, 2016 (A Forum on "*Gathering the Wisdom of Many Young People and Promoting the Spirit of the Silk Road*" was held in Ningxia), http://www.e-wzx.com/qianzhan/31145.html.

[103] 人社部组织实施 "赤子计划" 服务归国人才, 2018 (The Ministry of Human Resources and Social Security Organizes and Implements the *"Plan for Loyal Overseas Chinese"* to Serve Returned Talent, 2018), http://www.zgys.gov.cn/publicity_wqb/gzdt/gggs/41991.

[104] My research assistant, Chen Siru, collected data on each year, from 2010 to 2018, from a variety of sources. Those wishing to see those sources can contact me directly.

[105] Focus group in Vancouver, fall of 2008.

[106] For an earlier study of these groups, see "Chinese Academic Associations in the US: Bridges for Scholarly Discourse," *China Exchange News*, no. 19 (Spring 1991): 8–15.

[107] Annalee Saxenian, *Local and Global Networks of Immigrant Professionals in Silicon Valley*. San Francisco: Public Policy Institute of California, 2002, 5–8.

[108] Ryan Fedasiuk and Emily S. Weinstein, "Overseas Professionals and Technology Transfer to China," *CSET Issue Brief*, Center for Security and Emerging Technology, July 2020, https://cset.georgetown.edu/publication/overseas-professionals-and-technology-transfer-to-china/.

[109] For discussions of such associations in Germany, Europe, and South Korea, see chapters 7, 8, and 9 in Hannas and Tatlow, *China's Quest for Foreign Technology*.

[110] Fedasiuk and Weinstein, "Overseas Professionals and Technology Transfer," 13.

[111] Fedasiuk and Weinstein, "Overseas Professionals and Technology Transfer," 30.

[112] Qiang Zha, "What Factors Influence the Direction of Global Brain Circulation: The Case of Chinese Canada Research Chairholders," *Compare: A Journal of Comparative and International Education* 46 (2014), doi:10.1080/03057925.2014.916967.

[113] Zha, "What Factors."

[114] Personal comment to the author.

[115] These data were accessed on 4 October 2019 at http://www.1000plan.org.cn/qrjh/section/4/list. They are no longer online. For many public programs see Emily Weinstein's "Chinese Talent Program Tracker," https://chinatalenttracker.cset.tech/static/cset_chinese_talent_program_tracker.pdf.

[116] Hao Xin, "Frustrations Mount over China's High-Priced Hunt for Trophy Professors," *Science* 313, no. 22 (September 2006): 1721–1723.

[117] For Trump, see Annie Karni, "Trump Rants Behind Closed Doors with CEOs," POLITICO (Aug. 8, 2018), https://www.politico.com/story/2018/08/08/trump-executive-dinner-bedminster-china766609. For FBI Director Christopher Wray's speech to the *U.S. Senate Select Committee on Intelligence*, February 13, 2018, see Elizabeth Redden, "The Chinese Student Threat?" *Inside Higher Education*, February 14, 2018, https://www.insidehighered.com/news/2018/02/15/fbi-director-testifies-chinese-students-and-intelligence-threats.

[118] Li Ka Shing Foundation, "Mainland's Higher Education Reformed, Academic Leaders Nurtured as 'Cheung Kong Scholars Programme' Celebrates 10th Anniversary," December 5, 2008, https://www.lksf.org/20081205-2/.

[119] My research assistants collected data on them from the web.

[120] Interview number 1, Toronto, summer 2016.

[121] These findings were based on an interview in Shenzhen with a TTP recipient and with Dr Shi Yigong, then dean of the School of Life Sciences at Tsinghua University. See also Yigong Shi and Yi Rao, "China's Research Culture," *Science* 329, no. 5996 (September 3, 2010): 1128.

[122] Da-Hsiang Donald Lien, "Asymmetric Information and the Brain Drain," *Journal of Population Economics*, no. 6 (1993): 169–180.

[123] For a study of Li Yuanchao's effort to bring back the best overseas talent, see David Zweig and Huiyao Wang, "Can China Bring Back the Best? The Communist Party Organizes China's Search for Talent," *China Quarterly*, no. 215 (September 2013): 590–615.

[124] Miao, *Sixty Years of Overseas Study*, 957.

[125] 中央决定组织实施海外高层次人才引进计划 (Central Committee Decides to Organize and Bring into Effect a Plan to Bring in High-Quality Overseas Talent), 新华社 (Xinhua News Service), January 8, 2009, cited in Miao, *Sixty Years of Overseas Study*, 957.

[126] Tianjin University's party secretary strongly encouraged senior faculty to reach out overseas and find possible recipients of the full-time TTP. Interviews with administrators engaged in personnel at Tianjin University.

[127] See the case studies in chapter 4.

[128] Interview at a university in northwest China, October 2012.

[129] Cong Cao, personal communication with the author, August 8, 2011.

[130] J. E. Hirsch, "An Index to Quantify an Individual's Scientific Research Output," *Proceedings of the National Academy of Sciences* 102, no. 46 (2005): 16569–16572.

[131] Barry Bozeman and Elizabeth Corley, "Scientists' Collaboration Strategies: Implications for Scientific and Technical Human Capital," *Research Policy* 33, no. 4 (2004): 599–616, https://doi.org/10.1016/j.respol.2004.01.008.

[132] National Science Board, Science and Engineering Indicators, 2018.

[133] J. Sylvan Katz and Ben Martin, "What Is Research Collaboration?" *Research Policy* 26, no. 1 (1997): 1.

[134] B. K. Al Shebli, T. Rahwan, and W. L. Woon, "The Preeminence of Ethnic Diversity in Scientific Collaboration," *Nature Communications* 9, no. 5163 (2018), https://www.nature.com/articles/s41467-018-07634-8#citeas.

[135] Miller McPherson, Lynn Smith-Lovin, and James M. Cook, "Birds of a Feather: Homophily in Social Networks," *Annual Review of Sociology* 27 (2001): 415–444.

[136] Bozeman and Corley, "Scientists' Collaboration Strategies."

[137] Bihui Jin, et al., "The Role of Ethnic Ties in International Collaboration: The Overseas Chinese Phenomenon," in *Proceedings of the ISSI 2007*, edited by D. Torres-Salinas and H. F. Moed, CSIC, Madrid, 427–436.

[138] Interview presented in Zhen Zhang, *The Chinese Knowledge Diaspora and Diaspora Knowledge Network: Australia and Canada Compared*, University of Sydney PhD Thesis, August 2014, 147.

[139] Zhang, *The Chinese Knowledge Diaspora*, 248.

[140] Richard P. Suttmeier, "Structure and Identity in the Building of Sino-US Cooperation in S&T," paper prepared for the conference "People on the Move: The Transnational Flow of Chinese Human Capital," Center on China's Transnational Relations, The Hong Kong University of Science and Technology, Hong Kong, October 21–22, 2005.

[141] Koen Jonkers, *Mobility, Migration, and the Chinese Scientific Research System*. New York: Routledge Contemporary China Series, 2010, 88, 91.

[142] Jin, et al., "The Role of Ethnic Ties in International Collaboration."

[143] Jin, et al., "The Role of Ethnic Ties in International Collaboration."

[144] Hong Zhu, *Active Academic Communication across the Pacific: The Experience of Chinese Academic Diasporas in the United States*, PhD Thesis, Boston College, 2009.

[145] Zhu, *Active Academic Communication across the Pacific*, 132.

[146] Cai, "Deploying the Chinese Knowledge Diaspora," 136.

[147] Interview number 2, Toronto, summer 2016.

[148] Cai, "Deploying the Chinese Knowledge Diaspora," 136.

[149] Bozeman and Corley, "Scientists' Collaboration Strategies."

[150] Mary Frank Fox and Catherine A. Faver, "Independence and Cooperation in Research: The Motivations and Costs of Collaboration," *Journal of Higher Education* 55, no. 3 (May–June 1984): 347–359.

[151] Interview in Zhang, *The Chinese Knowledge Diaspora*, 151.

[152] Interview in Zhang, *The Chinese Knowledge Diaspora*, 149.

[153] Cai, "Deploying the Chinese Knowledge Diaspora," Interview OCS6, 376.

[154] Cai, "Deploying the Chinese Knowledge Diaspora," Interview DS2, 373.

[155] Cai, "Deploying the Chinese Knowledge Diaspora," Interview DS4, 376.

[156] Cai, "Deploying the Chinese Knowledge Diaspora," Interview DS4, 376.

[157] Interview with a senior professor from the mainland teaching at HKUST, 2002.

[158] Cai, "Deploying the Chinese Knowledge Diaspora," Interview OCS6, 376.

[159] https://www.ugc.edu.hk/eng/rgc/stat/award_statistics.html.

[160] Xiang, *Promoting Knowledge Exchange through Diaspora Networks*, 22.

[161] Kang Siqin, "Academic Returnee Policy and Knowledge Diffusion: A Case from Chinese National Talent Programs," MPhil thesis, The Hong Kong University of Science and Technology, 2018, doi: 10.14711/thesis-991012644468803412.

[162] Xiang, *Promoting Knowledge Exchange through Diaspora Networks*.

[163] Interview in Toronto, summer 2016.

[164] Interview in Vancouver, 2008.

[165] Hannas and Tatlow, *China's Quest for Foreign Technology*.

[166] https://idl-bnc-idrc.dspacedirect.org/bitstream/handle/10625/57464/IDL-57464.pdf?sequence=2&isAllowed=y.

[167] Interview No. 2 in Toronto, 2016.

[168] Interview No. 3, in Toronto, 2016.

[169] I am indebted to Dr. Kang Siqin for his assistance. Based on the QS World University ranking list, he selected fifty schools in the US, ten in the UK, five in Canada, and three in Australia. From this group, he then randomly selected eighteen American universities, four in the UK, three in Canada, and two in Australia (for the list, see appendix, table A.2). He found 1,010 scholars in science, engineering, and medical schools in these twenty-seven universities who had Chinese names (using the romanization system called *pinyin*), and from that list, he randomly selected 328. He was able to find background information (education, career, and connections to China) for 121 scholars.

[170] A journal's impact factor is based on how frequently articles in it are cited. We looked at the impact factor of the journals for all the articles a scholar published each year, and then we calculated the average yearly score. This is a good measure of the quality of their research.

[171] 王辉耀 (Wang Huiyao), 中国区域国际人才竞争力报告 (Report on China's Regional International Talent Competitiveness; Beijing: Social Sciences Academic Press, 2017), 11.

[172] Cheng Yingqi, "Xi offers support to overseas Chinese," *China Daily* (USA), October 22, 2013, https://usa.chinadaily.com.cn/epaper/2013-10/22/content_17050714.htm.

[173] See 习近平: 使留学人员回国有用武之地 留在国外有报国之门 ("Xi Jinping: Make Sure that Returned Students Have a Useful Place and That Those Who Stay Abroad Have a Channel Through Which to Contribute to the Nation"), http://news.xinhuanet.com/hr/2013-10/21/c_117808372.htm. This was Xi's speech to the meeting to commemorate the one hundredth anniversary of the Western Returnees Student Association.

[174] Spear, "Serve the Motherland," 22.

[175] "Xi Jinping: Make Sure that Returned Students Have a Useful Place."

[176] 习近平: 巩固发展最广泛的爱国统一战线 ("Xi Jinping: Consolidate and Develop the Broadest Patriotic United Front"), Xi Jinping speech at the CCP United Front Department meeting, May 20, 2015, https://www.xinhuanet.com/politics/2015-05/20/c_1115351358.htm, found at Wayback.

[177] 习近平在全国组织工作会议的讲话 (Xi Jinping's speech at the National Organizational Work Conference), July 3, 2018, www.12371.cn/2018/09/17/ARTI1537150840597467.shtml, found at Wayback.

[178] "Xi Jinping's speech at the National Organizational Work Conference."

[179] Alex Joske, "Reorganizing the United Front Work Department: New Structures for a New Era of Diaspora and Religious Affairs Work," *China Brief* 19, no. 9 (May 9, 2019), https://jamestown.org/program/reorganizing-the-united-front-work-department-new-structures-for-a-new-era-of-diaspora-and-religious-affairs-work/.

[180] Joske, "Reorganizing the United Front Work Department."

[181] Joske, "Reorganizing the United Front Work Department." According to Joske, the United Front Work Department continues to do business overseas under the name of the Overseas Chinese Affairs Office of the State Council.

[182] Shi, D., Liu, W. & Wang, Y. "Has China's Young Thousand Talents Program been successful in recruiting and nurturing top-caliber scientists?" *Science* 379, 6627 (2023): 62–65.

Chapter 3

[1] A draft of this chapter was presented at the 2019 Duke International Forum, "A New Age of Sino-US Higher Education Cooperation," Duke Kunshan University, Jiangsu Province, China, December 16–18, 2019. It was also published by the CSIS as an occasional paper: David Zweig and Siqin Kang, "America Challenges China's National Talent Programs," Center for Strategic and International Studies, no. 4 (May 2020), Washington, DC, https://www.csis.org/analysis/america-challenges-chinas-national-talent-programs.

[2] The science officer at the Chinese consulate in New York City emphasized this point. Interview by the author, February 2020.

[3] An excellent read on this issue is Mara Hvistendahl, *The Scientist and the Spy*. New York: Riverhead Books, 2020.

[4] Robin Cohen, *Global Diasporas: An Introduction*. Seattle: University of Washington Press, 1997, 517.

[5] Dr Chen told me that, unfortunately, a great deal of the settlement was used to pay for her legal fees. Conversation with Dr Chen, April 2024.

[6] Shawn Boburg, "Commerce Dept. Security Unit to Be Shut Down after Overstepping Legal Limits in Launching Probes, Officials Say," *Washington Post*, September 3, 2021, https://www.washingtonpost.com/investigations/commerce-disband-itms-investigations-unit/2021/09/03/43e1c8ee-0c0b-11ec-aea1-42a8138f132a_story.html.

[7] Committee Investigation Report, "Abuse and Misconduct at the Commerce Department," July 2021, https://www.commerce.senate.gov/services/files/C4ABC46A-7CB0-4D51-B855-634C26E7CF70.

[8] John Krige, "National Security and Academia: Regulating the International Circulation of Knowledge," *Bulletin of the Atomic Scientists*, March 1, 2014, doi: 10.1177/0096340214523249.

[9] Strategic Partnership Unit, "Chinese Talent Programs," September 2015, https://info.publicintelligence.net/FBI-ChineseTalentPrograms.pdf.

[10] Strategic Partnership Unit, "Chinese Talent Programs."

[11] Yongjun Zhu, et al., "Analyzing China's Research Collaboration with the United States in High-Impact and High-Technology Research," *Quantitative Science Studies* 2, no. 1 (2021): 363–75, https://doi.org/10.1162/qss_a_00098.

[12] For a list of cases brought against ethnic Chinese for spying in America, see https://en.wikipedia.org/wiki/List_of_Chinese_spy_cases_in_the_United_States_of_America.

[13] Michael J. Ybarra, *Washington Gone Crazy: Senator Pat McCarran and the Great American Communist Hunt.* Hanover: Steerforth Press, 2004.

[14] Philip Deery, "'Running with the Hounds': Academic McCarthyism and New York University, 1952–53," *Cold War History* 10, no. 4 (November 2010): 469–492, doi: 10.1080/14682740903527692.

[15] See Ellen W. Schrecker, *No Ivory Tower: McCarthyism and the Universities.* New York: Oxford University Press, 1986, and David R. Holmes, *Stalking the Academic Communist: Intellectual Freedom and the Firing of Alex Novikoff.* Hanover: University Press of New England, 1989.

[16] Deery, "'Running with the Hounds.'"

[17] Elizabeth Redden, "Reconsidering the China Initiative," *Inside Higher Education*, March 2, 2021, https://www.insidehighered.com/news/2021/03/02/criminal-initiative-targeting-scholars-who-allegedly-hid-chinese-funding-and.

[18] Andrew Chongseh Kim, "Prosecuting Chinese 'Spies': An Empirical Analysis of the Economic Espionage Act," *Cordoza Law Review* 40 (2019): 749–822, http://cardozolawreview.com/wp-content/uploads/2019/01/Kim.40.2.6.newcharts.pdf.

[19] See the "China Initiative Conference," sponsored by the DOJ and the FBI, Center for Strategic and International Studies, Washington, DC, February 6, 2020, https://www.csis.org/events/china-initiative-conference.

[20] Mike German, *Disrupt, Discredit, and Divide: How the New FBI Damages Democracy.* New York: New Press, 2019.

[21] Mara Hvistendahl, "The FBI's China Obsession: The US Government Secretly Spied on Chinese American Scientists," *Intercept*, February 2, 2020, https://www.linkedin.com/pulse/fbis-china-obsession-heros-de-moraes/.

[22] https://www.documentcloud.org/documents/6749526-1967-FBI-IS-CH1-OCR-SM-56-57-Redacted.html.

[23] "The Deemed Export Rule in the Era of Globalization," report for the secretary of commerce, December 20, 2007, 70, www.fas.org/sgp/library/deemedexports.pdf.

[24] "Deemed Export Rule in the Era of Globalization," 70-71.

[25] Harry Harding, "Has US China Policy Failed?" *Washington Quarterly* 38, no. 3 (2015): 95–122, http://dx.doi.org/10.1080/0163660X.2015.1099027.

[26] Lyle J. Goldstein, *Meeting China Halfway: How to Defuse the Emerging US-China Rivalry.* Washington, DC: Georgetown University Press, 2015; James Steinberg and Michael E. O'Hanlon, *Strategic Reassurance and Resolve: US-China Relations in the Twenty-First Century.* Princeton: Princeton University Press, 2014; Aaron L. Friedberg, "The Debate over US China Strategy," *Survival* 57, no. 3 (June–July 2015), 89–110; and

Robert A. Manning, "America's China Consensus Implodes," *National Interest*, May 21, 2015.

[27] Robert Zoellick, "Whither China: From Membership to Responsibility?" remarks to the National Committee on US-China Relations, New York, September 21, 2005.

[28] Jost Wübbeke, et al., "Made in China 2025: The Making of a High-Tech Superpower and Consequences for Industrial Countries," *MERICS: Papers on China, Mercator Institute for China Studies* (Berlin), no. 2 (December 2016).

[29] Kurt Campbell and Ely Ratner, "The China Reckoning: How Beijing Defied American Expectations," *Foreign Affairs* 97, no. 2 (2018): 60–70.

[30] David M. Lampton, "The Tipping Point: Can We Amplify What We Have in Common?" *Horizons: Journal of International Relations and Sustainable Development*, no. 4 (2015): 42–53, https://www.jstor.org/stable/48573556.

[31] Redden, "The Chinese Student Threat?"

[32] This analysis draws on Hvistendahl, *The Scientist and the Spy*, 100–110.

[33] Office of The United States Trade Representative, "Findings of the Investigation Into China's Acts, Policies, and Practices Related to Technology Transfer, Intellectual Property, and Innovation Under Section 301 of the Trade Act of 1974," March 22, 2018, https://ustr.gov/sites/default/files/Section%20301%20FINAL.PDF.

[34] Telephone interview with Michael Lauer, National Institute of Health, June 8, 2020.

[35] See US Permanent Subcommittee on Investigations, Committee on Homeland Security and Governmental Affairs, United States Senate, "Threats to the US Research Enterprise: China's Talent Recruitment Plans," https://www.hsgac.senate.gov/imo/media/doc/2019-11-18%20PSI%20Staff%20Report%20-%20China's%20Talent%20Recruitment%20Plans.pdf.

[36] Xu Lin, former Ministry of Education official, lecture at the Fairbank Center, Harvard University, December 1989.

[37] Anthony Carpaccio, "US Faces 'Unprecedented Threat' from China on Tech Takeover," https://www.bloomberg.com/news/articles/2018-06-22/china-s-thousand-talents-called-key-in-seizing-u-s-expertise.

[38] Carpaccio, "US Faces 'Unprecedented Threat.'"

[39] Carpaccio, "US Faces 'Unprecedented Threat.'"

[40] Office of Trade and Manufacturing Policy Report, "How China's Economic Aggression Threatens the Technologies and Intellectual Property of the United States and the World," June 19, 2018, https://trumpwhitehouse.archives.gov/briefings-statements/office-trade-manufacturing-policy-report-chinas-economic-aggression-threatens-technologies-intellectual-property-united-states-world/.

[41] Annie Karni, "Trump Rants behind Closed Doors with CEOs," *Politico*, August 8, 2018, https://www.politico.com/story/2018/08/08/trump-executive-dinner-bedminster-china766609.

[42] On this meeting in Texas, see Alyssa Rege, "FBI Informs Texas Hospital Officials of Classified Security Threats," *Becker's Hospital Review*, August 9, 2018, https://www.beckershospitalreview.com/hospital-management-administration/fbi-informs-texas-hospital-officials-of-classified-security-threats.html.

[43] According to APA Justice, "These secretive forums have been exclusionary, one-sided, and lacked transparency, and they are a major source of xenophobia, fear, and chilling effects for the Asian American and scientific communities." APA Justice, "Companion Notes: Addressing Immediate and Systemic Issues Implementation of NSPM-33," presentation to Office of Science and Technology Policy Subcommittee on Research Security, National Science and Technology Council, March 28, 2022, reference_notes_for_ostp_powerpoint_presentationb.pdf.

[44] Demetri Sevastopulo, "US Considered Ban on Student Visas for Chinese Nationals: White House Hawks Urged Trump to Tackle Espionage Threat from Beijing," *Financial Times*, October 2, 2018,

https://www.ft.com/content/fc413158-c5f1-11e8-82bf-ab93d0a9b321.

[45] "Attorney General Jeff Session's China Initiative Fact Sheet," November 1, 2018, https://www.justice.gov/opa/speech/file/1107256/download.

[46] Alex Joske, "'Picking Flowers, Making Honey:' The Chinese Military's Collaboration with Foreign Universities," *Policy Brief, Report No. 10/2018*, Australian Strategic Policy Institute, 18, https://s3-ap-southeast-2.amazonaws.com/ad-aspi/2018-10/Picking%20flowers%2C%20making%20honey_0.pdf?H5sGNaWXqMgTG_2F2yZTQwDw6OyNfH.u.

[47] https://dod.defense.gov/Portals/1/Documents/pubs/2018-National-Defense-Strategy-Summary.pdf.

[48] Dennis Normile, "China's Scientists Alarmed, Bewildered by Growing Anti-Chinese Sentiment in the United States," *Science*, July 31, 2019, https://www.sciencemag.org/news/2019/07/china-s-scientists-alarmed-bewildered-growing-anti-chinese-sentiment-united-states.

[49] Larry Diamond and Orville Schell, *China's Influence and American Interests: Promoting Constructive Vigilance*, November 29, 2018, Hoover Institution, Stanford University, https://www.hoover.org/research/chinas-influence-american-interests-promoting-constructive-vigilance.

[50] Diamond and Schell, *China's Influence and American Interests*, 7.

[51] Diamond and Schell, *China's Influence and American Interests*.

[52] OSTP has formal authority to convene all research funding agencies in the US on matters of policy through the National Science and Technology Council.

[53] The White House Office of Science and Technology Policy, *Enhancing the Security and Integrity of America's Research Enterprise*, https://trumpwhitehouse.archives.gov/wp-content/uploads/2020/07/Enhancing-the-Security-and-Integrity-of-Americas-Research-Enterprise.pdf.

54 "Department of Energy Foreign Government Talent Recruitment Programs," US Department of Energy, June 7, 2019, https://www.energy.gov/sites/default/files/2019/06/f63/DOE%20O%20486.1.pdf, accessed June 7, 2022.

55 Council on Foreign Relations, "A Conversation With Christopher Wray," April 26, 2019, https://www.cfr.org/event/conversation-christopher-wray-0.

56 https://www.washingtonpost.com/archive/politics/1999/12/12/china-prefers-the-sand-to-the-moles/5204a605-9184-4fe3-9bab-1d8a7e1e234d/.

57 "China Initiative Conference," February 6, 2020.

58 The White House Office of Science and Technology Policy (OSTP), "Letter to the United States Research Community," September 16, 2019, https://www.whitehouse.gov/wp-content/uploads/2019/09/OSTP-letter-to-the-US-research-community-september-2019.pdf.

59 US Permanent Subcommittee on Investigations, "Threats to the US Research Enterprise: China's Talent Recruitment Plans." The following section criticizes this report.

60 OSTP, "Enhancing the Security and Integrity of America's Research Enterprise."

61 OSTP, "Enhancing the Security and Integrity of America's Research Enterprise."

62 https://new.nsf.gov/news/nsf-creates-new-research-security-chief-position.

63 Interview with Dr. Kaiser, February 7, 2021.

64 Interview with Dr. Kaiser, February 7, 2021.

65 Elsa B. Kania and Lorand Laskai, "Myths and Realities of China's Military-Civil Fusion Strategy," *Center for a New American Security*, January 28, 2021, https://www.cnas.org/publications/reports/myths-and-realities-of-chinas-military-civil-fusion-strategy.

66 Elizabeth Redden, "Trump Proclamation Bars Entry of Certain Chinese Students," *Inside Higher Education*, June 1, 2020, https://www.insidehighered.com/quicktakes/2020/06/01/trump-proclamation-bars-entry-certain-chinese-students.

67 Redden, "Trump Proclamation Bars Entry of Certain Chinese Students."

68 Elizabeth Redden, "New Restrictions for Chinese Students with Military University Ties," *Inside Higher Education*, May 29, 2020, https://www.insidehighered.com/news/2020/05/29/us-plans-cancel-visas-students-ties-universities-connected-chinese-military.

69 The author attended that conference after presenting his own paper to CSIS critical of the CI.

70 "China Initiative Conference."

71 David Zweig, Chung Siu Fung, and Wilfried Vanhonacker, "Rewards of Technology: Explaining China's Reverse Migration," *Journal of International Migration and Integration* 7, no. 4 (November 2006): 449–471.

72 Strider Technologies Inc., *The Los Alamos Club: How the People's Republic of China Recruited Leading Scientists from Los Alamos National Laboratory to Advance Its Military Programs*, Strider-Los-Alamos-Report.pdf.

[73] National Science Board, "Chapter 5: Academic Research and Development," in *Science and Engineering Indicators 2018*, Alexandria, VA, 2018, https://nsf.gov/statistics/2018/nsb20181/assets/968/academic-research-and-development.pdf.

[74] William R. Kerr, *The Gift of Global Talent: How Migration Shapes Business, Economy, and Society*. Stanford: Stanford University Press, 2019.

[75] The analysis was based on output from November 1, 2016 to October 31, 2017. See "China and the United States Are Science Sweethearts," *Nature*, February 14, 2018, https://www.nature.com/nature-index/news-blog/china-and-the-united-states-are-science-sweethearts.

[76] British scientists probably published more in British journals, which generally have a lower impact factor than American journals, while Canadian scholars published in many US-based journals.

[77] Science and Engineering Indicators, https://ncses.nsf.gov/pubs/nsb20213.

[78] Peter Waldman, "Chinese scientists guilty of 'researching while Asian' in Trump's America," *South China Morning Post*, 29 Jun, 2019, https://www.scmp.com/magazines/post-magazine/long-reads/article/3016267/chinese-scientists-guilty-researching-while.

[79] After the CI began, the DOE forbade its employees from joining the TTP.

[80] See case study number 6 in the next chapter.

[81] Jeffrey Mervis, "NIH Letters Asking about Undisclosed Foreign Ties Rattle US Universities," *Science*, March 1, 2019, https://www.science.org/content/article/nih-letters-asking-about-undisclosed-foreign-ties-rattle-us-universities.

[82] http://www.fao.fudan.edu.cn/13/61/c1689a70497/page.htm.

[83] Waldman, "Chinese Scientists Guilty of 'Researching While Asian.'"

[84] https://www.apajustice.org/racial-profiling.html.

[85] US Permanent Subcommittee on Investigations, "Threats to the US Research Enterprise."

[86] Cited in US Permanent Subcommittee on Investigations, "Threats to the US Research Enterprise," 58.

[87] See United States Government Accountability Office, *Agencies Need to Enhance Policies to Address Foreign Influence*, GAO-21-130, December 2020, 16, https://www.gao.gov/assets/gao-21-130.pdf.

[88] United States Government Accountability Office, *Agencies Need to Enhance Policies*.

[89] United States Government Accountability Office, *Agencies Need to Enhance Policies*.

[90] United States Government Accountability Office, *Agencies Need to Enhance Policies*.

[91] https://grants.nih.gov/grants/guide/notice-files/NOT-OD-18-160.html.

[92] See https://researchservices.cornell.edu/policies/nih-disclosing-other-support-and-foreign-components.

[93] https://grants.nih.gov/grants/guide/notice-files/NOT-OD-19-114.html.

[94] Elias Zerhouni, "Chinese Scientists and Security," *Science* 365, no. 6448 (July 5, 2019): 9, doi: 10.1126/science.aay5212.

[95] Waldman, "Chinese Scientists Guilty of 'Researching While Asian.'"

[96] Harvey Lodish, Jianzhu Chen, and Phillip Sharp, "Clarity on the Crackdown," *Science* 371, no. 6532, (February 26, 2021): 867, doi: 10.1126/science.abh1627.

[97] Jeffrey Mervis, "NIH Reveals Its Formula for Tracking Foreign Influences," *Science and Policy,* September 27, 2019, https://www.sciencemag.org/news/2019/09/nih-reveals-its-formula-tracking-foreign-influences, doi:10.1126/science.aaz6589.

[98] Mervis, "NIH Reveals Its Formula for Tracking Foreign Influences."

[99] Michael S. Lauer, "Foreign Influences on Research Integrity: NIH Experience," Fourteenth Joint Meeting of the Board of Scientific Advisors and the National Cancer Advisory Board, December 3, 2019, slide 21, https://deainfo.nci.nih.gov/advisory/joint/1219/Lauer.pdf.

[100] Ruixue Jia, et al., "The Impact of US-China Tensions on US Science," National Bureau of Economic Research, Working Paper 29941, February 2023, http://www.nber.org/papers/w29941.

[101] Dr. Lauer agreed with the ballpark figure. Email to the author, September 14, 2020.

[102] Dr. Michael Lauer, email to the author, August 10, 2020.

[103] Mervis, "NIH Reveals Its Formula for Tracking Foreign Influences."

[104] Suzanne Murrin, *Vetting Peer Reviewers at NIH's Center for Scientific Review: Strengths and Limitations,* September 2019, OEI-01-19-00160, https://oig.hhs.gov/oei/reports/oei-01-19-00160.pdf.

[105] Dr. Michael Lauer, "Brief Summary of NIH Foreign Interference Cases," NIH, Office of Extramural Research, Patricia Valdez, NIH OER 2022-12-11 (December 11, 2022).

[106] Dr Michael Lauer, "ACD Working Group on Foreign Influences on Research Integrity Update," https://acd.od.nih.gov/documents/presentations/12132019ForeignInfluences.pdf.

[107] US Permanent Subcommittee on Investigations, "Threats to the US Research Enterprise," 58.

[108] Jeffrey Mervis, "Fired Cancer Scientist Says 'Good People Are Being Crushed' by Overzealous Probes into Possible Chinese Ties," *ScienceInsider*, March 11, 2020, https://www.sciencemag.org/news/2020/03/fired-cancer-scientist-says-good-people-are-being-crushed-overzealous-probes-possible.

[109] China Initiative, https://en.wikipedia.org/wiki/China_Initiative.

[110] "Moffitt's China Internal Investigation Abstract," January 17, 2020, 3, https://s3.documentcloud.org/documents/6661639/Moffitt-s-China-Internal-Investigation-Abstract.pdf.

[111] Mervis, "Fired Cancer Scientist Says 'Good People Are Being Crushed.'"

[112] Jeffrey Mervis, "NIH Probe of Foreign Ties Has Led to Undisclosed Firings—and Refunds from Institutions," *Science*, June 26, 2019, https://www.science.org/content/article/nih-probe-foreign-ties-has-led-undisclosed-firings-and-refunds-institution.

[113] Nidhi Subbaraman, "Universities Are Forging Ties with the FBI as US Cracks Down on Foreign Influence," *Nature*, March 12, 2020, https://www.nature.com/articles/d41586-020-00646-9.

[114] Subbaraman, "Universities Are Forging Ties with the FBI."

[115] Peter Waldman, "The U.S. Is Purging Chinese Americans From Top Cancer Research," *Bloomberg News*, June 13, 2019, https://news.bloomberglaw.com/pharma-and-life-sciences/the-u-s-is-purging-chinese-americans-from-top-cancer-research.

[116] Waldman, "The US Is Purging Chinese Cancer Researchers from Top Institutions."

[117] This information was in a new statement in the financial years of 2018, 2019, and 2020. Intelligence Authorization Act, Federation of American Scientists, Project on Government Secrecy, *Secrecy News 2019*, no. 45, December 16, 2019, https://fas.org/blogs/secrecy/.

[118] Jeffrey Mervis, "Pall of Suspicion," *Science* 379, no. 6638, March 23, 2023, https://www.science.org/content/article/pall-suspicion-nihs-secretive-china-initiative-destroyed-scores-academic-careers.

[119] Collin Binkley, "Feds Say US Colleges 'Massively' Underreport Foreign Funding," *NBC News*, October 20, 2020, https://www.nbcnewyork.com/news/national-international/feds-say-us-colleges-massively-underreport-foreign-funding/2678991/.

[120] Binkley, "Feds Say US Colleges 'Massively' Underreport Foreign Funding."

[121] https://www.apajustice.org/uploads/1/1/5/7/115708039/riceustatement_20190517.pdf.

[122] Statement supporting Stanford's international students and scholars, February 10, 2021, https://news.stanford.edu/report/2021/02/08/statement-president-marc-tessier-lavigne-support-stanfords-international-students-scholars.

[123] Redden, "Reconsidering the China Initiative."

[124] Mara Hvistendahl, "Exclusive: Major US Cancer Center Ousts 'Asian' Researchers after NIH Flags Their Foreign Ties," *ScienceInsider*, April 19, 2019, https://www.sciencemag.org/news/2019/04/exclusive-major-us-cancer-center-ousts-asian-researchers-after-nih-flags-their-foreign.

[125] US Permanent Subcommittee on Investigations, "Threats to the US Research Enterprise," 60.

[126] Office of the Vice President for Research, Texas Tech University, https://www.depts.ttu.edu/research/scholarly-messenger/Downloads/Talent-Programs-Legislation.pdf.

[127] Jodi Xu Klein, "US Academics Condemn 'Racial Profiling' of Chinese Students and Scholars over Spying Fears," *South China Morning Post*, https://www.scmp.com/news/china/diplomacy/article/3022413/us-academics-condemn-racial-profiling-chinese-students-and.

[128] "Stanford Professors Urge US to End Program Looking for Chinese Spies in Academia," *Thomson Reuters*, September 13, 2021, https://kfgo.com/2021/09/13/stanford-professors-urge-u-s-to-end-program-looking-for-chinese-spies-in-academia/.

[129] "Stanford Professors Urge US to End Program."

[130] For a list of DOJ cases under the CI, see Department of Justice, "Information about the Department of Justice's China Initiative," https://www.justice.gov/archives/nsd/information-about-department-justice-s-china-initiative-and-compilation-china-related.

[131] The following two paragraphs draw on Krige, "National Security and Academia."

[132] Panel on Scientific Communication and National Security, *Scientific Communication and National Security*. Washington, DC: National Academy Press, 1982, 41, www.nap.edu/catalog.php?record_id=253.

[133] Committee on Balancing Scientific Openness and National Security, *Balancing Scientific Openness and National Security Controls at the Nuclear Weapons Laboratories*. Washington, DC: National Academy Press, 1999, 11, www.nap.edu/catalog.php?record_id=9704.

[134] Krige, "National Security and Academia," 43–44.

[135] See Daniel Tenreiro, "Why American Scientists Take Chinese Money," *National Review*, February 3, 2020, https://www.nationalreview.com/2020/02/charles-lieber-case-why-american-scientists-take-chinese-money/.

[136] Tenreiro, "Why American Scientists Take Chinese Money."

[137] Elizabeth Redden, "Florida Lawmakers Probe 'Foreign Meddling' in Research," *Inside Higher Ed*, January 12, 2020, https://www.insidehighered.com/news/2020/01/13/florida-lawmakers-launch-investigation-foreign-meddling-state-research-universities.

[138] Science and Engineering Indicators, https://ncses.nsf.gov/pubs/nsb20213.

[139] Paul Goss, et al., "Challenges to Effective Cancer Control in China, India, and Russia," *Lancet Oncology* 15, no. 5 (April 2014): 489–538, https://www.thelancet.com/journals/lanonc/article/PIIS1470-2045%2814%2970029-4/fulltext.

[140] Matthew Bin Han Ong, "Moffitt CEO Alan List, Director Thomas Sellers Resign over Conflicts of Interests Involving China," *Cancer Letter* 46, no. 1, December 20, 2019, https://cancerletter.com/the-cancer-letter/20191220_2/.

[141] Cao, "China's Approaches to Attract and Nurture Young Biomedical Researchers."

[142] Waldman, "The US Is Purging Chinese Cancer Researchers."

[143] APA Justice, *Chinese Exclusion Act*, https://www.apajustice.org/exclusion-act.html.

[144] Shan Lu, et al., "Racial Profiling Harms Science," *Science* 363, no. 6433 (2019): 1290–1292, https://www.science.org/doi/10.1126/science.aaw6854.

[145] Spencer Ackerman, "FBI Taught Agents They Could 'Bend or Suspend the Law'," *Wired*, March 28, 2012, https://www.wired.com/2012/03/fbi-bend-suspend-law.

[146] Hvistendahl, *The Scientist and the Spy*, 76.

[147] German, *Disrupt, Discredit, and Divide*.

[148] German was quoted in Peter Waldman, "Suspected of Spying for Just Being Chinese: US Government Rejects Security Clearance for Chinese-Americans," *South China Morning Post*, January 31, 2020, https://www.scmp.com/magazines/post-magazine/long-reads/article/3048091/suspected-spying-just-being-chinese-us.

[149] German, *Disrupt, Discredit, and Divide*, 197.

[150] Peter Waldman, "Making Targets of Chinese Americans," *Magzter,* December 16, 2019, https://www.magzter.com/stories/Business/Bloomberg-Businessweek/Making-Targets-Of-Chinese-Americans.

[151] Hvistendahl, *The Scientist and the Spy*, 150.

[152] Grace Meng is quoted in Press Release, "Rep. Chu Joins Wrongly Accused Asian American Scientists to Call for Accountability from DOJ and an End to Profiling," November 17, 2015, https://chu.house.gov/press- release/rep-chu-joins-wrongly-accused-asian-american-scientists-call-accountability-doj-and.

[153] Matt Apuzzo, "After Missteps, US Tightens Rules for Espionage Cases," *New York Times*, April 26, 2016, http://www.nytimes.com/2016/04/27/us/after-missteps-us-tightens-rules-for- national-security-cases.htm.

[154] Kim, "Prosecuting Chinese 'Spies.'"

[155] Mulvenon attacked Kim's methodology arguing that it is unclear if the dataset Kim used, called PACER (Public Access to Court Economic Records), contained all the cases brought to court. If not, then Kim could not select a true "random sample" of all cases but only a random sample from the cases he found. Thus, many cases would never have had a chance to get into Kim's overall population from which he selected his sample. Still, in my view, even if Kim missed a significant number of cases, patterns found using the cases he found may still reflect the actual situation. Second, Mulvenon argues that ethnicity is not the reason that Chinese received tougher sentences than whites; in 57 percent of Kim's cases, the beneficiary of the technology transfer was a public, private, or government-owned Chinese firm, so the tougher punishments were because some spying or economic security was involved in these cases. See James Mulvenon, "Economic Espionage and Trade Secret Theft Cases in the US," in *China's Quest for Foreign Technology*, edited by Hannas and Tatlow, 292–306.

[156] Daniel C. Richman and William J. Stuntz, "Al Capone's Revenge: An Essay on the Political Economy of Pretextual Prosecution," *Columbia Law Review* 105, no. 8 (December 2005): 583, https://www.jstor.org/stable/4099318.

[157] Plea Agreement, *United States v. Huang*, No. 12-cr-01246 (DNM, August 25, 2014).

[158] Kim, "Prosecuting Chinese 'Spies.'"

[159] David A. Harris, "The Stories, the Statistics, and the Law: Why 'Driving While Black' Matters," *Minnesota Law Review* 84 (1999): 301, https://papers.ssrn.com/sol3/papers.cfm?abstract_id=199508.

[160] Bethany Allen-Ebrahimian, "ACLU Joins Chinese American Scientist's Lawsuit against US," *Axios: China*, November 9, 2021, https://www.axios.com/2021/11/09/aclu-joins-

chinese-american-scientist-lawsuit-against-us-sherry-chen. For a list of all groups of professors and civil rights organizations who sent petitions to the White House, calling on President Biden to end the CI, see https://sites.google.com/view/winds-of-freedom

[161] American Civil Liberties Union, "Civil Rights Organizations Appeal FBI's Refusal to Disclose Government Records on the 'China Initiative,'" July 16, 2021, para. 6, https://www.aclu.org/press-releases/civil-rights-organizations-appeal-fbisrefusal-disclose-government-records-china.

[162] For Li Yuanchao's efforts to improve the research culture in order to attract more returnees, see Zweig and Wang, "Can China Bring Back the Best?"

[163] I joined that meeting and found that attendance was sparse compared to the years when Li Yuanchao headed the Organization Department.

[164] Ryan Fedasiuk, "Putting Money in the Party's Mouth: How China Mobilizes Funding for United Front Work," *China Brief* 20, no. 16 (September 16, 2020), https://jamestown.org/program/putting-money-in-the-partys-mouth-how-china-mobilizes-funding-for-united-front-work/.

[165] "Xi Jinping: Consolidate and Develop a Broad-Based Patriotic United Front."

[166] Margaret Pearson, Meg Rithmire, and Kellee S. Tsai, "Party-State Capitalism in China," *Current History* (September 2021): 207–213.

[167] Zweig, Chung, and Vanhonacker, "Rewards of Technology."

[168] The restatement defines a trade secret as "any information that can be used in the operation of a business or other enterprise and that is sufficiently valuable and secret to afford an actual or potential economic advantage over others." *American Law Institute*, "Restatement (Third) of Unfair Competition," 39 (1995), https://wipolex-res.wipo.int/edocs/lexdocs/laws/en/us/us216en.pdf.

[169] Sheridan Prasso, "US Hunt for Chinese Spies Prompts Racism, Misconduct Claims," *Bloomberg Businessweek*, December 14, 2021, https://www.bloomberg.com/news/features/2021-12-14/doj-china-initiative-to-catch-spies-prompts-fbi-misconduct-racism-claims?sref=5rzJ02Bk#xj4y7vzkg.

[170] Kyle Swenson, "Zhang Yiheng - Virginia Tech professor accused of scamming National Science Foundation," https://www.washingtonpost.com/news/morning-mix/wp/2017/09/26/virginia-tech-professor-accused-of-scamming-national-science-foundation/?noredirect=on&utm_term=.3c56e1606101.

[171] Brendan J. Lyons, "GE engineer: This is not espionage," 7 August 2018, *Times Union,* https://www.timesunion.com/7dayarchive/article/GE-engineer-to-be-released-on-100K-bond-13127249.php.

[172] Ellen Barry, "Stolen Research: Chinese Scientist Is Accused of Smuggling Lab Samples," *The New York Times*, December 31, 2019, https://www.nytimes.com/2019/12/31/us/chinese-scientist-cancer-research-investigation.html.

[173] Rory Truex, "Addressing the China Challenge for American Universities," Working Paper for the Penn Project on the Future of U.S.-China Relations, Spring 2021, https://cpb-us-w2.wpmucdn.com/web.sas.upenn.edu/dist/b/732/files/2021/04/Rory-Truex_Addressing-the-China-Challenge-for-American-Universities_Updated.pdf.

[174] US Permanent Subcommittee on Investigations, "Threats to the US Research Enterprise."

[175] Zhu, et. al., "Analyzing China's research collaboration with the United States."

[176] Lili Yuan, et al., "Who Are the International Research Collaboration Partners for China? A Novel Data Perspective Based on NSFC Grants," *Scientometrics*, published online, April 20, 2018, https://doi.org/10.1007/s11192-018-2753-3.

[177] Jenny J. Lee & John P. Haupt, "Winners and losers in US-China scientific research collaborations," *Higher Education*, 7 Nov. 2019, https://doi.org/10.1007/s10734-019-00464-7.

[178] National Center for Science and Engineering Statistics; Science-Metrix; Elsevier, Scopus abstract and citation database, https://ncses.nsf.gov/pubs/nsb20214/international-collaboration-and-citations#.

[179] Kang Siqin, *Whether State Efforts Increase the Diaspora's Academic Collaboration? Evidence from China's National Talent Programs*, MPhil Thesis, Division of Social Science, The Hong Kong University of Science and Technology, July 2018.

[180] 严瑜 (Yan Yu), "美国'中国行动计划'引发激烈反对" (The China Initiative Launched by the United States Has Sparked Strong Opposition), 人民日报 (*People's Daily*), https://s.cyol.com/articles/2022-01/22/content_DaRYB8Uz.html.

[181] 申杨, 杨弘杨, 杨毅 (Shen Yang, Yang Hongyang, and Yang Yi), "美司法部2018年已正式启动'中国行动计划' 外交部: 纯属政治操弄" ("The US Department of Justice Formally Launched the 'China Initiative' in 2018, Ministry of Foreign Affairs: It Is Purely Political Manipulation"), 央视新闻 (CCTV News), http://news.cyol.com/content/2020-10/31/content_18834657.htm. See also 付随鑫 (Fu Suixin), "美国政府应停止损人不利己的'中国行动计划'" ("The US Government Should Stop the 'China Action Plan' that Harms Others but Does Not Benefit Itself"), http://www.china.com.cn/opinion2020/2022-01/26/content_78011715.shtml.

[182] 胡文利 (Hu Wenli), "华裔学者胡安明被判无罪引发美国社会反思和声讨" ("The Acquittal of Chinese-American Scholar Anming Hu Triggers Reflection and Condemnation in American Society"), 中国青年报 (*China Youth Daily*), http://news.cyol.com/gb/articles/2021-09/16/content_wwgpEsRVJ.html.

[183] 马子倩 (Ma Ziqian), "赵立坚：在美华裔遭歧视和不公是美国民主的耻辱" ("Zhao Lijian: Discrimination and Injustice against Chinese Americans in the United States Are a Disgrace to American Democracy"), 中国青年报 (*China Youth Daily*), https://s.cyol.com/articles/2021-12/15/content_DaMWOKCz.html.

[184] 朱瑞卿 (Zhu Ruiqing), "'中国行动计划'凸显美对华扭曲心态" ("The China Initiative Highlights the Distorted Mindset of the United States toward China"), 新华网 (*Xinhuanet*), http://news.cyol.com/gb/articles/2021-12/29/content_JRX47fZyb.html.

[185] Zhu, "The China Initiative Highlights the Distorted Mindset."

[186] 陈小茹 (Chen Xiaoru), "*FBI* 探员承认曾诬告华裔教授为 '中国间谍,' 赵立坚: 美方通过情报机构搞政治操弄的又一例证" ("FBI Agent Admits Falsely Accusing Chinese-American Professor as a 'Chinese Spy:' Zhao Lijian: Another Example of the US Using Intelligence Agencies for Political Manipulation"), 中国青年报 (*China Youth Daily*), https://s.cyol.com/articles/2021-06/22/content_rya3oPuR.html.

[187] Smriti Mallapaty, "China Hides Identities of Top Scientific Recruits amidst Growing US Scrutiny," *Nature*, October 22, 2018, https://www.natureindex.com/news-blog/china-hides-identities-of-top-scientific-recruits-amidst-growing-us-scrutiny.

[188] Information shared with the author, 2019.

[189] Yuan Yang and Nian Liu, "China Hushes Up Scheme to Recruit Overseas Scientists," *Financial Times*, January 10, 2019, https://www.ft.com/content/a06f414c-0e6e-11e9-a3aa-118c761d2745.

[190] Zweig interview with officials at Chinese consulate in New York City, February 2020.

[191] National Institute of Allergy and Infectious Diseases, "US-China Collaborative Biomedical Research Program," January 4, 2023. https://www.niaid.nih.gov/research/us-china-collaborative-biomedical-research-program.

[192] Lu, et al., "Racial Profiling Harms Science."

[193] Yang and Liu, "China Hushes Up Scheme to Recruit Overseas Scientists."

[194] Yang and Liu, "China Hushes Up Scheme to Recruit Overseas Scientists."

[195] Hua Ran, "美国政府新申明对华人血脂和 中国有什么印象" ("The Uproar: What Was the Impact on Chinese Scholars and on China of the American Government's New Statement?"), 知识分子 (The Intellectual), http://zhuanlan.zhihu.com/p/42960810.

[196] Hua, "The Uproar."

[197] 窦贤康, 国家自然科学基金委员会党组书记, 主任窦贤康: 加强基础研究是世界科技强国建设的必由之路 (Dou Xiankang, Secretary of the Party Leadership Group and Director of the National Natural Science Foundation of China: "Strengthening basic research is the only way to build a world power in science and technology"), 学习时报 (*Study Times*), 14 August 2023, https://www.nsfc.gov.cn/publish/portal0/tab440/info90018.htm.

[198] Truex, "Addressing the China Challenge for American Universities."

[199] Prasso, "US Hunt for Chinese Spies Prompts Racism, Misconduct Claims."

[200] Lewis is quoted in Prasso, "US Hunt for Chinese Spies Prompts Racism, Misconduct Claims."

[201] Kolata, "Scientists with Links to China May Be Stealing Biomedical Research."

[202] US Permanent Subcommittee on Investigations, "Threats to the US Research Enterprise."

203 Betsy Woodruff Swan, "Inside DOJ's Nationwide Effort to Take on China," *Politico*, April 7, 2020, https://www.politico.com/news/2020/04/07/justice-department-china-espionage-169653.

204 Lam's interview with the author, February 24, 2022.

205 Swan, "Inside DOJ's Nationwide Effort to Take On China."

206 Lam's interview with the author, February 24, 2022.

207 Lam's interview with the author, February 24, 2022.

208 Lam's interview with the author, February 24, 2022.

209 Presidential Memorandum on United States Government-Supported Research and Development National Security Policy, January 14, 2021, https://trumpwhitehouse. archives.gov/presidential-actions/presidential-memorandum-united-states-government-supported-research-development-national-security-policy/.

210 Presidential Memorandum on United States Government-Supported Research.

211 Statement of Michael German, fellow, Brennan Center for Justice at NYU Law School.

212 Henry Ren, "Ivy League's Brown Rues 'Big Mistake' on US-China College Ties," *Bloomberg*, February 3, 2022, https://www.bloomberg.com/news/articles/2022-02-03/ivy-league-s-brown-rues-big-mistake-on-u-s-china-college-ties.

213 Ren, "Ivy League's Brown Rues 'Big Mistake.'"

Chapter 4

1 Mulvenon, "Economic Espionage and Trade Secret Theft Cases in the US."

2 Ellen W. Schrecker, "Foreword," in Holmes, *Stalking the Academic Communist*, vii–ix.

3 Eileen Guo, Jess Aloe, and Karen Hao, "We Built a Database to Understand the China Initiative," *MIT Technology Review*, December 2, 2022, https://www.technologyreview.com/2021/12/02/1039397/china-initiative-database-doj/.

4 Moffitt's China Internal Investigation Abstract, January 17, 2020, https://www.documentcloud.org/documents/6661639-Moffitt-s-China-Internal-Investigation-Abstract.

5 Justine Griffin, "Moffitt Cancer Center Shakeup: CEO and Others Resign over China Ties," *Tampa Bay Times*, December 18, 2019, https://www.tampabay.com/news/health/2019/12/18/moffitt-cancer-center-shakeup-ceo-and-others-resign-over-china-ties/.

6 It is unclear if this was an annual payment or a one-off event.

7 Ulf Leonhardt, a UK professor, discovered that the institute that granted him a TTP award was taking a significant amount of the monies due to him. Mara Hvistendahl, "Show Me the Money," *Science*, April 23, 2015, 411–415, https://www.science.org/doi/10.1126/science.346.6208.411.

8 Griffin, "Moffitt Cancer Center Shakeup."

9 Griffin, "Moffitt Cancer Center Shakeup."

[10] News 5, Cleveland, "Fed. Prosecutors Dismiss Criminal Case Involving Former Cleveland Clinic Doctor with Ties to China," July 15, 2021, https://www.news5cleveland.com/news/local-news/investigations/fed-prosecutors-dismiss-criminal-case-involving-former-cleveland-clinic-doctor-with-ties-to-china.

[11] Mervis, "Pall of Suspicion."

[12] NIH Deputy Director Michael Lauer, "US Senate Committee on Health, Education, Labor & Pensions Hearing," April 22, 2021, https://www.help.senate.gov/hearings/protecting-us-biomedical- research-efforts-to-prevent-undue-foreign-influence.

[13] Mervis, "NIH Probe of Foreign Ties."

[14] Mervis, "NIH Probe of Foreign Ties."

[15] Interview by the author with Jeremy Wu, co-organizer of APA Justice.

[16] Mervis, "NIH Probe of Foreign Ties."

[17] I was an expert witness for the defense and signed a nondisclosure agreement.

[18] Dr. Huang shared this information with me as he wants to publicize his case.

[19] Phone interview with Dr. Huang.

[20] Mervis, "Pall of Suspicion."

[21] I never presented my views at the hearing, as the panel, after reading my submission, reportedly decided that they knew what I would say, that Dr Huang had joined the TTP when collaborative cancer research was seen positively, and that Li Yuanchao had orchestrated a campaign environment that pressured Chinese in the US to join the program; the panel simply did not want to hear any compelling defense of Dr Huang.

[22] "Arkansas Professor Pleads Guilty to Lying about China Patents to FBI," *Associated Press*, January 22, 2022, https://www.scmp.com/news/world/united-states-canada/article/3164392/arkansas-professor-pleads-guilty-lying-about-china?module=hard_link&pgtype=article.

[23] Comments from Dr. Ang, May 2023. Personal email to the author.

[24] vcfa.uark.edu/fayetteville-policies-procedures/vcri/404-appendix-d-2021.docx.

[25] University of Arkansas, Fayetteville, UAF Memorandum, November 15, 2011.

[26] UAF Memorandum, October 28, 2011.

[27] Jaime Adame, "Ex-UA Professor Admits False Statement: Fraud Case Dropped," *Arkansas Democrat Gazette*, January 22, 2022, https://www.arkansasonline.com/news/2022/jan/22/former-ua-professor-pleads-guilty-to-making-false/.

[28] "Research Opportunities in Space and Earth Sciences—2016" (Roses-2016), NASA Research Announcement (NRA) Soliciting Basic and Applied Research Proposals, Nnh16zda001n.

[29] https://science.nasa.gov/researchers/sara/faqs/prc-faq-roses.

[30] Email with the author, May 2023.

31 Josh Campbell, "FBI Arrests Researcher for NASA Who Allegedly Failed to Report Ties to China," *CNN*, May 12, 2020, https://www.cnn.com/2020/05/12/us/nasa-researcher-arrest-china/index.html.

32 Jamie Adame, "UA Memo Says Ang Profited Off Research," *Kansas Democratic Gazette*, September 7, 2020, https://www.pressreader.com/usa/northwest-arkansas-democrat-gazette/20200907/281921660450087.

33 https://ualr.edu/techlaunch/files/2011/10/Patent-Policy.pdf.

34 https://uasys.edu/board-policy/210-1/.

35 https://www.uasys.edu/wp-content/uploads/sites/16/2019/08/BP-210.1-Patent-and-Copyright-Policy-8.21.19.pdf.

36 Jaime Adame and Bill Bowdon, "Fired UA Professor Sentenced for FBI Lie," *Arkansas Democratic Gazette*, June 17, 2020, https://www.pressreader.com/usa/arkansas-democrat-gazette/20220617/281547999556979.

37 https://www.bop.gov/resources/news/20221118_first_step_act_time_credits_policy.jsp.

38 "MIT Professor Arrested and Charged with Grant Fraud," January 14, 2021, https://www.justice.gov/usao-ma/pr/mit-professor-arrested-and-charged-grant-fraud.

39 Gang Chen, "We Are All Gang Chen," *Science* 375, no. 6583 (February 24, 2022): 797, doi: 10.1126/science.abo6697.

40 Robert Delany, "MIT President Criticizes Washington for 'Unfounded Suspicions' about Chinese Academics," *South China Morning Post*, June 26, 2019, https://www.scmp.com/news/china/article/3016078/mit-president-criticises-washington-unfounded-suspicions-about-chinese.

41 MIT News Office, "Letter to the MIT Community: Immigration Is a Kind of Oxygen," June 25, 2019, http://news.mit.edu/2019/letter-community-immigration-is-oxygen-0625.

42 See L. Rafael Reif, "Letter to the MIT Community, and Professor Chen," *Letters to the MIT Community*, January 22, 2021, https://reif.mit.edu/speeches-writing/letter-community-re-sustech-relationship-and-professor-chen.

43 "Faculty Letter to President Reif in Support of Professor Gang Chen," January 21, 2021, *MIT Faculty Newsletter XXXIII*, no. 3 (January/February 2021), https://fnl.mit.edu/january-february-2021/faculty-letter-to-president-reif-in-support-of-professor-gang-chen/.

44 "Dismissal of Indictment," January 20, 2022, https://fingfx.thomsonreuters.com/gfx/legaldocs/klvykqyjzvg/gangchen_dropped.pdf.

45 Nate Raymond, "US Drops Criminal Case against MIT Professor over China Ties," *Reuters*, January 20, 2022, https://www.reuters.com/world/us/us-drops-criminal-case-against-case-mit-professor-over-china-ties-2022-01-20/.

46 Kirk Carapezza, "MIT Takes Steps to Stop Foreign Espionage, but Some Faculty Say It Goes Too Far," *GBH News*, October 19, 2023, https://www.WGBH.Org/News/Education-News/2023-03-01/Mit-Takes-Steps-To-Stop-Foreign-Espionage-But-Some-Faculty-Say-It-Goes-Too-Far.

[47] "Defendant Gang Chen's Motion for Sanctions for US Attorney Lelling's Repeated Violations of Local Rule 83.2.1," https://www.universalhub.com/files/gangchen-sanctions.pdf.

[48] APA Justice, Meeting Summaries, https://www.apajustice.org/meeting-summaries.html.

[49] *United States of America v. Anming Hu*, Clerk, US District Court, Eastern District of Tennessee at Chattanooga, February 25, 2020, Case No. 3:20-CR- 21.

[50] This article describes many of the events in great detail. 刘栋 (Liu Dong), "诬陷, 滥权, 钓鱼执法, 美司法部 '中国行动计划' 第一案败诉始末" ("Framing, Abuse of Power, Fishing for Law Enforcement: The Whole Story of the Failure of the First Case of the US Department of Justice's 'China Action Plan'"), 澎湃新闻 (*The Paper*), http://news.cyol.com/gb/articles/2021-09/27/content_0N89yfvQB.html.

[51] Jamie Satterfield, "Trump Administration's First 'China Initiative' Prosecution Sputters as Jurors Deadlock," *Knoxville News Sentinel*, June 16, 2021, https://www.knoxnews.com/story/news/crime/2021/06/17/anming-hu-case-jurors-trump-china-initiative-trial-deadlocked/7712463002/.

[52] Satterfield, "Trump Administration's First 'China Initiative' Prosecution Sputters."

[53] Mara Hvistendahl, "'Ridiculous Case': Juror Criticizes DOJ for Charging Scientist with Hiding Ties to China," *Intercept*, June 23, 2021, https://theintercept.com/2021/06/23/anming-hu-trial-fbi-china/?fbclid=IwAR1nrN_uNPgx-R8_5IMF2yjPQRzNHgiwoUckp7xd5VxVF8lVR-ze8MGirzg.

[54] Aruna Viswanatha, "Judge Thomas Varlan said the US Government Failed to Make Its Case in a Bellwether Trial over Alleged Research Grant Fraud," *Wall Street Journal*, September 9, 2021, https://www.wsj.com/articles/federal-judge-acquits-professor-accused-of-hiding-china-ties-11631230728.

[55] Joseph Choi, "Federal Agents Admit to Falsely Accusing Chinese Professor Being a Spy," *The Hill*, June 14, 2021, https://thehill.com/regulation/court-battles/558345-federal-agents-admit-to-falsely-accusing-chinese-professor-of-being/.

[56] Jamie Satterfield, "Trial Reveals Federal Agents Falsely Accused a UT Professor Born in China of Spying," *Knoxville News Sentinel*, June 13, 2021, https://www.knoxnews.com/story/news/crime/2021/06/14/federal-agents-falsely-accused-university-of-tennessee-professor-spying-china/7649378002/.

[57] Professor X agreed to allow me to report this case, but only if no names were included.

[58] The description of the events that follows is based on the chronological narrative supplied to me by Professor X. This version was current as of March 15, 2023.

[59] Letter of December 13, 2021.

[60] Document L9, September 27, 2021.

[61] Interview with the author.

[62] German, *Disrupt, Discredit, and Divide.*

[63] Telephone interview with Mike German, March 1, 2023.

Chapter 5

[1] https://en.wikipedia.org/wiki/Matthew_G._Olsen.

[2] Jeffrey Mervis, "Controversial US China Initiative Gets New Name, Tighter Focus on Industrial Espionage," *Science* 375, no. 6584, February 28, 2022, https://www.science.org/content/article/controversial-u-s-china-initiative-gets-new-name-tighter-focus-industrial-espionage.

[3] Mervis, "Controversial US China Initiative."

[4] Vanessa Romo, "Biden Appoints Erika Moritsugu to Asian American Liaison Role," *National Public Radio*, April 14, 2021, https://www.npr.org/2021/04/14/987520356/biden-appoints-erika-moritsugu-to-asian-american-liaison-role.

[5] Shawna Chen, "DOJ Drops Cases against 5 Chinese Researchers," *AXIOS*, July 24, 2021, https://www.axios.com/2021/07/24/doj-chinese-researchers-china-initiative.

[6] Melissa Korn and Aruna Viswanatha, "Justice Department Weighs Amnesty for Academics to Disclose Foreign Funding," *Wall Street Journal*, January 22, 2021, https://www.wsj.com/articles/justice-department-weighs-amnesty-for-academics-to-disclose-foreign-funding-11611345451.

[7] Elizabeth Redden, "Republican Senators Oppose Amnesty for Nondisclosures," *Inside Higher Ed*, May 7, 2021, https://www.insidehighered.com/quicktakes/2021/05/07/republican-senators-oppose-amnesty-nondisclosures.

[8] Shawna Chen, "Exclusive: Lawmakers Urge Probe into DOJ's Alleged Racial Profiling of Asians," *AXIOS*, July 30, 2021, https://www.axios.com/2021/07/30/china-asians-racial-profiling-doj-congress.

[9] "Rep. Lieu Exchange with AG Garland on Racial and Ethnic Prof," https://www.facebook.com/watch/?v=565286837867354.

[10] Vincent Ni, "'You're Treated Like a Spy': US Accused of Racial Profiling over China Initiative," *Guardian*, February 9, 2022, https://www.theguardian.com/us-news/2022/feb/10/youre-treated-like-a-spy-us-accused-of-racial-profiling-over-china-initiative.

[11] Natasha Gilbert, "I Lost Two Years of My Life," *Nature* 603 (March 17, 2022): 371–372, https://www.nature.com/articles/d41586-022-00528-2.

[12] https://www.advancingjustice-aajc.org/petition-delivered-end-china-initiative.

[13] https://www.committee100.org/initiatives/racial-profiling-among-scientists-of-chinese-descent-and-consequences-for-the-us-scientific-community/.

[14] Yu Xie, Xihong Lin, Ju Li, Qian He, and Junming Huang, "Caught in the Crossfire: Fears of Chinese-American Scientists," *PNAS* 120, no. 27 (June 27, 2023), https://doi.org/10.1073/pnas.2216248120.

[15] Sheridan Prasso, "China Initiative Set Out to Catch Spies. It Didn't Find Many," *Bloomberg, Businessweek*, December 14, 2021, https://www.bloomberg.com/news/features/2021-12-14/doj-china-initiative-to-catch-spies-prompts-fbi-misconduct-racism-claims.

[16] APA Justice, "Addressing Immediate and Systemic Issues Implementation of NSPM-33," Presentation to Office of Science and Technology Policy, Subcommittee on Research Security, National Science and Technology Council, March 28, 2022.

[17] Xi Xiaoxing, "The US Should Listen to Scientists about How to Counter Influence from China," *Nature Review of Physics* 3 (2021): 384–85, https://doi.org/10.1038/s42254-021-00316-3.

[18] Ni, "You're Treated Like a Spy."

[19] Xi, "The US Should Listen."

[20] Elizabeth Redden, "Reconsidering the China Initiative."

[21] Elizabeth Redden, "Reconsidering the China Initiative."

[22] Jeffrey Mervis, "US Judge Lectures the Government on How Academic Research Works," *Science* (January 20, 2023), doi: 10.1126/science.adg7875.

[23] Jeffrey Mervis, "No Jail Time for Kansas Professor Convicted for Undisclosed Research Ties to China," *Science* (January 18, 2023), https://www.science.org/content/article/no-jail-time-kansas-professor-convicted-undisclosed-research-ties-china.

[24] George Pence, "While China Initiative May Have Ended, Foreign Influence Remains DOJ Enforcement Priority," *Reuters*, March 28, 2022, https://www.reuters.com/legal/legalindustry/while-china-initiative-may-have-ended-foreign-influence-remains-doj-enforcement-2022-03-28/.

[25] Associated Press, "FBI Chief: Threat from China 'More Brazen' Than Ever Before," February 1, 2022, https://www.asahi.com/ajw/articles/14537375.

[26] Sarah N. Lynch, "US Justice Department to End Trump-Era Program Targeting Threats Posed by China," *Reuters*, February 23, 2022, https://www.reuters.com/world/us/us-justice-department-end-trump-era-program-targeting-threats-posed-by-china-2022-02-23/.

[27] Lynch, "US Justice Department to End Trump-Era Program."

[28] This section draws on Ken Dilanian, "FBI director defends investigations of Chinese academics in front of university audience," *NBC News*, December 2, 2022, https://www.nbcnews.com/politics/national-security/fbi-director-wray-defends-investigations-chinese-academics-rcna59864.

[29] Dilanian, "FBI director defends investigations of Chinese academics."

[30] Josh Gerstein, "DOJ Shuts Down China-Focused Anti-Espionage Program," *Politico*, February 23, 2022, https://www.politico.com/news/2022/02/23/doj-shuts-down-china-focused-anti-espionage-program-00011065.

[31] Gerstein, "DOJ Shuts Down China-Focused Anti-Espionage Program

[32] Pence, "While China Initiative May Have Ended."

[33] Pence, "While China Initiative May Have Ended."

[34] Carapezza, "MIT Takes Steps to Stop Foreign Espionage."

[35] Carapezza, "MIT Takes Steps to Stop Foreign Espionage."

[36] Carapezza, "MIT Takes Steps to Stop Foreign Espionage."

[37] Ryan Gallagher and Henrik Moltke, "The Wiretap Rooms: The NSA's Hidden Spy Hubs in Eight US Cities," *Intercept*, June 25, 2018, https://theintercept.com/2018/06/25/att-internet-nsa-spy-hubs/.

[38] https://www.advancingjustice-aajc.org/publication/national-asian-american-coalition-letter-led-asian-american-scholar-forum-asian.

[39] https://www.advancingjustice-aajc.org/publication/national-asian-american-coalition-letter-led-asian-american-scholar-forum-asian.

[40] Noa Yachot, "News & Commentary: 'Do Everything They Ask So They Don't Shoot Me,'" American Civil Liberties Union, December 8, 2017, https://www.aclu.org/news/national-security/do-everything-they-ask-so-they-dont-shoot-me.

[41] https://www.advancingjustice-aajc.org/publication/national-asian-american-coalition-letter-led-asian-american-scholar-forum-asian.

[42] The online survey received responses from 617 grantees, for a response rate of 79.8 percent. See Suzanne Murrin, Deputy Inspector General for Evaluation and Inspections, "Opportunities Exist to Strengthen NIH Grantees' Oversight of Investigators' Foreign Significant Financial Interests and Other Support," June 2022, OEI-03-20-00210, https://oig.hhs.gov/oei/reports/OEI-03-20-00210.pdf.

[43] Murrin, "Opportunities Exist."

[44] Lauer, "Brief Summary of NIH Foreign Interference Cases."

[45] See APA Justice newsletter, #256 which offers access to the draft bill through https://bit.ly/3UOqbLr.

[46] Natasha Gilbert, "China Initiative's Shadow Looms Large for US Scientists," *Nature* 615, no. 7951 (2023): 198–199.

[47] "Consistent Posting of Investigative Results and Publish Statistical Summaries," see NSF Office of the Inspector General website, https://bit.ly/3KYEKFP.

[48] APA Justice, "Companion Notes: Addressing Immediate and Systemic Issues Implementation of NSPM-33," Presentation to Office of Science and Technology Policy Subcommittee on Research Security, National Science and Technology Council, March 28, 2022, reference_notes_for_ostp_powerpoint_presentationb.pdf.

[49] Remco Zwetsloot and Zachary Arnold, "Chinese Students Are Not a Fifth Column: Indiscriminate Bans Will Hurt—Not Protect—US Innovation," *Foreign Affairs*, April 23, 2021, https://www.foreignaffairs.com/articles/united-states/2021-04-23/chinese-students-are-not-fifth-column.

[50] Graham Allison and Eric Schmidt, "The US Needs a Million Talents Program to Retain Technology Leadership," *Foreign Policy*, July 16, 2022, https://foreignpolicy.com/2022/07/16/immigration-us-technology-companies-work-visas-china-talent-competition-universities/.

51 Minxin Pei, "Cultural Decoupling from China Will Hurt the US," *Project Syndicate*, August 18, 2020, https://www.project-syndicate.org/commentary/cultural-decoupling-will-hurt-america-more-than-china-by-minxin-pei-2020-08.

52 饶毅 (Rao Yi), "中国研究生的一个新趋势" ("New Trend among China's Graduate Students"), 饶毅科学 (Rao Yi's Science), June 27, 2022, https://mp.weixin.qq.com/s/J6iSIQF7nNOEt5jIRRecHQ.

53 Heather Timmons and Mimi Dwyer, "Explainer: What 1.1 Million Foreign Students Contribute to the US Economy," *Reuters*, July 8, 2020, https://www.reuters.com/article/us-usa-immigration-students-economy-expl-idUSKBN2492VS. An official at Purdue University told *Reuters* that foreign students had paid an extra USD 10 million in tuition to the school in 2015.

54 Ann Scott Tyson, "Colleges, Officials Try to Thaw Effects of the US-China Chill," *Christian Science Monitor*, November 20, 2019, https://www.csmonitor.com/USA/2019/1120/Colleges-officials-try-to-thaw-effects-of-the-US-China-chill.

55 Scott Tyson, "Colleges, Officials Try to Thaw Effects of the US-China Chill."

56 See Poormina Weerasekara, "Put Off by US, Chinese Students Eye Other Universities," *Yahoo News*, July 7, 2019, https://news.yahoo.com/put-off-us-chinese-students-eye-other-universities-033810321.html.

57 Elizabeth Redden, "US to Limit Visa Length for Some Chinese Students," *Inside Higher Education*, May 30, 2018, https://www.insidehighered.com/quicktakes/2018/05/30/us-limit-visa-length-some-chinese-students.

58 Tribune News Service, "Nine Chinese Students from Arizona State University Detained at Los Angeles Airport and Sent Back to China," *South China Morning Post*, September 6, 2019, https://www.scmp.com/news/china/article/3025949/nine-chinese-students-arizona-state-university-detained-los-angeles.

59 "Top 10 Places of Origin of International Students in the United States, 2012–2022," https://www.iie.org/research-initiatives/project-atlas/explore-data/united-states-2/.

60 Sha Hua, "Chinese Student Visas to US Tumble from Pre-Pandemic Levels," *Wall Street Journal*, August 11, 2022, https://www.wsj.com/articles/chinese-student-visas-to-u-s-tumble-from-prepandemic-levels-11660210202.

61 Weerasekara, "Put Off by US."

62 Jack Corrigan, James Dunham, and Remco Zwetsloot, "The Long-Term Stay Rates of International STEM PhD Graduates," Center for Security and Emerging Technology, April 2022, https://doi.org/10.51593/20210023.

63 These are the findings of Xie et al., who used the school that authors of over 2.3 million scientific papers listed as their home institution to determine how many people had returned to China. See Xie, et al., "Caught in the Crossfire."

64 Xie, et al., "Caught in the Crossfire."

[65] David Armstrong, Annie Waldman, and Daniel Golden, "The Trump Administration Drove Him Back to China, Where He Invented a Fast Coronavirus Test," *ProPublica*, March 18, 2020, https://www.propublica.org/article/the-trump-administration-drove-him-back-to-china-where-he-invented-a-fast-coronavirus-test.

[66] Armstrong, Waldman, and Golden, "The Trump Administration Drove Him Back."

[67] Xie, et al., "Caught in the Crossfire."

[68] R. V. Noorden, "The Number of Researchers with Dual US-China Affiliations is Falling," *Nature* (May 30, 2022), https://www.nature.com/articles/d41586-022-01492-7.

[69] The list of grantees is available at https://report.nih.gov/award/index.cfm#tabpi. We determined who was a China-born researcher in the US based on family names using the *pinyin* romanization system—which is used only in the PRC.

[70] Qian He and Yu Xie, "The Moral Filter of Patriotic Prejudice: How Americans View Chinese in the COVID-19 Era," *PNAS*, November 14, 2022, https://doi.org/10.1073/pnas.2212183119.

[71] Committee of 100, "New Research Reveals Racial Profiling among Scientists of Chinese Descent and the Consequences for the US Scientific Community," October 28, 2021, https://www.committee100.org/wp-content/uploads/2021/10/release-C100-UA-survey-data-FINAL.pdf.

[72] Committee of 100, "New Research Reveals Racial Profiling."

[73] Jeffrey Mervis, "Two Surveys Document Harmful Impact of China Initiative on Researchers: Chinese Faculty Describe Heightened Anxiety, Fewer Collaborations, Loss of Trust," *Science,* October 28, 2021, https://www.science.org/content/article/two-surveys-document-harmful-impact-china-initiative-researchers.

[74] https://www.gofundme.com/f/Legal-Defense-Fund-for-Franklin-Tao/topdonations.

[75] Roy Murphy, "Convictions Overturned for US Chemical Engineer Accused of Hiding Ties to China," *Washington News*, September 22, 2022, https://localtoday.news/wa/convictions-overturned-for-us-chemical-engineer-accused-of-hiding-ties-to-china-60338.html.

[76] Jenny J. Lee and John P. Haupt, "Winners and Losers in US-China Scientific Research Collaborations," *Higher Education*, November 7, 2019, https://doi.org/10.1007/s10734-019-00464-7.

[77] Stuart Winkler, "Chinese Cash that Powered Silicon Valley Is Suddenly Toxic," *Wall Street Journal*, June 11, 2019, https://www.wsj.com/articles/chinese-cash-is-suddenly-toxic-insilicon-valley-following-u-s-pressure-campaign-11560263302.

[78] Daniel Flatley and Janet Lorin, "Congress Takes Aim at China's Recruitment of Talent in the US," *Bloomberg*, July 18, 2021, https://www.bloomberg.com/news/articles/2021-07-18/congress-takes-aim-at-china-s-recruitment-of-talent-in-u-s.

[79] Dennis Normile, "China's Scientific Treasures Tempt Foreign Collaborators," *Science* 372, no. 6537 (April 2, 2021): 17–18, doi: 10.1126/Science.372.6537.17

[80] Ren, "Ivy League's Brown Rues Big Mistake."

[81] Jenny J. Lee, "How China-US Collaborations Still Happen, Despite Politics," *Nature* 607, no. 423 (July 19, 2022), https://www.nature.com/articles/d41586-022-01957-9.

[82] Jenny J. Lee and John P. Haupt, "Scientific Collaboration on COVID-19 amidst Geopolitical Tensions between the US and China," *Journal of Higher Education* 92, no. 2 (2021): 303–329, doi: 10.1080/00221546.2020.1827924.

[83] Stephen Chen, "Chinese, US Scientists Still Working Together Despite Donald Trump's Hostility," *South China Morning Post*, October 22, 2020, https://www.scmp.com/news/china/science/article/3106531/chinese-us-scientists-still-working-together-despite-trump.

[84] Rory Murphy, "Nanjing University and the American Chemical Society Sign a Memorandum of Understanding and Collaborate on the New Open Access Journal Chemical & Biomedical Imaging," *Washington News*, August 16, 2022, https://localtoday.news/wa/nanjing-university-and-the-american-chemical-society-sign-a-memorandum-of-understanding-and-collaborate-on-the-new-open-access-journal-chemical-b-iomedical-imaging-30232.html.

[85] Committee of 100, "New Research Reveals."

[86] Committee of 100, "New Research Reveals."

[87] Xie, et al., "Caught in the Crossfire."

[88] Xie, et al., "Caught in the Crossfire."

[89] Dennis Normile, "A Beijing Think Tank Offered a Frank Review of China's Technological Weaknesses. Then the Report Disappeared," *Science*, February 8, 2022, https://www.science.org/content/article/beijing-think-tank-offered-frank-review-china-s-technological-weaknesses-then-report.

[90] Xu Qiyuan, Dong Weijia, and Lang Pingping, "中美科技博弈变局下的中国视角" ("A Chinese Perspective on the Changing Landscape of the US-China Science and Technology Game"), 开放导报 (Open Guide) 224, no. 05 (2022): 64–71, doi:10.19625/j.cnki.cn44-1338/f.2022.0071.

[91] These are the views of Dr. Joy Zhang at the University of Kent, who studies global scientific governance. Eanna Kelly, "Viewpoint: Chinese Scientists Caught in a Cycle of Mistrust with the World," *Science/Business*, April 8, 2021, https://sciencebusiness.net/viewpoint/viewpoint-chinese-scientists-caught-cycle-mistrust-world.

[92] Li Tang, et al., "A Collateral Damage beyond Deteriorating US–China Relations," *Science and Public Policy* 48, no. 5 (2021): 630–634, https://doi.org/10.1093/scipol/scab035.

[93] Coco Feng, "Xi Jinping Calls for International Tech Cooperation to Tackle Global Challenges, amid Simmering US Tensions," *South China Morning Post*, September 24, 2021, https://www.scmp.com/tech/tech-war/article/3150042/president-xi-calls-international-tech-cooperation-tackle-global.

[94] Yojana Sharma, "COVID-19 Research Checks Could Deter Global Collaboration," *University World News*, April 15, 2020, https://www.universityworldnews.com/post.php?story=20200415141352492.

[95] Xie, et al., "Caught in the Crossfire."

[96] Committee of 100, "New Research Reveals Racial Profiling."

[97] Jenny J. Lee, and Xiaojie Li, "Neo-Racism, Neo-Nationalism, and the Costs for Scientific Competitiveness: The China Initiative in the United States," *Review of Higher Education* 46, no. 3 (2023): 285–309, doi:10.1353/rhe.2023.0000.

[98] Caroline S. Wagner and Xiaojing Cai, "Drop in China-USA International Collaboration," *ISSI Newsletter* 18, no. 1 (2022), https://www.issi-society.org/media/1434/newsletter69.pdf#page=6.

[99] Joy Y. Zhang, Sonia Ben Ouagrham-Gormley, and Kathleen M. Vogel, "Creating Common Ground with Chinese Researchers," *Research Culture* (Summer 2022): 45–48.

[100] Charles Hutzler, "US, China Poised to Drift Farther Apart," *Wall Street Journal*, August 11, 2023, A7. See also Jami Miscik, Peter Orszag, and Theodore Bunzel, "The US-Chinese Economic Relationship Is Changing—But Not Vanishing," *Foreign Affairs*, May 24, 2023, https://www.foreignaffairs.com/united-states/us-chinese-economic-relationship-changing-not-vanishing.

[101] Jeffrey Mervis, "US-China Tensions Could Complicate Effort to Renew Key Research Pact," *Science* 381, no. 6661 (September 1, 2023): 931–932, https://www.science.org/content/article/u-s-china-tensions-could-complicate-effort-renew-key-research-pact.

[102] Congressional Research Service, "US-China Science and Technology Cooperation Agreement," October 16, 2023, https://crsreports.congress.gov/product/pdf/IF/IF12510.

[103] James Mitchell Crow, "US-China Partnerships Bring Strength in Numbers to Big Science Project," *Nature* 603, S6-S-8 (2022), doi: https://www.nature.com/articles/d41586-022-00570-0.

[104] Mervis, "US-China Tensions Could Complicate Effort to Renew Key Research Pact."

Conclusion

[1] Peter S. Li, "Immigration from China to Canada in the Age of Globalization: Issues of Brain Gain and Brain Loss," *Pacific Affairs* 81, no. 2 (2008): 217–239.

[2] The world average was 5.2. See www.theglobaleconomy.com/rankings/human_flight_brain_drain_index/.

[3] Bang, "Reverse Brain Drain in South Korea State Led Model," and Shirley L. Chang, "Causes of the Brain Drain and Solutions: The Taiwan Experience," *Studies in Comparative International Development* 7, no. 1 (Spring 1992): 27–43.

[4] Miao, *Sixty Years of Studying Abroad.*

[5] Zweig, Kang, and Wang, "The Best Are Yet to Come."

[6] Meyer, et al., "Turning Brain Drain into Brain Gain."

[7] Didi Kirsten Tatlow, "Exclusive: US Gave $30 Million to Top Chinese Scientist Leading China's AI 'Race'," *Newsweek*, November 1, 2023, https://www.newsweek.com/us-gave-30-million-top-chinese-scientist-leading-chinas-ai-race-1837772.

[8] Spear, "Serve the Motherland While Working Overseas."

[9] Zweig and Chen, *China's Brain Drain to the United States*, 71.

[10] Zweig, Chung, and Han, "Redefining the 'Brain Drain': China's Diaspora Option."

[11] Hannas and Tatlow, eds., *China's Quest for Foreign Technology.*

[12] Jin Bihui, Ling Li, and Ronald Rousseau, "Long-Term Influences of Interventions in the Normal Development of Science: China and the Cultural Revolution," *Journal of the American Society for Information Science and Technology* 55, no. 6 (April 2004): 544–550.

[13] Telephone interview by the author with Mike German, March 1, 2023.

[14] German, *Disrupt, Discredit, and Divide.*

[15] Mervis, "Pall of Suspicion." See also H. Holden Thorp, "Lauer Opens Up," *Science* 380, no. 6647 (May 25, 2023): 775, doi: 10.1126/science.adi8239.

[16] Gina Kolata, "Scientists with Links to China May Be Stealing Biomedical Research, US Says," *New York Times*, October 30, 2019, https://www.nytimes.com/2019/11/04/health/china-nih-scientists.html.

[17] Letter from Francis Collins, director, NIH, August 20, 2018, https://www.aau.edu/sites/default/files/Blind-Links/NIH_Foreign_Influence_Letter_to_Grantees_08-20-18.pdf.

[18] *Secrecy News*, from the Federation of American Scientists Project on Government Secrecy 2019, no. 45, December 16, 2019, https://fas.org/irp/agency/dod/jason/fundamental.pdf.

[19] *Secrecy News 2019*, no. 45.

[20] *Secrecy News 2019*, no. 45.

[21] Deemed Export Advisory Committee, 2007: 26, cited in Krige, "National Security and Academia."

Appendix A

List of Fifty-Two Asian American and Allied Organizations that Signed the September 23, 2023, Letter to US Congress in Opposition to Reauthorizing Section 702 without Comprehensive Reforms

AAPI Equity Alliance

AAPI Victory Alliance

Action Against Hate

API Equality-LA

ASATA—Alliance of South Asians Taking Action

Asian American Academy of Science and Engineering (AAASE)

Asian American Federal Employees for Nondiscrimination

Asian Americans for Civil Rights and Equality

Asian American Legal Defense and Education Fund (AALDEF)

Asian American Scholar Forum

Asian Americans Advancing Justice—AAJC

Asian Americans Advancing Justice-Asian Law Caucus

Asian Americans Advancing Justice-Atlanta

Asian Americans Advancing Justice Southern California

Asian Americans Leadership Council

Asian Law Alliance

Asian Pacific American Labor Alliance (APALA), AFL-CIO

Asian Pacific Partners for Empowerment, Advocacy, and Leadership (APPEAL)

Asian Student Alliance

Asian Texans for Justice

Association of Chinese Americans

Aurora Commons

Chinese American Citizens Alliance Portland Lodge

Chinese for Affirmative Action

Coalition of AAPI Churches Los Angeles

Communities United for Status and Protection (CUSP)

Empowering Marginalized Asian Communities

Grassroots Asians Rising

Muslim Advocates

Muslims for Just Futures

National Asian Pacific American Families against Substance Abuse (NAPAFASA)

National Asian Pacific American Women's Forum

National Council of Asian Pacific Americans (NCAPA)

National Korean American Service and Education Consortium (NAKASEC)

OCA-Asian Pacific American Advocates

OCA San Diego Asian Pacific American Advocates

OCA Greater Seattle-Asian Pacific American Advocates

OCA Asian Pacific American Advocates-Pittsburgh Chapter

OCA Columbus

OCA Greater Chicago

OCA Greater Cleveland-Asian Pacific American Advocates

OCA Silicon Valley

OCA Central Virginia Chapter

OCA Greater Houston

Restore the Fourth

Rising Voices

South Asian American Policy and Research Institute (SAAPRI)

South Asian Public Health Association

Stop AAPI Hate

Tulane Association of Chinese Professionals

Vincent Chin Institute

Woori Juntos

Appendix B

Statistical Appendix

The first dataset used in the chapter on the diaspora option compares full-time returnees under the Changjiang Scholars Plan (长江学者计划—CJSP) who may have returned before receiving the award with those who joined the Changjiang Visitors Program (CJVP) and remained abroad. I compare their scientific productivity, measured by the h-index and the number of citations, controlling for the number of years since their PhD.[1] We do need to be wary of a problem of self-selection, where lower-quality scholars may be predisposed to return full-time because they cannot get good jobs overseas or can get better jobs back in China, while the best scholars stay abroad, following Lien's argument that offering incentives, such as talent awards, to encourage people to return, increases the flow of people of moderate quality but not the most talented.[2]

The results (table A.1) show that part-time participants are better than full-timers, as the negative and statistically significant results for three of these results show that part-time returnees are cited more frequently than full-time returnees and have a higher h-index. And when we divide their citations and h-index by the number of years since these scholars received their PhD (the variables are "h-index_phd" and "Citation_phd*1000," where the latter variable adjusts for the fact that many of these people had thousands of citations), their h-index and their citations are highly significant. Particularly, in the case of their citations, the strong correlation of -0.842 shows that part-time returnees are almost twice as productive as those who returned full-time. No doubt, some full-time returnees may publish mostly in Chinese to enhance their domestic influence, so they are not necessarily weaker scholars.[3] But full-time returnees can get sidetracked by administrative obligations and interpersonal politics within their unit, particularly compared to the situation abroad, where they could throw themselves into full-time research.

I use both age and the log of age (age^2) because previous literature found a nonlinear relationship between age and migration decisions, where middle-aged people were more likely to return full-time than either younger or older scientists.

People in the social sciences are more likely to be part-time than people in the natural sciences, as a hedge in case they get into political trouble. They may also prefer working in a less political environment. On the other hand, there is no significant difference between people in the life sciences and the natural sciences or between engineers and natural scientists.

Variables	(1) Full-Time	(2) Full-Time	(3) Full-Time	(4) Full-Time	(5) Full-Time
Citations	-0.050*** (0.012)	-0.048*** (0.017)			
h-index			-0.002 (0.003)		
h-index_phd				-0.000*** (0.000)	
Citation_ phd*1000					-0.842** (0.390)
male		-0.792* (0.423)	-0.578 (0.388)	-0.535 (0.404)	-0.724* (0.425)
year_award		0.262*** (0.074)	0.290*** (0.072)	0.284*** (0.077)	0.250*** (0.078)
age		2.540*** (0.537)	2.618*** (0.527)	2.935*** (0.496)	2.816*** (0.508)
age2		-0.026*** (0.005)	-0.027*** (0.005)	-0.030*** (0.005)	-0.029*** (0.005)
social science	-1.674*** (0.406)	-1.694*** (0.603)	-1.503*** (0.512)	-1.798*** (0.524)	-2.068*** (0.655)
engineering	0.146 (0.229)	0.181 (0.302)	0.170 (0.305)	0.084 (0.314)	0.062 (0.312)
life science	-0.171 (0.309)	-0.207 (0.401)	-0.386 (0.387)	-0.389 (0.410)	-0.242 (0.423)
constant	1.158*** (0.228)	-586.926*** (148.686)	-646.407*** (146.515)	-641.722*** (154.919)	-569.406*** (156.060)
observations	481	391	391	374	373

Table A.1. Comparing Academic Productivity
between CJSP and CJVP, 2012–2017.

Notes:

(1) For the dependent variable, "Type of Plan," full-time participants = 1 and part-time participants = 0.

(2) The baseline for the regression for field of research is science.

(3) The baseline is participants in the CJVP.

(4) The number of full-time returnees is 292, and the number of part-time participants is 192. Due to missing results, the total is less than the total participants in each program.

(5) Robust standard errors in parentheses. *** p<0.01, ** p<0.05, * p<0.1.

Source: List of all participants in the CJSP was online from 2012 to 2017.

I created the data set for comparing China-born scientists in the US, Hong Kong, and Canada at the turn of the millennium. In 2001 and 2002, my research team of MPhil students at HKUST interviewed twenty-eight mainland academics in Hong Kong. In 2005, I sent 401 mainland professors teaching in Hong Kong an email exploring their engagement with the mainland. I received seventy responses, for a response rate of 17 percent.[4] Among this total of ninety-eight academics, 66 percent were full or associate professors (11 percent were full professors), 56 percent received their degree in the US and 19 percent in Canada. Most were trained at top overseas universities: of the forty-one for whom I have data, eight studied at the University of Toronto, four at Princeton, three at MIT, four at Columbia, five at the University of British Columbia, three at the Ohio State University, and four within the University of California system. The majority had been in Hong Kong for over ten years, making them quite capable of working with mainland colleagues.

For the US dataset, Dr. Kang Siqin, who was then my research assistant and MPhil student, divided the wealthiest three hundred American universities, based on their endowments, into three groups of one hundred and then selected twenty schools randomly from each group of one hundred.[5] From each school's website, he compiled a list of faculty members with *pinyin* (Chinese romanization) names. Through email, we invited 756 academics in sixty universities to complete an online survey. We received ninety-four answers for a response rate of 12.5 percent. Half of these academics were only assistant professors, 88 percent were trained in the US, and 71 percent were engineers or natural scientists.

Finally, in 2005, Dr. Kang selected twenty-three Canadian universities based on their size and adopted the same methodology as in the US survey. We contacted 428 academics and received fifty-nine answers, a response rate of 14 percent. Among the fifty-nine academics, half were full or associate professors (13 percent were full professors).

Kang and I spent an enormous amount of time, energy, and money to collect the dataset of participants in the CJSP and the TTP, which we date from 2008 to 2013. We hired undergraduate students at Zhongshan University, in Guangzhou, who came to work in the South China Global Talent Institute, where I was associate dean. Though it was time-consuming, using these scholars' CVs we calculated their h-index, their average annual impact factor (AAIF), and the average number of papers per year, which we used as three dependent variables. Our independent variables were their age when they joined the plan (age_plan), their gender, the number of years they worked before joining the respective program, which program they joined, whether they joined full- or part-time, and their scientific field.

The logit regression analyses of these full- and part-time participants of the CJSP and the TTP reveal that for both programs, participants who kept their overseas positions and only joined the talent plan on a part-time basis were superior researchers (table A.2, rows 1 and 3). So China has sound reasons to engage ethnic Chinese scientists in the diaspora, as they can help domestic scientists link with the world and bring cutting-edge research being carried out (perhaps by them) in laboratories in the West into Chinese institutions.

Variables	h-index	AAIF	No. Papers
Changjiang Part-Time	0.593*** (0.147)	0.555** (0.256)	0.673*** (0.188)
1,000 Talents Full-Time	-0.172 (0.199)	0.040 (0.265)	-0.096 (0.212)
1,000 Talents Part-Time	0.581*** (0.165)	0.760*** (0.255)	0.524*** (0.200)
Year joined plan	0.015 (0.020)	0.040 (0.031)	0.043* (0.025)
Female	-0.050 (0.205)	-0.047 (0.226)	-0.047 (0.188)
Age_plan	-0.059 (0.040)	-0.140** (0.059)	-0.087* (0.049)
Age_plan^2	0.001 (0.000)	0.001* (0.001)	0.001 (0.000)
Fields of Research	YES	YES	YES
Constant	-26.320 (39.792)	-75.437 (61.741)	-83.739* (49.942)
Observations	833	833	833
R-squared	0.117	0.154	0.079

Table A.2. Comparing Full-Time Returnees and China-Born
Scholars in the Diaspora, Changjiang Scholars and
the Thousand Talent Plan Awardees, 2011–2013.

Note: * p<0.1, ** p<0.05, *** p<0.01. The baseline is Changjiang Scholars Full-Time. Source: Data collection was supervised by Dr. Kang Siqin, who managed a team of students from Zhongshan University, Guangzhou. Work was done at the South China Global Talent Institute, Guangzhou.

US Universities
Harvard University
University of California, Berkeley
Princeton University
University of California, Los Angeles
University of Pennsylvania
The Johns Hopkins University
University of Illinois at Urbana-Champaign
Northwestern University
University of Colorado Boulder
University of California, Santa Barbara
The University of Texas Southwestern Medical Center at Dallas
University of California, Davis
Pennsylvania State University-University Park
Purdue University
The Ohio State University
Boston University
Indiana University, Bloomington
Baylor College of Medicine
UK Universities
University of Oxford
The Imperial College of Science, Technology, and Medicine
University of Bristol
London School of Economics and Political Science
Canadian Universities
University of Toronto
University of British Columbia
McGill University
Australian Universities
University of Melbourne
The Australian National University

Table A.3. The Universities of My Top 121 China-Born
Scholars Working Overseas, 2016.

Here I present the multiple regression analysis which explains the involvement of
these 121 world class professors in lecturing, coauthoring, or holding an adjunct
position in China. Their characteristics appear in Chapter 2, table 2.13 and their

level of involvement is shown in table 2.14. The statistical analysis presented below shows that full professors, as compared to associate professors, were more likely to have joint positions in China, were much more likely to coauthor with researchers in China, and were more likely to have joint positions. It also shows that engineers, as compared to academics in medical schools or those in basic sciences, were more likely to be involved with China.

Independent Variables	Lectures in China	Hold a Joint Position	Coauthorship (No. of Papers)
Gender (Male)	.051	.151	7.64*
Age	-.000	.030***	.374
Academic Position[1]	.215**	.191**	8.15**
Medical School[2,3]	-.451***	-.192*	1.29
Science[2,3]	-.124	-.240***	-3.04
Constant	.460***	-.103***	-15.5***
Observations	110	110	110

Table A.4. Explaining Modes of Participation,
121 Top Global China-Born Scholars, 2016.

Notes:

[1] Professor =1; Associate Professor = 0. * $p<0.1$, ** $p<0.05$, *** $p<0.01$.

[2] The subject information is coded based on the title of a scholar's department.

[3] The baseline group for subject (medical school and science) is engineering.

Source: Data collection was supervised by Dr. Kang Siqin, who managed a team of students from Zhongshan University, Guangzhou. Work was done at the South China Global Talent Institute, Guangzhou.

In the analysis that follows, we try to explain the quality of the work only by our TTP participants, measured by their h-index, their AAIF, and the number of scholarly papers published.

First, I compare full-time and part-time participants in the TTP who received an American PhD (table A.5), where the former returned full-time to China, while the latter kept positions in the US and were expected to participate in the TTP for no more than two to three months a year. As of 2011, among 501 cases we collected from the web, only 26.5 percent of scientists and professors who joined the TTP returned full-time, while three-quarters joined the part-time program (table 2.7). The data show that part-time participants are significantly better than full-time returnees on all three of our quality measures (table A.5, row 1). It also shows that the scores used for measuring the impact factor varied by field of study. Age also had a slightly negative influence on their AAIF.

Variables	h-index #	AIIP #	Papers/yr.
Part-time	0.414*** (0.116)	0.781*** (0.176)	2.851*** (0.547)
Year joined plan	0.027 (0.036)	0.030 (0.060)	0.024 (0.323)
Gender (female)	0.119 (0.150)	0.057 (0.264)	-1.646* (0.957)
Age	-0.022 (0.053)	-0.147* (0.082)	0.063 (0.245)
Age^2	0.000 (0.000)	0.001* (0.001)	-0.001 (0.002)
Field of study	-0.116	-0.547***	-0.933
Constant	-50.352 (71.406)	-55.044 (119.711)	-48.078 (647.329)
Observations	337	337	337
R-squared	0.085	0.194	0.049

Table A.5. Quality of Part-Time vs. Full-Time
TTP Participants with US PhDs, 2011–2013.

Notes: Robust standard errors in parentheses. *** $p<0.01$, ** $p<0.05$, * $p<0.1$. # We use the log of these two dependent variables. The comparative group is full-time returnees to China.

Source: Data collection was supervised by Dr. Kang Siqin, who managed a team of students from Zhongshan University, Guangzhou. Work was done at the South China Global Talent Institute, Guangzhou.

Our data also show that working in the US enhanced the research of TTP participants. While getting a PhD in the US, without working there, did not significantly enhance the quality of their research (table A.6, row 1), receiving an American PhD *and* working in the US had a significant impact (table A.6, row 3) on whether their work was cited (h-index) and on the AAIF of the journals in which they published ($p<0.05$). It did not affect the number of papers they published each year. Age, again, had a significant but negative influence on the impact factor of the journals in which they published, as the younger people were publishing in better journals.

Variables	h-index #	AAIF #	Average Number of Papers/Year
US PhD	0.030 (0.023)	0.056 (0.045)	0.260 (0.177)
US work experience	0.214*** (0.075)	0.355*** (0.136)	0.752 (0.524)
Year joined plan	-0.024 (0.030)	-0.044 (0.053)	-0.095 (0.260)
Gender (Female)	0.125 (0.121)	0.075 (0.237)	-0.896 (1.020)
Age	-0.030 (0.043)	-0.130** (0.057)	0.065 (0.237)
Age^2	0.000 (0.000)	0.001** (0.001)	-0.001 (0.002)
Field of study	Controlled	Controlled	Controlled
Constant	53.086 (59.122)	93.396 (106.894)	194.118 (521.839)
Observation	470	470	470
R-squared	0.046	0.138	0.018

Table A.6. Quality of TTP Participants Who Studied and/or Worked in the US versus Other Countries, 2011–2013.

Notes: Robust standard errors are in parentheses. # We used the log of their h-index and of their AAIF. Level of statistical significance: *** $p<0.01$, ** $p<0.05$, * $p<0.1$. The baseline group is those with PhDs and/or work experience from countries other than the US.

Source: Data collection was supervised by Dr. Kang Siqin, who managed a team of students from Zhongshan University, Guangzhou. Work was carried out at the South China Global Talent Institute, Guangzhou.

Table A.7 compares full-time and part-time participants in the TTP, all of whom had worked in the US before joining the program, decreasing the number of observations to 322. This way, we look only at the impact of staying abroad versus returning to China on the quality of their publications (though the results could be stronger for those who worked longer in the US). Among participants who had worked in the US, those who stayed abroad produced higher quality scholarship than those who returned to China full-time (row 1). Men also published more papers, as the value for female was negative.

Variables	h-index #	AAIF #	Average Number of Papers/Year
Part-Time	0.332*** (0.100)	0.556*** (0.191)	2.831*** (0.637)
Year joined plan	0.050 (0.032)	0.014 (0.061)	-0.020 (0.328)
Gender (Female)	0.121 (0.138)	-0.071 (0.244)	-2.114** (1.038)
Age	-0.027 (0.050)	-0.165*** (0.056)	-0.011 (0.265)
Age^2	0.000 (0.000)	0.001** (0.001)	-0.001 (0.003)
Field of study	-0.186*	-0.678***	-1.813***
Constant	-96.241 (63.958)	-21.209 (122.917)	44.947 (658.994)
Observations	322	322	322
R-squared	0.067	0.152	0.049

Table A.7. Quality of Full-Time and Part-Time Participants
in TTP Who Worked in the US, 2011–2013.

Notes: Robust standard errors in parentheses. *** p<0.01, ** p<0.05, * p<0.1. Baseline group is full-time returnees who had worked in the US. # We use the log for both dependent variables.

Source: Data collection was supervised by Dr. Kang Siqin, who managed a team of students from Zhongshan University, Guangzhou. Work was carried out at the South China Global Talent Institute, Guangzhou.

While the TTP drew part-time participants from the UK, Japan, the EU, Canada, and other countries, part-time participants in the US were better than part-time participants from most other countries (table A.8). Still, TTP part-time participants in the UK and Canada were high-quality. Part-time participants in the UK were as well-cited (p<.05) as those who stayed in the US,[6] while Canadian part-time participants published in high-quality journals (AAIF, p<.01) and were widely cited (h-index, p<.10).

Variables	h-index #	AAIF #	Average No. Papers/Year
US	0.279** (0.122)	0.412** (0.201)	1.092 (0.675)
Canada	0.310* (0.173)	0.734*** (0.281)	1.507 (1.032)
UK	0.341** (0.150)	0.335 (0.264)	1.012 (0.839)
Japan	0.136 (0.199)	0.063 (0.376)	0.497 (1.126)
Europe	0.111 (0.157)	0.160 (0.283)	0.152 (0.807)
Others	0.289 (0.207)	0.378 (0.419)	3.228* (1.780)
Year joined plan	-0.020 (0.029)	-0.037 (0.054)	-0.085 (0.262)
Age	-0.027 (0.045)	-0.125** (0.058)	0.091 (0.248)
Age^2	0.000 (0.000)	0.001* (0.001)	-0.001 (0.002)
Field of study	Controlled	Controlled	Controlled
Constant	43.224 (57.911)	79.539 (107.376)	173.826 (525.340)
Observations	470	470	470
R-squared	0.048	0.139	0.024

Table A.8. Quality of TTP Part-Time Participants, by Country, 2011–2013.

Notes: Robust standard errors in parentheses. *** $p<0.01$, ** $p<0.05$, * $p<0.1$. The baseline group is those with Chinese PhDs. # We use the log of these two variables.

Source: Data collection was supervised by Dr. Kang Siqin, who managed a team of students from Zhongshan University, Guangzhou. Work was carried out at the South China Global Talent Institute, Guangzhou.

Notes

[1] The number of citations includes papers published in journals that are ranked in the SSCI system. The h-index is based on the set of a scholar's most-cited papers and the number of citations that they have received in other publications. For example, an h-index of forty means that the scholar has published forty papers that have been cited forty times.

[2] Lien, "Asymmetric Information and the Brain Drain."

[3] The dean of the School of Economics at Southwest University of Finance and Economics, who was a part-time returnee under the Changjiang program, told me that he published

domestically to increase his influence on government policy on poverty alleviation and income distribution.

[4] I found 401 of them by searching university websites for names in *pinyin* romanization. Amy Liu Mei-hwa, who wrote a book about mainlanders in Hong Kong, estimated at that time that there were 450 China-born academics in Hong Kong's eight universities, so I had found most of them.

[5] The survey was online from May 9 to July 9, 2004.

[6] However, their lower impact factor score is probably because they publish more in British journals, which generally are cited less, so they have a lower impact factor than US journals.

Appendix C

Key Events in US War on China's Talent Programs

Date	US Actor	Event or Activity
2014	Investigations and Threat Management Service (ITMS), Commerce Dept.	Dr. Sherry Chen, US government employee, arrested (all charges dropped in 2015)[1]
May 2015	FBI	Xi Xiaoxing Arrested; all charges dropped four months later[2]
Sept 2015	FBI	FBI memo attacks TTP[3]
2015	NIH and NSFC National Defense Strategy	Agreement to fight cancer extended[4]
Jan 19, 2018	DOD, National Defense Strategy	"China is a strategic competitor using predatory economics to intimidate its neighbors while militarizing features in the South China Sea." It "seeks Indo-Pacific regional hegemony in the near-term and displacement of the United States to achieve global pre-eminence in the future."[5]
Feb 13, 2018	FBI Director Wray at Senate Intelligence Committee	China using "non-traditional collectors" in academia in "whole-of-society" attack on US[6]
Mar 8, 2018	White House and USTR	Beginning of Trade War with China[7]
Mar 2018	USTR	China's "unreasonable" trade practices criticized under Section 301—"[a] range of tools may be appropriate to address these serious matters"[8]
Mar 2018	NIH, NOTOD-18-160	Clarifies conflict of iterest and conflict of commitment, demands stricter disclosure of overseas engagements[9]
Apr 2018	FBI	Gives NIH list of 3,000 scientists to investigate for links to Chinese talent programs[10]
Apr 2018	US House of Representatives	Holds hearing called "Scholars or Spies"[11]
Apr 2018	National Intelligence Council	No. of TTP "recruits" in US said to be 2,629[12]

Jun 2018	Peter Navarro, director, White House Office of Trade and Manufacturing Policy	Publishes "How China's Economic Aggression Threatens the Technologies and Intellectual Property of the United States and the World"[13]
Aug 2018	NIH Director Collins	Wrote to 10,000 US institutions about "systematic programs to influence NIH researchers and peer reviewers," leading to "unacceptable breaches of trust"[14]
Aug 2018	President Trump	"Almost every student that comes over to this country [from China] is a spy"[15]
Aug 2018	NIH	Reports that 55 institutions had conducted investigations in response to its inquiries[16]
Nov 2018	Attorney General Sessions	Announces the "China Initiative"[17]
Nov/Dec 2018	NIH	Letters and emails sent to hundreds of schools, listing "cases of concern"[18]
Apr 2019	NIH	Reports probing 250 China-born academics[19]
May 2019	White House Office of Science and Technology Policy (OSTP)	Creates Joint Committee on the Research Environment (JCORE), whose target is China[20]
Aug 2019	19 research universities and associations	Urged US government to "tread carefully"[21]
Sept 2019	Director of OSTP	Letter to US Research Community highlights foreign talent programs, calls for catching those who "abuse" the open scientific environment in the US[22]
Nov 2019	US Senate report	"Threats to the US Research Enterprise: China's Talent Recruitment Plans"[23]
Dec 2019	OSTP conference	"Enhancing the Security and Integrity of America's Research Enterprise" defines conflicts of commitment[24]
Dec 2019	NIH	Preliminary report, "ACD Working Group on Foreign Influences on Research Integrity Update"[25]
Jan. 2020	FBI	Charles Lieber of Harvard arrested[26]
Feb. 2020	FBI	Hu Anming arrested[27]
March 2020	National Science Foundation (NSF)	Creates Chief of Research Security and Policy (CRISP)[28]
March 2020		COVID-19 rips through US
May 2020	White House	Students/scholars with institutional ties to "military-civil fusion strategy" banned from US[29]

Dec 2020	Government Accountability Office (GAO)	Reports that government funding agencies of university research "moved the goalposts" as to what overseas ties researchers must report[30]
Jan 2021	White House	National Security Presidential Memorandum-33[31]
Jan 14, 2021	FBI	Arrest of Chen Gang of MIT[32]
Jan 20, 2021	White House	Joe Biden becomes president
Feb 2021	DOJ, FBI (meeting at CSIS)	Wray claims FBI opening new case on China "every 10 hours"[33]
July 2021	Members of Congress	Nearly one hundred members of Congress urged Attorney General Garland to investigate the DOJ's alleged racial profiling of Asians[34]
Sept 2021	DOJ	Hu Anming acquitted[35]
Jan 2022	DOJ	Olsen replaced Demers as director of NSD,[36] charges against Chen Gang dropped[37]
Feb/2022	DOJ	Biden Administration ends the CI[38]
Aug/2022	White House and Congress	Chips and Science Act[39]
Dec 2022	NIH (final report)	246 cases, with 103 fired or resigned[40]
Jan 2023	Judge Julie Robinson	Franklin Tao sentenced to time served, Judge Robinson lectures DOJ on CI[41]
Jul 2023	US Congress	Section 702 of Foreign Intelligence Surveillance Act (FISA) is up for debate[42]
Aug/2023	President Biden	Presidential Executive Order forbids US investment in Chinese firms producing advanced semiconductors and quantum computers. US citizens and permanent residents barred from taking part in any of these prohibited deals[43]
Apr 2024	US Congress	Section 702 renewed[44]
Jul 2024	DOJ	Courts overturn conviction of Franklin Tao[45]

Notes

[1] https://www.nbcnews.com/news/asian-america/falsely-accused-spying-china-sherry-chen-wins-significant-settlement-rcna56847.

[2] https://www.aclu.org/news/privacy-technology/chilling-surveillance-and-wrongful-arrest-chinese.

[3] https://info.publicintelligence.net/FBI-ChineseTalentPrograms.pdf.

[4] https://www.niaid.nih.gov/research/uschina-collaborative-biomedical-research-program.

[5] https://dod.defense.gov/Portals/1/Documents/pubs/2018-National-Defense-Strategy-Summary.pdf.

[6] https://www.insidehighered.com/news/2018/02/15/fbi-director-testifies-chinese-studentsand-intelligence-threats.

[7] https://www.npr.org/sections/thetwo-way/2018/01/22/579848409/trump-slaps-tariffs-on-imported-solar-panels-and-washing-machines.

[8] https://ustr.gov/sites/default/files/Section%20301%20FINAL.PDF.

[9] https://grants.nih.gov/grants/guide/notice-files/NOT-OD-18-160.html.

[10] https://www.science.org/content/article/record-settlement-over-china-funding-puts-u-s-research-institutions-notice.

[11] https://www.hsgac.senate.gov/imo/media/doc/2019-11-18%20PSI%20Staff%20Report%20-%20China's%20Talent%20Recruitment%20Plans.pdf.

[12] https://www.bloomberg.com/news/articles/2018-06-22/china-s-thousand-talents-calledkey-in-seizing-u-s-expertise.

[13] https://trumpwhitehouse.archives.gov/briefings-statements/office-trademanufacturing-policy-report-chinas-economic-aggression-threatens-technologiesintellectual-property-united-states-world/.

[14] https://www.science.org/content/article/nih-lettersasking-about-undisclosed-foreign-ties-rattle-us-universities.

[15] https://www.politico.com/story/2018/08/08/trump-executive-dinner-bedminsterchina766609.

[16] https://www.sciencemag.org/news/2019/09/nih-reveals-itsformula-tracking-foreign-influences.

[17] https://www.justice.gov/opa/speech/file/1107256/download.

[18] https://www.science.org/content/article/nih-lettersasking-about-undisclosed-foreign-ties-rattle-us-universities.

[19] https://www.sciencemag.org/news/2019/09/nih-reveals-itsformula-tracking-foreign-influences, doi:10.1126/science.aaz6589.

[20] https://insight.ieeeusa.org/articles/ostp-establishes-joint-committee-on-the-research-environment/.

[21] https://www.scmp.com/news/china/diplomacy/article/3022413/us-academics-condemn-racial-profiling-chinesestudents-and.

[22] https://www.whitehouse.gov/wpcontent/uploads/2019/09/OSTP-letter-to-the-US-research-community-september-2019.pdf.

[23] https://www.hsgac.senate.gov/imo/media/doc/2019-11-18%20PSI%20Staff%20Report%20-%20China's%20Talent%20Recruitment%20Plans.pdf.

[24] https://trumpwhitehouse.archives.gov/wpcontent/uploads/2020/07/Enhancing-the-Security-and-Integrity-of-Americas-Research-Enterprise.pdf.

[25] https://acd.od.nih.gov/documents/presentations/12132019ForeignInfluences.pdf.

[26] https://www.justice.gov/opa/pr/harvard-university-professor-and-two-chinese-nationals-charged-three-separate-china-related.

[27] https://www.justice.gov/opa/pr/researcher-university-arrested-wire-fraud-and-making-false-statements-about-affiliation.

[28] https://new.nsf.gov/news/nsf-creates-new-research-security-chief-position.

[29] https://www.insidehighered.com/quicktakes/2020/06/01/trump-proclamation-bars-entry-certain-chinese-students.

[30] GAO-21-130, December 2020, 16, https://www.gao.gov/assets/gao-21-130.pdf.

[31] https://trumpwhitehouse.archives.gov/presidential-actions/presidential-memorandum-united-states-governmentsupported-research-development-national-security-policy/.

[32] https://www.justice.gov/usao-ma/pr/mit-professor-arrested-and-charged-grant-fraud.

[33] https://www.csis.org/events/china-initiative-conference.

[34] https://www.axios.com/2021/07/30/china-asians-racialprofiling-doj-congress.

[35] https://www.science.org/content/article/u-s-judge-acquits-academic-accused-deceiving-nasa-about-his-china-ties.

[36] https://www.science.org/content/article/controversial-u-s-china-initiative-gets-new-name-tighter-focus-industrialespionage.

[37] https://www.nytimes.com/2022/01/20/science/gang-chen-mit-china-initiative.html.

[38] https://www.scientificamerican.com/article/the-controversial-china-initiative-is-ending-and-researchers-are-relieved/.

[39] https://acd.od.nih.gov/documents/presentations/12132019ForeignInfluences.pdf.

[40] https://new.nsf.gov/chips.

[41] https://www.science.org/content/article/no-jailtime-kansas-professor-convicted-undisclosed-research-ties-china.

[42] https://www.wsj.com/articles/u-s-and-china-poised-to-drift-further-apart-after-investment-ban-1e37427d.

[43] https://www.nbcnews.com/politics/congress/section-702-foreign-intelligence-surveillance-act-congress-what-know-rcna96259.

[44] https://www.npr.org/2024/04/20/1246076114/senate-passes-reauthorization-surveillance-program-fisa.

[45] https://apnews.com/article/china-initiative-university-kansas-9ac9a1177feca187a0d314 24e1fb56fb.

INDEX